McLaren
THE EPIC YEARS

McLaren

THE EPIC YEARS

ALAN HENRY

FOREWORD BY KEKE ROSBERG

Haynes Publishing

First published in July 1998

British Library Cataloguing in Publication Data
A catalogue record for this book is
available from the British Library

ISBN 1 85960 431 5

Library of Congress catalog card no. 98-70520

Haynes Publishing, Sparkford, Nr Yeovil,
Somerset, BA22 7JJ.
Tel: 01963 440635 Fax: 01963 440001
Int. tel: +44 1963 440635 Fax: +44 1963 440001

E-mail: sales@haynes-manuals.co.uk
Web site: http://www.haynes.com

Haynes North America, Inc.
861 Lawrence Drive, Newbury Park,
California 91320 USA

Designed & typeset by
G&M, Raunds, Northamptonshire
Printed in Great Britain by
J. H. Haynes & Co., Ltd, Sparkford

Contents

Foreword

by Keke Rosberg, 1982 World Champion

RACING FOR THE McLaren Formula 1 team was a very special part of my professional life. I led my very last grand prix – the Australian race at Adelaide – driving one of their TAG turbo-engined cars which, although a punctured tyre prevented me from finishing the job, was an enormously satisfying experience. I also led the German Grand Prix at Hockenheim where I had the additional enjoyment of starting from pole position, so the fact that I did not manage to add another grand prix win to the five I had achieved with the Williams team did not alter the fact that 1986 was an extremely memorable experience for me.

Much of the motivation for making the switch of team stemmed from my insistence to Frank Williams that if he signed Nigel Mansell to drive for him, then I would leave. But Frank signed him at the start of 1985 and I duly left once my contract expired at the end of that season.

Once I took that decision there was clearly only one place I could go and, since I knew that it would be my final season in F1, driving for McLaren could be considered my one last priority as a front-line racing driver. Driving for McLaren is an enormous privilege. Ron Dennis and his colleagues run a fine racing team in which attention to even the smallest detail is one of the key hallmarks.

In my role now as Mika Hakkinen's manager, I have continued my links with McLaren. I am happy to say that Mika's relationship with the team is one of the most deep-rooted partnerships on the current F1 stage. People say you should never do business with friends, but working with McLaren seems to have proved that theory to be incorrect . . .

May 1998

Acknowledgements

THIS BOOK HAS been produced with the knowledge, although not the official collaboration, of McLaren International. However, I am greatly indebted to various members of the McLaren family past and present for help over the years in my general news-gathering role as a Formula 1 journalist. They have contributed enormously to what I hope offers an accurate, fair perspective and understanding about this leading grand prix team.

So thanks to Ron Dennis, Martin Whitmarsh, Jo Ramirez, Creighton Brown, Gordon Murray, Tyler Alexander, Adrian Newey, Neil Oatley, Steve Nichols, Davey Ryan, Anna Guerrier, Justine Blake, Stuart Wingham, Shaune and Bob McMurray, Steve Hallam, David Brown, Ekrem Sami, Peter Burns, Peter Stayner and others too numerous to mention. Outside McLaren, my appreciation is directed towards its former team drivers Alain Prost, Keke Rosberg, Niki Lauda and John Watson for sharing their memories; to John Barnard, whose efforts at the design helm of McLaren International helped lay the foundations of what the team is achieving today; to Norbert Haug, the Mercedes-Benz motorsport manager, and Mario Illien of Ilmor Engineering for some fascinating background information; to Nigel Roebuck, Maurice Hamilton, Eoin Young, Martin Hines and Eric Silberman for comparing and checking McLaren anecdotes; to John Townsend of Formula One Pictures and David Phipps, plus both Wolfgang Schattling and Xander Heijnen of Daimler-Benz Motorsport Communications, who contributed to the superb selection of photographs between these covers.

I would also like to thank Peter Foubister for permission to quote from *Motoring News*, and Richard Poulter, of Hazleton Publishing, for permission to quote from the *Autocourse* annual.

Finally to Darryl Reach, Flora Myer and Alison Roelich at Haynes, whose patience seemingly knows no bounds. Let's hope.

Alan Henry
May 1998

Introduction

GRAND PRIX MOTOR racing teams are like extended families. They reflect the characters of the pivotal personalities who exert the most influence within them, but the sum total of their parts is inevitably more significant than those key individuals concerned.

Yet the very nature of this intensely, some would say brutally, competitive sport requires that such families evolve and develop to adapt to the ever-changing environment in which they operate. If they don't, they risk fading away into the sepia-tinted pages of the motor racing history books.

The McLaren team stands out as one of the most glitteringly successful such operations in the sport's history. Founded by the late Bruce McLaren as Bruce McLaren Motor Racing Limited as long ago as 1964, it may seem strange to readers not versed in motor racing folklore that the company still carries the name of the man who was killed in a testing accident at Goodwood back in June 1970.

Although Bruce set the team's original tone, establishing its corporate identity almost as an extension of his own free-wheeling personality, many others have played a key role in the company's subsequent development. This volume does not, in the main, concern itself with those fledgling years. Nor with the team's gradual rise to the forefront of F1 competitiveness, which reached its zenith with James Hunt's World Championship in 1976, followed by a subsequent gentle decline.

The sub-title 'The Epic Years' signals that here we are concerned with mainly the portion of McLaren history extending from 1984 through to the present day, an era that saw McLaren International, as the company became in 1980, win the 1984, '85, '86, '88, '89, '90 and '91 World Championships, thanks to a combination of brilliant engineering, pin-sharp managerial focus and the driving genius of Niki Lauda, Alain Prost and the late Ayrton Senna.

In addition, it examines the painful three-year dearth of victories between Ayrton Senna's final win with the team at Adelaide in 1993 and David Coulthard's triumph at Melbourne at the start of 1997, an event that marked the team's return to winning ways. It also heralded the dawn of what looks set to be a new era of sustained success with its present engine partner, Mercedes-Benz.

This volume also stands as a singular testimony to the vision of Ron Dennis, the man who took over at the management helm in 1980, and fashioned the Championship years before enduring that painful slump from which the team re-emerged at the start of the 1997 season. You will read much about Dennis, and the diversity of his company's business activities, in these pages, although this is in no sense an officially sanctioned account of the McLaren team's efforts throughout this golden era.

I have known Dennis since 1971 and count him as a friend, although the fact that I am also a journalist means that, even when at his most relaxed, the McLaren boss is always slightly on his guard. Despite the best efforts of his engine partners over the years – Honda, Peugeot, and particularly Mercedes-Benz – he has always reacted to the media like a poker player who wants to keep his best hand until last; and even then is reluctant to play it at all.

Like all such driven men he can be generous, warmly perceptive and immensely considerate. His success has bought him considerable material wealth, yet, despite a reputation within F1 as something of an egotist, Ron ensures family life with his wife Lisa and their three children is conducted privately and away from the spotlight of attention. That is an attractive quality.

Professionally, I have found him to be of considerable assistance on many occasions. He has risked taking me into his confidence on various matters in a way that I am not certain I would have been bold enough to emulate had the positions been reversed. I would like to think that I have not knowingly let him down.

Ken Tyrrell, the grandfather of F1 team owners, says of Dennis: 'First of all, Ron is a guy who loves his motor racing. He really likes his racing. He is absolutely straightforward and honest. I would trust him with my life, if that is not too much of an exaggeration.'

By the same token, my colleagues and I have also experienced moments when Ron has appeared to be stubborn, confrontational, exasperatingly tactless and frustratingly aloof. Like most human beings, in fact.

Yet without Ron Dennis there would almost certainly have been no McLaren story of any consequence to tell after James Hunt won his World Championship 22 years ago. He may not agree with the interpretations that I have put on some the events of the past decade or more, but I would like to think that he and his McLaren colleagues will conclude that this is a fair assessment and analysis of what, by any standards, has been a quite remarkable era of sustained achievement at the centre of this most demanding, uniquely 20th-century pastime.

Straight
from the grid

IT WAS THE end of lap 45 in the 1998 Spanish Grand Prix and suddenly everybody froze. Mika Hakkinen's McLaren-Mercedes had come in to make the second refuelling stop of the Finn's dominant run to victory in the fifth round of the 1998 World Championship. Yet for a split-second it looked as though his car had developed a problem.

The seconds ticked by as the silver and black machine stood motionless. Then Mika was accelerating back into the race after being stationary for 10.8 seconds. Under pressure, such a stop should have been managed in seven or eight seconds. But Hakkinen was not under pressure at all. McLaren could service his car at their own pace, not allowing themselves to be hurried. They knew they were the class of the field.

After 65 laps Hakkinen took the chequered flag to score his third win so far out of the first five races of this glittering season. David Coulthard crossed the line in second place, completing the third McLaren-Mercedes 1–2 of the year. Mika now led the championship with 36 points to David's 29 and Ferrari team leader Michael Schumacher's 24.

In the Constructors' points table, McLaren-Mercedes had accumulated 65 points – more than its total for the whole of 1997 – to Ferrari's 35 while Williams, McLaren's long-established and closest rivals for F1 domination over the previous decade, were trailing with 14 points. The rest were nowhere. After three years of pain and application, the 1998 season was unfolding into pay-off time for McLaren and its partners.

Hakkinen was delighted, but characteristically controlled in response to this latest win. 'With a lead like that, you might imagine that it is easy, but it never is,' he grinned.

'You have to make sure that you are concentrating hard, you have to be careful when overtaking and although it is enjoyable to be passing other drivers, it is also demanding because the situation and the timing are not always ideal.

'At the beginning of the race I was pushing quite hard. I guess there is always a little room for improvement in your lap times during a race, especially when you are leading, but certainly there was no point in taking any risks at that early stage when damaging your tyres.'

He also acknowledged that Coulthard had kept him on his toes all the way through to the chequered flag. 'I now realise that David's pit stops were very good and he got close to me,' he admitted. 'But the way I was coming into the pits was to make sure that I didn't take any risks, and the difference between us fell to four seconds after the second stop. So maybe I was taking it a bit too easy.'

For his part, Coulthard openly conceded that he hadn't been totally happy with the feel of his car from the outset. 'My first set of tyres were not so good,' he explained, 'and I had made changes to the chassis set-up both after the morning warm-up and then again just before the start. The car's front end felt a little "pointy" from the start, but its handling got progressively better throughout the race and was at its best on the last set of tyres.

'But you always have to push, and I pushed as hard as I could through the whole race. You never know what the strategy is of the people behind you and, secondly, if anything was to have happened to Mika in traffic or at a pit stop, there was always a chance of me being able to sneak through. I tried hard, but I just wasn't quick enough this weekend.'

Nevertheless, prior to the race, David's former Williams sparring partner Damon Hill still rated him as favourite to win the 1998 World Championship. 'Standing here now I would put money on David who has looked stronger than Mika at Beunos Aires and Imola,' said Hill. 'I think he has an excellent chance of cracking it. Now he just has to keep his head and get on with it.

'It's fun to battle with your team mate and certainly makes meal times together more interesting. I had a very healthy relationship with Jacques Villeneuve (in his championship year at Williams in 1996).

'In those conditions you simply have to do a better job as a driver because, whatever you do with the car, the other guy knows the same information.'

It had been clear that McLaren would be in a class of their own since the previous week's test session at the Circuit de Catalunya where Hakkinen and Coulthard had again set the pace. Come qualifying for the race, the Finn was simply out of reach, demonstrating once more that remarkable capacity to deliver quick laps at will. Each time Imola winner Coulthard came close, Hakkinen just sliced off a couple more tenths.

Qualifying at Barcelona had seen the two McLaren-Mercedes comfortably out-run their opposition. Hakkinen's pole position lap was really special and the mild-mannered Finn seemed able to pull out an extra advantage over Coulthard almost at will. Yet the initiative had ebbed and flowed between the two men from the start of the year with Coulthard perhaps having the edge in two races, Hakkinen the same, and shared honours in the remaining one.

There was another particularly nice touch to follow at the end of the Spanish race. Rather than team boss Ron Dennis attending the rostrum ceremony as the representative of the winning constructors, Mansour Ojjeh, the Chairman of the TAG McLaren Group, attended to do the honours. Also the Chief Executive Officer of TAG (Techniques d'Avant-Garde), Ojjeh's presence served as an almost symbolic reminder of the contribution his family's company had made to McLaren fortunes ever since Ron Dennis approached them to finance the original TAG turbo V6 back in the early 1980s.

The resultant McLaren-TAGs scored a hat-trick of World Championships from 1984 to 86 in the hands of Niki Lauda and Alain Prost (twice) and this period of sustained success effectively underpinned all that McLaren would subsequently achieve.

McLaren has a magnificent track record. The Woking team's 111 race victories over 24 seasons make it the most consistent winner in the history of Formula 1. Indeed, a decade ago Ayrton Senna and Alain Prost, driving McLaren MP4/4s, were the all-conquering duo who famously clocked up 15 victories in the 16-round 1988 season. The Marlboro red and white cars looked insuperable then, just as the silver ones – reliveried for the change of sponsorship to West last year – are appearing to a frustrated grid this season.

Yet watching Hakkinen and Coulthard dominating proceedings at the Circuit de Catalunya, it was almost impossible to believe just how far McLaren had come in the previous decade, expanding from its initial role as purely a grand prix motor racing team into a high technology group with a workforce of nearly 700, and business interests as diverse as aviation and electronics.

Away from the pure grand prix world McLaren has sustained a reputation for innovative and imaginative engineering. In 1989 Ron Dennis and McLaren Cars technical director Gordon Murray embarked on a programme to build the world's most ambitious super performance road car. It came to fruition as the McLaren F1. One hundred examples of this were built, with a price tag of £650,000, until production ceased in May 1998.

To mark the end of its production, distinguished sports car racer Andy Wallace took the car to Volkswagen's Ehra-Lessien test track near Wolfsburg in Germany, and achieved over 240mph to set a new production car world speed record.

To occupy McLaren Cars after the end of the F1 production run and before the next long-term innovative project, Gordan Murray and his engineers turned their minds to developing a unique two-

seater grand prix car. Unveiled in 1998, the MP4-98T will be used
for promotional and charity events to enable lucky sponsors,
partners, prize winners – and even trembling members of the media
– to sample as a passenger riding behind Hakkinen or Coulthard
what goes on in the high g, 190mph world of grand prix action.

McLaren also developed the TAG Electronics Company to
research and build high performance electronic systems for
production and racing cars, and now has an interest in the
Farnborough aerodrome, which it intends developing into the
biggest private jet centre in Europe.

In the pure racing environment, McLaren has spread its wings to
encourage young talent up through the grass roots of the sport by
means of its Driver Support Programme, which encompasses
everything from karting through Formula 3 to Formula 3000.

Yet its core business remains Formula 1. For the 1998 season
McLaren and Mercedes, its long-term engine partner, made a terrific
effort to break through to the old winning ways established to such
consistent effect from the mid-1980s to the early 1990s. Ron Dennis,
TAG McLaren's Managing Director and co-founder, had always said
that his ambition with Mercedes was to dominate just as the team's
cars had done with TAG and Honda engines in the past.

Now it seemed as though that ambition was close to being
realised.

Nothing is ever taken for granted by the McLaren team, but for
the moment they could bask contentedly in the knowledge of a job
well done.

Barely five hours after Hakkinen and Coulthard had taken the
chequered flag at the Circuit de Catalunya, many of the team's
engineers, mechanics and other personnel were strapped aboard a
British Airways Boeing 737 bound for London's Gatwick airport and
home.

Yet the relentless pressure which always lurks behind the scene of
an F1 team was brilliantly crystallised by McLaren old sweat Tyler
Alexander as we left the airport's baggage hall. Why, asked the
author, hadn't he got any luggage?

'Hell,' he said, 'I just threw it in the back of the transporter back at
the track. I've got to be out at Magny-Cours for a test on Tuesday,
leaving on a flight almost before dawn.'

That was barely 30 hours after the wheels of the jet had touched
down in England. It was a salutory reminder that, like the iceberg
that sank the *Titanic*, nine-tenths of the grind behind the glory takes
place below the surface, out of sight of prying eyes.

Watching Mika and David take the chequered flag at races like the
Spanish Grand Prix is simply the icing on the cake, the end result of
all that toil and team work.

1

Beginnings, 1958–70

BRUCE McLAREN ARRIVED in Britain, a fresh-faced 21-year-old New Zealander, in April 1958, just in time to drive a Formula 2 Cooper in the Aintree 200, one of several important non-championship motor races that acted as a curtain-raiser to the main business of the grand prix season.

Ron Dennis at that time was 10 years old, Niki Lauda barely nine and Alain Prost just two. In far-away Brazil, something of a distant and mysterious land for most people in those days, newly-weds Milton and Neyde da Silva were settling down to married life together. Their first-born would not arrive for almost another two years. By the time their son Ayrton was born on 21 March 1960, Bruce McLaren would have two grand prix victories to his credit at the wheel of a Cooper-Climax. The Brazilian boy would eventually win 41, all but six achieved at the wheel of a car bearing the name of the man who was born in Auckland on 30 August 1937.

Bruce McLaren was the son of a successful garage owner, by all accounts growing up as a popular child with a sunny, outgoing disposition. Struck down in his youth by Perthes disease, a potentially debilitating hip condition, he spent almost three years in a home for crippled children between the ages of nine and 12. There was the unspoken fear that he might never walk again, but that happily turned out not to be the case.

Les McLaren, Bruce's father, was a keen amateur competition driver who tracked down an Austin Seven Ulster, which he rebuilt for circuit racing in 1951. It took him the best part of a year to rebuild the machine into something vaguely approaching a competitive proposition, but the Old Man was so appalled at the Seven's primitive and wayward handling when he first gave it a test run on the local Auckland roads that he vowed he would sell it immediately.

Bruce, by then still a year away from the age of 15 at which he would be permitted to take his own driving test, persuaded his father to keep the car. Les gave into his son's wishes, the only condition being that Bruce looked after the car himself. Eventually he would team up with a pal, Phil Kerr, who was also racing an old Austin, and the two youngsters were permitted to prepare their cars out of 'Pop' McLaren's garage premises.

It wasn't long before Bruce wangled his way into the driving seat of his father's Austin Healey 100S – one of the very first such cars to arrive in New Zealand – and eventually acquired the centre-seat 'bob-tailed' 1.5-litre Cooper in which Jack Brabham had made his F1 debut in the 1955 British Grand Prix at Aintree.

He corresponded regularly with Brabham during the course of the following year and the Australian suggested that he might be able to arrange to bring out a pair of single-seater Coopers for the early 1958 New Zealand racing season, one of which could be earmarked for Bruce's use.

As a result of his efforts in this car Bruce found himself the first recipient of an award from the New Zealand International Grand Prix Association of a trip to Europe and a grant to cover his expenses during the season. The Cooper was duly transported to Sydney, where it would be loaded on to the Orient Line steamship *Orantes* for the six-week trip to Britain, a journey time that seems almost impossible to grasp in this era of Boeing 747 freighters capable of transporting an entire grand prix grid from one side of the world to the other in little more than 24 hours.

In the event, Bruce had to fly on ahead of his own car in an effort to make that date at the Aintree 200 in a chassis furnished by Cooper. A succession of promising F2 performances followed, as a result of which he was promoted to the Cooper works F1 team in 1959, driving as number two to Jack Brabham, and he rounded off the year on a suitably upbeat note with victory in the United States Grand Prix at Sebring.

The 1960 season opened on a similarly successful note for Bruce as he survived the broiling heat in Buenos Aires to win the Argentine Grand Prix. For the rest of the year he continued to play an unobtrusive, but supremely effective, supporting role to Brabham, finishing second in the Monaco, Belgian and Portuguese Grands Prix, third in the French and US races and fourth in Britain.

Brabham successfully retained Cooper's World Championship title by the end of the year, but Bruce took second place in the points standings. Perhaps surprisingly, although he would score points every year thereafter through to his death in the summer of 1970, Bruce would never again achieve such a high position in the title points table.

When Jack Brabham left to establish his own F1 team at the end of the 1961 season, McLaren duly assumed the Cooper team leadership, but life in the once-proud British equipe was becoming hard work. Cooper had slipped from the competitive high wire, a situation exacerbated by the acute conservatism of the company founder Charles Cooper.

There was an irony here. Cooper had pioneered the technically advanced concept of central-engined grand prix cars, at a stroke rendering their front-engined opposition obsolete. But it would take Lotus boss Colin Chapman to develop successfully that audacious design theme and progress to scale fresh heights of achievement. Cooper, by contrast, would be left behind.

Finally, when Charles Cooper refused to sanction the construction of two special cars for the 1963/64 Tasman Championship, Bruce decided to go it alone and build the cars himself. To complete this project, he established Bruce McLaren Motor Racing, and this decision was the catalyst that led him to quit Cooper at the end of 1965 in order to pursue his own ambitious plans in a variety of racing formulae.

That Tasman adventure at the start of 1964 would also contain an unexpectedly tragic dimension, for Bruce's talented team-mate Timmy Mayer was killed in practice for the final round at Longford, Tasmania. Mayer had raced in Europe as a member of the Tyrrell Formula Junior team in 1963 and had been signed as Bruce's number two in the Cooper F1 squad for the following year.

'Timmy was an absolutely lovely fellow,' recalled Ken Tyrrell more than 30 years later. 'He was the apple of his brother's eye, partly because I think Teddy saw in Timmy everything he'd wanted to be and to achieve. Timmy was very bright, very intelligent and was definitely F1 material. A lovely guy with a gorgeous wife; they made the perfect couple.'

What Timmy Mayer might have achieved in F1 has gone down in history as one of the sport's many tantalising 'might have beens', but his family name would certainly continue to be associated with front-line motor racing for many years. His brother Teddy, who had abandoned a career as a lawyer to manage Timmy's career, threw in his lot with McLaren to bring some much-needed finance and considerable mental dexterity on the management side.

When Mayer joined the company in May 1964 the financial structure of professional motor racing was extremely different from what we know today.

'We paid our top two mechanics, Tyler Alexander and Wally Willmott, £30 a week and we reckoned that was a tremendous amount of money,' he told me in 1983. 'I began by concentrating on the business administration side of the company.

'You've got to remember that there were none of the outside commercial sponsors we know today. Virtually all the sponsorship came from oil and tyre companies, and most of the negotiations were carried out via the old pals' act. It was as if you waved a mystic magic wand and the finance appeared.'

It would be no exaggeration to say that McLaren Racing blew a breath of fresh air through the rather stuffy and conservative British motor racing establishment during the mid-1960s, a time during which the sport was primed for lift-off into a dramatically expanded commercial era.

In that respect McLaren and Mayer formed something of a double act, Bruce's outward tolerance and reservoir of goodwill often acting as a timely foil to Mayer's sometimes abrasive business edge. The company developed into a well-balanced organisation that always thrived on hard work and radiated a practical, no-nonsense approach to any task it tackled.

After Bruce won the 1962 Monaco Grand Prix at the wheel of a Cooper-Climax, six years would pass before he took the chequered flag again in an F1 event. By 1968 the team's F1 cars were powered by Cosworth Ford DFV engines, Bruce emerging triumphant from both the Race of Champions at Brands Hatch and the Belgian Grand Prix at Spa-Francorchamps.

By this time his compatriot Denny Hulme, who had won the '67 Championship for Jack Brabham's team, had been signed to drive as Bruce's team-mate. The affable New Zealander was content to let his friend set the F1 pace, but both men also enjoyed the domination exerted by the team's rumbling, ground-shaking Chevrolet-engined sports cars in the financially lucrative Can-Am sports car series in North America, a category that the McLaren team made virtually its own private stamping ground in the second half of that decade.

Hulme, recalled Mayer, was a major asset to the team at that time. 'A good driver, always very calm and a guy who got on extremely well with his mechanics,' he reflected. 'Also, he was extremely observant. He always knew what was going on in the F1 world and didn't miss much. He was a bit moody, but when he felt he was in with a chance he was a bloody good driver.

'Most of the time Denny was as quick as he needed to be, which, I think, was a little bit quicker than Bruce. He was also a better test driver. He didn't care how or why you might come to a conclusion about the way in which the car was handling – as long as it worked he was happy.

'With Bruce, it was rather different. If Bruce latched on to a "pet theory" it was enormously difficult to shake it away from him. He would go out of his way to justify the theory, even if it clearly wasn't the way to go.'

By 1970 Bruce McLaren was firmly established as a successful and prosperous businessman. There was talk that he might be considering retirement from race driving, a road car project was close to completion and the company as a whole had successfully evolved into a financially viable business entity, expanding to launch an assault on that bastion of US motor racing, the Indianapolis 500.

Bruce may not have been the fastest driver of his era, but he had nurtured a reputation for consistency and dependability that could rightly be described as second to none. Yet on 2 June 1970 all those plans were ripped apart with a dreadful finality.

While at Goodwood testing one of the latest McLaren-Chevrolet M8Ds in preparation for the forthcoming Can-Am series, an improperly secured rear body section flew backwards off the car as Bruce was lapping the Sussex circuit at high speed. The car was abruptly pitched out of control and slammed into a disused marshals' post, killing its driver instantly.

Bruce McLaren had achieved a great deal during the 32 years and nine months that he had lived. Yet not even his most ardent admirers could have imagined that his name would endure so prominently on the front-line international motor racing scene, still carried by one of the most formidably competitive F1 teams of all time 28 years after his untimely death.

2

After Bruce, 1970–80

THE FIRST McLAREN F1 car had made its race debut in the 1966 Monaco Grand Prix driven by the company founder. Powered by a linered-down version of the four-cam Indy Ford V8, it proved to be the wrong choice; heavy and unreliable, it was not a long-term option. The team also briefly flirted with an Italian Serenissima V8, which powered Bruce to sixth place in that year's British Grand Prix at Brands Hatch, but then it was back to the Ford power unit for the rest of the year.

For the 1967 season the team marked time with a 2.1-litre V8 BRM-powered version of its little M4A Formula 1 chassis, pending the arrival of customer versions of BRM's full 3-litre V12. Installed in the new McLaren M5 chassis, the smooth power curve of the new engine helped Bruce to dominate the early stages of the Canadian Grand Prix at Mosport Park, but the real aim was the Cosworth Ford DFV package, which came on stream for McLaren in 1968 and enabled the company to consolidate its position as a serious F1 player.

The team also had a management structure well in place. Teddy Mayer was in effect 'senior investor' in the company alongside Bruce, while Phil Kerr arrived to take the position as Joint Managing Director alongside Teddy, dealing mainly with the operational administration of the team. The final member of the management quartet was Tyler Alexander, an American from Hingham, Massachussets, who had trained as an aircraft engineer before getting involved in motor racing, and eventually landed up preparing various of Timmy Mayer's racing cars. Throughout the 1970s he would be responsible for McLaren's USAC (Indycar) operation based out of Livonia, on the outskirts of Detroit.

When the quartet became a trio after the tragic events of 2 June 1970, McLaren continued to sustain its competitive edge on both sides of the Atlantic. Testing at Indianapolis a month before McLaren's death, Denny Hulme had suffered painful burns to his hands in a methanol fire caused when fuel leaked from a partially secured filler cap. British driver Peter Gethin was signed up to deputise for the rugged New Zealander while Denny recovered, and was scheduled to test the McLaren M14 Formula 1 car at Goodwood on the day of Bruce's fatal accident.

Mustering a superhuman effort, Hulme forced himself back into the cockpit of a grand prix car long before he was really fit, the two men picking up the threads of the McLaren F1 challenge in time for the Dutch Grand Prix at Zandvoort.

Veteran American ace Dan Gurney was also invited into the team in an effort to strengthen morale, but the popular Californian knew that his best days were already behind him and he quietly bowed out of the equation after only three races.

'Dan was a great guy to work with, enormous fun,' said Mayer, 'but, God, could he fiddle about with a car during practice!' The Jo Marquart-designed M14 design had certainly not been an unqualified success. In 1971 a new F1 designer, Ralph Bellamy, penned a more promising replacement, the M19, after Marquart left to start his own enterprise in other categories of motor racing. The M19's most interesting feature was rising rate suspension, and the new car proved extremely promising from the moment it rolled out for its very first test run.

On its debut outing in the South African Grand Prix, Hulme pushed the new McLaren confidently into the lead, fending off a strong challenge from Mario Andretti's Ferrari 312B1. If only a bolt hadn't fallen out of the M19's rear suspension, Denny might well have won the car's first race. As it was, Andretti sailed past to take the victory and Hulme limped his crippled machine home a disappointed sixth.

That was effectively the high point of the McLaren F1 year. Mid-season Peter Gethin switched to BRM, for whom he would score a split-second victory in the Italian Grand Prix at Monza, but for McLaren there were only thin pickings. Prospects revived slightly at the Canadian Grand Prix where the second works car was fielded in the dark blue livery of the Penske team for Indianapolis ace Mark Donohue, who brought it through to third place at the chequered flag behind Jackie Stewart's Tyrrell and Ronnie Peterson's March.

Ralph Bellamy left McLaren to join the rival Brabham team at the end of 1971. The M19s were uprated to 'A' specification, retaining their rising rate suspension only at the front, and Peter Revson was signed up to drive alongside Hulme, the McLarens now benefiting from title sponsorship from the Yardley cosmetics firm. Hulme made up for his disappointment the previous year by winning at Kyalami, this time beating the Lotus 72 of Emerson Fittipaldi, the man who would go on to win that year's World Championship.

Thereafter the best results achieved by Peter and Denny were second and third in the Austrian Grand Prix, although the team also gave a chance to the young South African ace Jody Scheckter to demonstrate his remarkable talent with a debut in the US Grand Prix at Watkins Glen.

By this stage in the company's history, McLaren were firmly perceived as solid performers, but Lotus was continuing to dominate the scene with the radical Type 72, despite the fact that this machine was well into its third full racing season. But McLaren really raised the stakes in 1973 when Gordon Coppuck pencilled the superb side-radiator M23, which Hulme used to score the sole pole position of his F1 career in South Africa.

Denny should have won that race, but in a painful echo of his experience with the first M19, he was delayed by a puncture while leading and could only finish fifth. But the M23 was clearly a winning proposition, as Revson later proved with victories in the British and Canadian Grands Prix. Denny Hulme would add a third such success to this tally with an heroic spurt in the final stages to win the Swedish Grand Prix at Anderstorp.

A member of the Revlon cosmetics family, Peter Revson had initially dipped his toes into the swirling F1 maelstrom as long ago as 1964, when he became ensnared with the under-financed Reg Parnell Racing outfit. Paying for the privilege of slogging round at the tail of the pack in one of their uncompetitive Lotus-BRMs understandably was not to his taste, so he scampered back across the Atlantic to build his reputation in Can-Am and other US-based categories.

By 1972 he was back in the grand prix mainstream with McLaren and bagged a strong third behind Emerson Fittipaldi and Jackie Stewart in the British Grand Prix at Brands Hatch at the wheel of the trusty M19A. But it was only when the M23 appeared the following year that Revson and his team-mate Denny Hulme could seriously think in terms of winning from the front.

In terms of their opposition, the 1973 season saw them ranged primarily against the Tyrrells of Stewart and François Cevert and the formidable Lotus 72s, one of which bagged pole position in stupendous, tyre-smoking style for the British Grand Prix driven by the redoubtable Ronnie Peterson.

Flanking Ronnie on the front row were the works M23s of Hulme and Revvie, with Jackie Stewart's Tyrrell ahead of Fittipaldi's Lotus 72 tucked in behind them. The third row was headed by the fiery, inexperienced South African new boy Jody Scheckter, whose presence in the cockpit of a third works McLaren was calculated, however unintentionally, to put pressure on the team's two senior drivers.

At the start, Ronnie eased into the lead as the pack jostled through Copse Corner, but Stewart, who was running a slightly softer Goodyear tyre compound, out-fumbled the Swede brilliantly to take the lead going into Becketts. At the end of the first lap Jackie came hurtling through Woodcote about six lengths in the lead ahead of Peterson, with Carlos Reutemann's Brabham BT42 third and chasing hard. Then all hell broke loose . . .

In fourth place coming up into the Woodcote right-hander before the pits – taken near flat in a contemporary F1 car – Hulme saw Scheckter edging his M23 alongside his own. The craggy New Zealander, whose gruff outward manner had caused him to become known as 'The Bear', moved over cautiously to allow Jody, dubbed 'Baby Bear', to go flying by on the inside. There was no way Scheckter would make the corner.

Sliding wide on to the grass, Jody's McLaren came spearing back across the middle of the pack before slamming into the pit wall on the right-hand side of the circuit. Cars dodged left and right, shedding wheels and bodywork as they slammed into each other like billiard balls. When the dust settled, no fewer than nine cars had been eliminated, including the entire three-car Surtees team.

Amazingly, the sole casualty was Andrea de Adamich. It took the best part of an hour to cut the bespectacled Italian from his wrecked Brabham with a broken right ankle and left leg. The commentator on the scene was right: it certainly looked like the scene of an air crash. But calling it 'the end of grand prix racing as we know it' was a little over the top.

Of course the race was stopped and, after a long delay, restarted. Ronnie Peterson's Lotus made much of the early running, but after the track surface was brushed by a light rain shower, Revson pressed home his challenge, expertly snatched the lead from Ronnie on lap 39 of the 67, and never looked back. At the chequered flag he was almost 3 seconds ahead.

That Silverstone victory was a success that surprised many of Revson's critics. Up to '72 he had been perceived as a solid, reliable performer, but his turn of speed with the superb McLaren M23 proved quite an eye-opener. Later that year he added the Canadian Grand Prix at Mosport Park to his tally of victories, and also hit the society headlines when he began dating the then Miss World, American model Marjorie Wallace.

Yet despite this success, he had a slightly strained relationship with Teddy Mayer, with whose late brother Timmy he had been a classmate at Cornell and, later, a fledgling Formula Junior team-mate in the early 1960s.

'He was something of a funny guy,' said Teddy. 'I'd known him for all those years and formed the impression that he'd got a bit of a chip on his shoulder. He had a very short fuse and I had a few run-ins with him, but by the end of his time at McLaren he was very quick indeed.

'That victory in the British Grand Prix was really quite impressive.

But I remember one big row centred round whether he would run one particular F1 race or go to Pocono to run the Indianapolis car. I had to put my foot down and point out that our sponsor, Gulf Oil, wanted him at Pocono and that was where he was going. So he went to Pocono and absolutely flew . . .'

As a result of the tensions that built up, Revson switched to the promising Shadow team only to be killed during testing in preparation for the South African Grand Prix when his car suffered a front suspension failure and he ploughed into the guard rail at the old Kyalami circuit's tricky downhill Barbecue bend.

By the end of the '73 season McLaren concluded that Scheckter might be a little too expensive to keep on a long-term basis. It was not a perspicacious decision. They let him go, he signed for Tyrrell and won two races in 1974, the first step on a path that would take him to a World Championship for Ferrari five years later.

This would not be the first occasion on which the post-Bruce management team made the wrong decision; in 1977, having given Gilles Villeneuve his F1 debut at Silverstone, they let the Canadian slip through their fingers and sign for Ferrari the following year. The justification for that particular move – that he might be expensive in terms of damaged cars while he learned the F1 trade – seems no less crassly inexplicable today than it did 20 years ago.

Teddy Mayer was firmly established in the McLaren commercial driving seat by the end of the 1973 season. The American lawyer with the nasal twang could be a prickly little customer. Incredibly motivated and single-minded, he was as much a perfectionist in his own way as Ron Dennis would become a decade further down the line. And, like Dennis, there were times when Mayer could also make his workforce climb the walls in frustration.

With Bruce gone, some said, there was no softening Mayer's asperities. His priorities were the McLaren team first, second and last. He also had little time for the press at a time when F1 was barnstorming its way into a high-profile, supposedly media-friendly era. Yet, paradoxically, Bruce would probably have approved of his attitude; he was very much Keeper of the McLaren Flame. And when you got to know him, Teddy was nowhere near as intolerant and dismissively aggressive as he appeared at first glance. Not quite, anyway.

McLaren had a three-year sponsorship deal with Yardley, but as cost inflation in F1 rocketed out of control towards the end of 1973, it was clear that the deal was grossly inadequate if the team's finances were to sustain a fully competitive effort the following year. Ironically, just as McLaren had inherited Yardley in the role of a disillusioned former BRM sponsor at the end of 1971, so the company that replaced them – the Philip Morris Marlboro cigarette brand – was hard on their heels at the end of 1973.

McLaren simply couldn't turn Marlboro away. Their package would enable the transfer of 1973 World Champion Emerson Fittipaldi from key rivals Lotus, and the budget would be supplemented by additional backing from the Texaco oil company. At the time there was talk of the whole Marlboro/Texaco/McLaren package being worth more than £600,000 sterling for a single year – perhaps four times as much as Yardley could afford. Yet the cosmetics company was determined not to have its F1 involvement with McLaren swept aside so lightly.

Towards the end of 1973 Yardley issued a robust press statement outlining its dissatisfaction with the situation. I was working on the editorial staff of *Motoring News* at the time, very much feeling my way in my first season as an F1 reporter, when the Yardley missive landed on my desk.

Within a couple of hours of its arrival, Mayer – with whom I'd scarcely exchanged more than a couple of words up to that point – rang up all pally and told me that it really wouldn't be very helpful if we published the Yardley statement. When I voiced mild reservations, he came on quite strong, hinting that perhaps legal action might follow if we didn't tow the line. He was trying it on.

Not then fully understanding how F1 worked, I caved in cravenly and acquiesced to his request. I feel ashamed about that. But it was certainly an instructive lesson in the politics of grand prix motor racing, and I came to enjoy a quite cordial – if combative – relationship with Mayer over subsequent years.

Many years later Teddy would tell my fellow author Doug Nye: 'Though we had a very good relationship with Yardley we just could not afford to fulfil the deal for '74. The money they wanted to pay was just sufficient for one car and they were insisting we run two.

'Marlboro had taken over when Yardley had opted out of BRM and they had a similar experience, and now they were courting us, asking if we'd be free to run with them for '74 and '75. To say that Yardley weren't happy with what was happening would be putting it mildly, and contractually we were sailing very close to the wind, that's true.'

This increasingly untenable situation was eventually resolved when the team finalised an arrangement to run two Marlboro/Texaco-sponsored M23s for Emerson Fittipaldi and Denny Hulme, plus a single Yardley-backed car for Mike Hailwood. As things transpired, it all worked our remarkably well, with near enough absolute parity of equipment between the two teams.

Mayer later admitted that there were some other complexities to the deal that were not obvious from the outside, not least the fact that Bernie Ecclestone was bidding hard to sign Marlboro as title sponsor for his own Brabham F1 team.

'I went down to Bernie's country house one Sunday and I can

remember we were playing gin rummy as Bernie pumped me endlessly as to what I was doing,' he said. 'The whole business was further hampered by the fact that Yardley's Dennis Matthews lived close by Bernie's place and I had to excuse myself for an hour or so while I nipped over there and signed the final deal providing for the single Yardley car in 1974.

'Bernie never let up pumping me for information . . . and I think he felt slightly annoyed that McLaren eventually pulled off the Marlboro deal as well, leaving Brabham without a major sponsor in 1974.'

In fact Hailwood only got the Yardley-backed drive after Chris Amon, an old McLaren hand who'd driven with Bruce in the team's Can-Am sports cars back in the mid-1960s, had been asked to return to the team. However, by then Amon – with an admirable, if misplaced, sense of loyalty – had committed himself to the disastrous F1 project bearing his own name, which later foundered without trace. It was the story of the likeable New Zealander's career.

Fittipaldi drove brilliantly throughout 1974, balancing sheer speed with great tactical acuity to win his second World Championship in the face of a strong Ferrari challenge. Sadly, the genial Mike Hailwood's F1 career ended when he crashed the Yardley McLaren at Nurburgring during the German Grand Prix, sustaining serious leg injuries. His place in the car was taken by the young German Jochen Mass, who then transferred to the Marlboro/Texaco line-up as Fittipaldi's number two in 1975.

The completion of the 1974 season also saw the curtain fall on another link back to the pioneering days of Bruce McLaren, when Denny Hulme finally quit F1 at the age of 37. His dry, laconic humour would be greatly missed in the pit lane, although he remained close to the sport for the rest of his life, sadly dying of a heart attack at the wheel of a BMW saloon while racing at Bathurst, Australia, in the autumn of 1992.

Fittipaldi finished second to Ferrari's Niki Lauda in the 1975 World Championship, having won five grands prix across two seasons with McLaren. Mayer and his colleagues desperately wanted him to continue with them in 1976, but Emerson eventually succumbed to the blandishments of his elder brother Wilson and left to join the much-touted 'all Brazilian' F1 operation that Wilson had started in '75 with backing from the Copersucar sugar marketing cartel. It was the end of the younger Fittipaldi as a front-line grand-prix-winning force.

Within minutes of being told that Emerson was leaving, Mayer was on the telephone to British driver James Hunt to open negotiations for 1976. Hunt, who won the 1975 Dutch Grand Prix in Lord Hesketh's F1 car, had been rendered apparently unemployed when Hesketh closed its doors at the end of the season. Now Mayer signed him for a £40,000 retainer, a bargain considering what was to follow.

In 1976 Hunt drove the three-year-old M23 to victory in the World Championship by a single point over Niki Lauda, helped in no small measure by his Austrian friend's absence from three races recovering from the burns he sustained when his Ferrari crashed at the Nurburgring.

James was just the tonic McLaren needed. Youthful, aggressive and highly motivated, he was at his own personal peak through the second half of 1976 and the first part of 1977, by which time the old M23 had been supplanted by the new M26, essentially a tidied-up, lightened and more sophisticated version of its immediate predecessor.

Yet by the middle of 1977 it was clear that McLaren's technical capability was starting to drift. Colin Chapman's innovative design team at Lotus had already produced the Type 78 wing car, harnessing the air flow beneath the chassis for added downforce, and was working hard on the full ground effect Type 79 for the 1978 season. Hunt would become frustrated as he attempted to combat these superior rival machines, first over-driving to keep up and eventually losing his motivation.

By the end of 1978 McLaren's fortunes had faded dramatically and there seemed no obvious way out. After three seasons Mayer made it clear that he would not be renewing Hunt's contract for 1979, by now satisfied that James's competitive spark was all but extinguished. It was an accurate, if obvious, conclusion. Hunt switched to Walter Wolf's team for the following season – and quit racing for good after only seven races.

There was worse to come. At the end of '78 McLaren had signed a deal for the dynamic Swede Ronnie Peterson to lead the team as Hunt's replacement. But Ronnie died of complications that set in after he broke both his legs in a pile-up at Monza seconds after the start of the 1978 Italian Grand Prix. Poignantly, it was James Hunt who risked his life plunging into the flaming wreckage in an effort to help the injured Swedish driver.

As a result of this, the popular Ulsterman John Watson was signed to partner Frenchman Patrick Tambay – who'd replaced Mass at the end of 1977 – in the McLaren line-up for 1979. Gordon Coppuck pencilled a new ground-effect chassis, the M28, as the team's own interpretation of the Lotus 79 concept. The car was ready early and well tested before the first race. But it proved to be a hopelessly uncompetitive proposition. And Marlboro, the team's loyal sponsors, were becoming ever so slightly uneasy as McLaren made heavy weather of this latest setback.

Watson arrived at McLaren in an upbeat and positive mood. A mild-mannered fellow from Hollywood, just outside Belfast, he'd been raised in a family that had always been keen on motor racing. His father Marshall, a Belfast car dealer, had won the first saloon car race to be held in Northern Ireland on the Newtownards airfield at the wheel of a Citroën Light 15.

John's own racing career progressed through club racing to international Formula 2 from the start of the 1970 season, driving a Brabham BT30 financed by his father. Despite breaking a leg and an arm in a practice shunt at the spectacular Rouen-les-Essarts road circuit in northern France, he eventually battled his way into full-time F1 in 1974 driving a private Brabham entered by Paul Michaels, the North London businessman who owned Hexagon of Highgate, the luxury car dealers.

In 1975 John drove briefly for Team Surtees before switching to the new F1 operation established by Roger Penske, taking the place of his original driver Mark Donohue who had died of brain injuries sustained when a tyre failure caused him to crash during the race morning warm-up prior to the 1975 Austrian Grand Prix.

Watson would earn the team a superb, if poignant, victory in that same race a year later, forfeiting his beard in a personal wager with Penske, the millionaire Ivy League team boss clearly having disapproved of this hirsute appendage from the outset.

After Penske withdrew from F1 at the end of that season, 'Wattie' moved to the Bernie Ecclestone-owned Brabham-Alfa squad, where he raced for two season, the second as team-mate to Niki Lauda. In terms of sheer natural talent, there has never been any doubt in my mind that John was amongst the very best drivers I have been fortunate enough to watch during 25 years of grand prix reporting. He was one of those guys who literally had ability dancing like static electricity from his fingertips. Yet in an era when driving talent alone was increasingly becoming only part of the complex F1 package, he was less and less able to string together any sustained success.

One of the problems was that he projected the image of a 'softie' when he was out of the cockpit. Watson might have been every bit as uncompromising a competitor in the technical sense when it came to outbraking a rival at 170mph for the *Ostkurve* at the old Osterreichring, but as soon as he undid his belts and removed his helmet, he tended to come across as a bit of a fusspot. And I say that as a friend.

By the end of the 1978 season, Ecclestone was keen to replace Watson with new boy Nelson Piquet. Peterson's untimely death left McLaren facing a driver crisis, so Watson was the obvious man. At least, he would have been had the McLaren M28 not turned out to be the most appalling dog imaginable.

McLaren designer Gordon Coppuck reasoned that the best way to develop the ground-effect theme pioneered by Lotus was to build a car with a larger plan area in an effort to produce more aerodynamic downforce. The result was an obviously huge machine that set a promising pace in early testing. But once the racing started, the sun went in.

The M28 suffered from major structural shortcomings stemming from problems with the bonding of its cast magnesium beams with the Nomex honeycomb monocoque. The 1979 season opened on a disappointing note, with Watson held responsible for triggering a multiple accident at the start of the Argentine Grand Prix at Buenos Aires for which he was duly fined. At least he finished the restarted race in third place, but that was as good as the M28 got.

The second race, in Brazil, saw the McLaren team's fortunes evaporate in acute despair. The M28 generated insufficient grip and it was too heavy and slow on the straight as a result. By 1 May, with only four rounds of the World Championship completed, Mayer sanctioned the construction of a completely new car.

'That M28 was ghastly, a disaster,' he remembered. 'It was ludicrous, quite diabolical. Gordon's track record was not looking too clever with the M28 following on behind the M26. I'm afraid we ignored all the crucial design precepts that a car should be as light, agile and compact as possible. And its failure came at a particularly difficult time for the team.

'Interestingly, the M28's uncompetitiveness didn't unduly get on top of Watson. It was so obvious that the car was hopeless that he didn't worry about it. It was later that we had problems, in 1980, when he got his hands on the M29.'

The first M29, a more conventional aluminium sheet monocoque with a single central fuel cell, was completed in time for John Watson to finish a strong fourth in the British Grand Prix at Silverstone. The new car at least enabled the team to hold its own to the end of the year, but it was now becoming clear that the existing McLaren management was swimming against an unstoppable tide.

For 1980, although Watson was retained, the team decided to replace Patrick Tambay, whose confidence by now had been completely undermined by a bruising two years with the team. At Watkins Glen in 1970, Marlboro's Paddy McNally introduced Mayer to a compact young Frenchman with a distinctive bent nose and a cheeky grin. This confident little Charles Aznavour lookalike would eventually carve a niche in F1 history as the most successful grand prix driver of all time. It was Alain Prost.

A month later Mayer invited him to test the McLaren M29. 'I watched for ten laps, then ran to my car to get a draft contract from my briefcase,' he later recounted. Prost would be signed as the team's new driver for 1980. He finished sixth on his debut in Buenos Aires, fifth on his second outing at Interlagos. Within no time at all he established himself firmly as de facto team leader.

Yet in Prost's mind he was having too many accidents in the M29.

He broke a bone in his wrist when he shunted in practice for the South African Grand Prix at Kyalami, and the suspension broke again in Spain, pitching him into the barrier, thankfully this time without harm. He was also involved in the multiple shunt on the first corner at Monaco, a race at which Watson suffered the indignity of failing to qualify.

The McLaren team was getting rather bored with John's lacklustre performances, but their disapproval came with a cruel edge. John was increasingly regarded as a figure of fun, something that this dignified gentleman certainly did not deserve. In practice for one race, a decal reading 'John WhatsWrong' was placed on the side of his car. It was all slightly asinine, on reflection, and Prost certainly felt uncomfortable about all these cheap shots.

To this day Alain has varied memories of the team-mates for whom he has driven over the past two decades, and he rates Watson very highly. Despite the embarrassment he was obviously causing to John professionally, he never found the Ulsterman anything but cordial and supportive.

'John was under no real obligation to be helpful with me or forthcoming with technical information,' recalls Alain. 'But I have a great affection for him. He was always available to give me helpful advice and, of course, knew every circuit on the Championship trail very well. He did all this despite the fact that I was making life pretty difficult for him in all manner of ways.

'In all honesty, I was much better than John when it came to setting up the cars and I was faster. This caused a lot of gossip within the team. I didn't appreciate some of the facetious remarks that were made about him. But John was very long-suffering and gentlemanly about all this. I wouldn't have put up with it in the way he did.'

However, McLaren was by now in deep trouble and not even Prost could extricate the team from this dilemma. Marlboro had been telling the team that something had to be done ever since the middle of the 1979 season. When John Barnard, formerly a member of the McLaren design team in the early 1970s, returned from the US and his stint as designer of the successful Chaparral Indycar, Mayer offered him a job.

His idea was that Barnard could work with Gordon Coppuck to raise the level of McLaren's technical game. Marlboro and Barnard wanted Mayer to dismiss Coppuck, but he wasn't prepared to do that, so the deal fell through. As a result, Barnard went off and began to forge a partnership with Ron Dennis, whose Project Four team was by then running a ProCar BMW M1 for Niki Lauda with Marlboro sponsorship.

By mid-1980 Dennis and Barnard had an F1 design under way. The previous year Marlboro had 'suggested' to Mayer that McLaren might consider an amalgamation with Project Four, but the

McLaren boss simply wasn't interested. In the summer of 1980 the cigarette sponsor came back with the same suggestion, this time couched more firmly in the form of a thinly veiled instruction. The message was quite simple: if McLaren wanted to retain Marlboro backing, they'd better get into bed with Dennis and Barnard. And sharpish.

The new company, McLaren International, formally came into being in September 1980. Ron and Teddy were joint Managing Directors of the new company, but with Mayer already owning 85 per cent of the original McLaren shareholding, he now became the biggest single shareholder in the new concern, holding 45 per cent of the McLaren International equity. Gordon Coppuck was not part of the new arrangement, and although it pained Mayer to break the news to his long-time employee, he recalled that his former Chief Designer seemed almost relieved at the news.

Almost immediately there was a crisis over Prost's future with the team, which came to a head in practice for the United States Grand Prix at Watkins Glen.

'That car, the M29, was always breaking,' reflected Alain. 'Over the season I had six or seven serious accidents. You know, if your car loses a wheel in every race, I think it's not good and I don't think any driver can accept that.

'The worst was at the end of the year, in qualifying at Watkins Glen, where the suspension broke in a fourth-gear corner. I hit the wall very hard, and got a big bang on the head. That was something, I can tell you. I was knocked out.

'When I got back to the pits eventually, I heard people in the team telling journalists I had made a mistake, gone too fast on cold tyres – even though I'd already done eight laps. The following day they wanted me to race, even though I knew after the warm-up I wasn't fit. My head ached like hell, and I hadn't been able to sleep all night.

'After their remarks to the press after the accident, I made up my mind to leave. I said, "OK, if you want to say things like that, it's finished. I have a three year contract with you, but I won't drive for you any more. If you won't release me, OK. I stop Formula 1."'

A Renault deal was offered to the Frenchman for 1981, which made many people at McLaren feel bitter, reasoning that the French national team had used its financial muscle to poach their new young talent. But Alain didn't see it that way at all.

'When I sign a contract, I mean it,' he insisted. 'When I give my word, I mean it. Whatever people say, I did not leave McLaren because I got a better offer. After Montreal [1980], with one race left, I didn't know what to do. I felt I should stay with McLaren, because of my contract with them, but at the same time I was getting more and more worried about suspension failures all the time.

'You reach a point where you *expect* the car to break, where you are waiting for it to happen. And in those circumstances you can't drive properly. But what happened at the Glen really made up my mind for me.'

This glitch in the relationship took place before Dennis and Barnard took day-to-day management control of the team. 'John Barnard and I went to Canada and Watkins Glen just to watch, having no active involvement in the team,' said Dennis.

'In Canada I had some good conversations with Alain and he'd pretty much committed to staying with the team, then we went to Watkins Glen and the car broke. Effectively Teddy told the world that it was a driving mistake – and it was very clearly not a driving mistake – and it was Alain's disenchantment with the management that was functioning at that point which caused him to leave.'

This breach between McLaren and Prost would not prevent the two of them being thrown together again as unexpected partners some three years later. By then, the fortunes of McLaren International would have changed quite dramatically. For the better.

3

Ron Dennis and McLaren International, 1980–82

TODAY THERE ARE many routes by which an enthusiastic and committed young person can enter the professional motor racing business. The club racing scene is crammed to overflowing with bright-eyed young racers all hoping to follow in the footsteps of Mika Hakkinen and David Coulthard, and indeed McLaren has actively supported the advancement of bright new talent since 1989, when the first Young Driver of the Year award was presented, appropriately enough to Coulthard, as part of a programme run in conjunction with *Autosport* magazine.

Yet for those who want to be involved in this professional and wide-ranging sport, competing at the sharp end is not the only option. Highly qualified mechanical and automotive engineers will always have a chance of making a good career in motorsport, whether in F1, Indycars, touring cars or rallying, and there is also plenty of scope for good administrators, mechanics and PR people. In short, the opportunities have never been greater or more wide-ranging.

In the mid-1960s motor racing was not like that at all. 'It was a bit like walking round a building with no windows and only two doors,' reflects Ron Dennis. 'The only ways in were as a driver – which meant you had to have private means – or as a mechanic.'

Dennis entered F1 as a mechanic, attending his first grand prix working on Jochen Rindt's Cooper-Maserati in the summer of 1966. He was just 19 years old.

The fact that Dennis was once a mechanic has become a curious issue in contemporary grand prix racing. The more successful he became in his role as McLaren's MD, the more people remarked, 'Of course he started out as a mechanic.' Most were full of admiration for what he had achieved, but a minority used it as a pejorative stick with which, if not to beat him, then at least occasionally to give him a provocative prod.

In turn, this has made Ron a trifle over-defensive about his modest starting point within the sport. Most of us on the touchlines, in the pit lane, press room and paddock, genuinely admire and respect what he has achieved. Why he should sometimes appear to be so unduly sensitive about it remains a puzzle.

Dennis worked on Rindt's Cooper, then shadowed the Austrian driver's switch to Brabham in 1968. Ron admits that he wasn't taken with him, agreeing with journalist Denis Jenkinson's assessment that Rindt was too big for his boots.

'Yes, he was arrogant and really didn't treat people properly,' Dennis told me in 1990, 'especially the mechanics. I recall at the 1967 German Grand Prix Roy Salvadori [the team manager] telling him that he'd better hurry up and get ready, because it was almost time for the start.

'Rindt just replied, "They won't dare start the German Grand Prix without me." So one of the other mechanics looked up and muttered rather acidly, "Why don't you pop down the road with your helmet and fill it with ten pounds of potatoes?"

'I left Cooper at the end of 1967 and it was several months to the first grand prix of the next year. I only went to Brabham on the express condition that I didn't work in the production shop, and was therefore involved in building the prototype F1 car for the 1968 season. I just developed a good relationship with Jack and, before the season actually started, he asked me to work on his car. So I said "OK, but you break the news to Rindt."'

Dennis shed few tears when Rindt switched to Lotus at the end of the '68 season, after which he was promoted to Chief Mechanic. Yet it was in the paddock at Zandvoort that Ron struck up one of the most personally important and enduring friendships of his professional career when he met up with Neil Trundle.

'We don't do things like that at Brabham's.' Trundle, who'd recently arrived in the team, glanced up from cleaning out the gearbox bellhousing on Rindt's Brabham BT26 and found Dennis addressing him with what he took to be a disapproving stare.

'How would you like a punch on your nose?' was Trundle's considered response. It may have seemed like an unpromising start, but the two men soon became close friends. To this day Neil continues to work at McLaren International on gearbox development, long since reconciled to the differing fortunes that he and his former partner have experienced.

At the end of the 1970 season Jack Brabham took the decision to retire, and, having effectively run his F1 team in the season's-end races in North America, Dennis felt sufficiently confident to strike out in partnership with Trundle. By the end of the year they had decided that they would establish their own operation to contest the highly competitive European Formula 2 Trophy series the following season. The team was titled 'Rondel Racing Ltd' – with hindsight, an incredibly corny acronym, but one that would not easily be forgotten.

It was originally decided that the team's effort should concentrate on a single Brabham BT36 to be driven by up-and-coming Australian Tim Schenken. But then Dennis hit on a means of further enhancing the planned team's commercial viability.

The financial structure of F2 at the time meant that any team running a driver with a proven record of achievement in either grands prix or international sports car events would benefit financially from the race organisers. In 1970 the Swiss driver Clay Regazzoni had not only won the European F2 Trophy for the Italian Tecno team, but had also won the Italian Grand Prix at the wheel of a works Ferrari.

Regazzoni was available to Rondel and it initially appeared that there was a good chance of gaining valuable backing from Meubles Arnold, a French furniture manufacturer owned by passionate racing enthusiast Marcel Arnold, who had supported Clay's racing efforts in F3 back in 1967.

Negotiations went ahead, but then Ferrari works driver Ignazio Giunti was killed in an appalling accident at the wheel of one of the factory 312P sports cars during the Buenos Aires 1000km race in January 1971. Enzo Ferrari got a fit of the jitters about releasing his contracted drivers to compete for any other team, so the proposed deal fell through. Dennis went back to the drawing board to explore other options.

The scheme thus reverted to plans for a single car for Schenken. But then Bob Wollek, a young French F3 rising star (who would later carve a reputation as a successful sports car racer), got wind of Rondel's plans and arrived with sufficient backing from the Motul oil company to get things moving.

It is perhaps instructive to reflect how budgets have multiplied in geometric progression over the past 27 years. 'Ron Tauranac loaned us three F2 chassis, we sold them at the end of the year and paid him the difference,' remembers Dennis. 'So he effectively created a cashflow, but it was also good for him because we were the only ones running his cars really competently. We bought the engines from Bernie Ecclestone which had come back from the South American F2 Temporada series as deck cargo. They were covered in corrosion, but we tidied them up a bit and then went on to use them.'

The cars were transported around Europe in a smart pale blue transporter. 'It's worth between four and five thousand pounds now,' Dennis told me proudly just before Christmas, 1971, 'but it was in a positively dreadful mess when we acquired it. It had previously been owned by Ron Harris [one-time Lotus F2 team owner] and had stood gently decomposing behind the premises of Mike Spence Limited in Maidenhead since the end of 1968. The paintwork was peeling off, the woodwork rotten, but mechanically the thing wasn't too bad.'

Even so, it looked as though Rondel might be unable to afford its restoration until Dennis and Trundle hit on a novel solution to their problems. Gathering around all their friends from the local pub, they transported them down to the Brabham factory en masse where they were put to work stripping, spraying and generally refurbishing the truck in return for liberal supplies of liquid refreshment.

The total expenditure on six Cosworth FVA engines in 1971 was around £10,500, added to which had to be added £2,500 for routine rebuilding during the course of the season. In addition to Dennis and Trundle, who did more than their fair share of hands-on work with the cars, the team had just two others on its workforce. They were 27-year-old Clive Walton, like Dennis a Cooper old sweat, and 23-year-old Preston Anderson, an ex-Brabham lad who'd worked on Jochen Rindt's Formula 2 Lotus 69s during the 1970 season.

Rondel benefited from a lucky break when the lads were down at the Brabham factory building up the BT36 earmarked for Bob Wollek. Graham Hill, then a member of the Brabham F1 squad, wandered in and Dennis asked him whether he'd be interested in doing some of the early-season races.

He did just that, finishing second in the European Trophy season-opener at Hockenheim and following it up with a great victory in the Easter Monday Thruxton F2 international, always a major prestige event in the spring calendar.

In an effort to attract potential sponsors, Dennis and Trundle prepared a brochure outlining Rondel's aims and objectives – in itself something of an advanced move in the early 1970s – and an extraordinary sequence of events brought them into contact with somebody well equipped to help the fledgling team.

The father of Dennis's ex-fiancée owned a large antique dealers and told Ron about a Ferrari owner who was something of an antique connoisseur and regularly visited his premises. Ron promptly despatched a copy of the brochure to the individual concerned, who turned out to be Tony Vlassopulos, a City ship broker who was also a great racing enthusiast and a regular commentator at club meetings organised by the British Automobile Racing Club. He helped a great deal in smoothing out the financial ups and downs of Rondel's maiden racing season, taking over the role of company Chairman.

Vlassopulos always had faith that Dennis would go far, and remains a staunch fan of his former protégé to this day. Now a practising Solicitor Advocate, one got a taste of Tony's continuing respect for Dennis as recently as November 1995 when the local planning authorities were considering McLaren International's plans to move its factory to a new site.

In a letter to a local newspaper, he described Ron as 'a genius' and went on to make it clear that he regarded McLaren in the same light as Ferrari in terms of the team's importance to the British motor racing industry. 'Ron Dennis,' he continued, 'apart from being one of the most successful businessmen in the land, is a very reasonable and logical man.'

Of course, Rondel's operating costs seem puny in the extreme when viewed from a distance of more than a quarter of a century. 'Each time the transporter leaves for a race meeting, its basic running costs can be reckoned at £150,' said Dennis at the time. A set of four Firestone YB24 slicks cost around £130 and there was always around £1,200 worth of rubber in the back of the team's transporter at any one race.

Armstrong shock absorbers for the Brabhams came in at about £10 apiece, brake pads were £30 a race and an engine rebuild £150 a time, assuming that nothing was wrong.

On the face of it, Rondel Racing was just another F2 team surfing the intensely competitive waves of the European Championship. Yet, if you looked closer, it was clearly a great deal more than that. In 1971 many racing cars had been prepared in a grimy lock-up garage – and looked as though they had. Rondel's machines were spick and span in a way that was almost unheard of.

Dennis, who admits he's 'a bit of an old woman' when it comes to immaculate preparation, had effectively brought F1 standards down into F2. Yet it was even more than that; looking back, he was effectively laying down a marker in terms of preparation that would eventually set the tone for McLaren International in F1 – a standard at which other teams would eventually have to aim.

Tim Schenken finished fourth in the 1971 European Trophy series in the Rondel Brabham and the team continued with success through 1972 using Brabham BT38s. In 1973, with added backing from Motul oil, the team built its own Motul F2 chassis, designed by Ray Jessop, and Ron's ambitions also extended towards making an early F1 bid.

Unfortunately the economic climate at the end of 1973, highlighted by the Arab–Israeli war, did nothing for commercial confidence. The Jessop-designed F1 car was eventually taken over by Vlassopulos and his friend Ken Grob after Dennis had left the organisation, briefly emerging as the Token F1 challenger in 1974 when it was driven by Tom Pryce, David Purley and Ian Ashley. Rondel ceased trading.

Meanwhile, John Hogan of Philip Morris approached Dennis to run a couple of unknown Ecuadorian drivers in Formula 2. Hogan, who had earlier worked as a Coca Cola promotions man in the UK and helped get sponsorship for Rondel Racing, was another great admirer of Ron's focused professionalism. The duration of the subsequent Marlboro McLaren link would largely be down to his sustained confidence.

Dennis remained in F2 for much of the 1970s. In 1974 he

established a new company called Project Three, then Project Four started operating from 1976. It remained a significant F2 player through to the end of the decade and fielded the winning 1980 British F3 Championship car for Swede Stefan Johansson. But by then a more important turn of events had taken place.

In 1979 BMW introduced its new M1 super-car and Project Four was one of the companies commissioned to prepare a number of these machines for the one-make 'ProCar' series that would be staged as support events at key European grands prix in 1979. More significantly, Project Four ran its own Marlboro-backed M1 for Niki Lauda in the 1979 ProCar series – and won the title. Now Ron wanted to make the step forward into grand prix racing on his own account.

Dennis, whose company was now based in Pool Road, Woking, barely a mile from McLaren International's current headquarters, was keen to get a deal together with a top F1 designer. He wanted John Barnard to come aboard, although he also approached Gordon Murray at Brabham and Patrick Head at Williams, just on the off-chance that they might be considering a move.

Barnard, recalls Dennis, didn't seem to be terribly interested at first glance, but when Ron made it clear that he would have an absolutely free hand on the technical side, the two men began to make progress. Dennis showed him a carbon-fibre rear wing from one of the BMW M1 racers. It set Barnard thinking.

Within weeks John came back and suggested making the whole monocoque out of this novel material on the basis that its supreme rigidity would be hugely advantageous when it came to making a slender ground-effect chassis. Ron then went to work to try and raise the finance, an estimated £80,000. It wasn't enough. But events were going their way. By the end of 1980 Marlboro would have brokered the marriage with McLaren with the result that McLaren International came into being.

Teaming up with John Barnard would turn out to be one of the most perspicacious decisions Dennis ever made. Their partnership lasted barely six years, but laid the hard core of McLaren International's foundations. In many ways they were very similar characters; motivated, uncompromising in their quest for excellence and, in their own way, absolute perfectionists. Their professional relationship was volatile and explosive, giving rise to rows of heroic decibel proportions that have long since been written into Formula 1 legend.

Born at Wembley in 1946, John had initially studied engineering at Brunel Technical College and Watford Technical College, ending up in the GEC design department working on machinery for producing electric light bulbs. For a life-long car enthusiast, this was understandably a short-term project, and in 1969 he joined Lola

Cars at Huntingdon as a junior in the drawing office.

At the turn of the 1970s Lola was producing a wide range of proprietary racing cars for every imaginable international and national formula. Moreover, by curious coincidence it was in the Lola design office that John met up with a like-minded engineer called Patrick Head. Over a decade later, Head's Williams F1 designs would spearhead the battle for the World Championship against the Barnard-designed McLaren-TAGs.

In 1972 Barnard received an invitation to join McLaren as number two designer to Gordon Coppuck, who was then in the final stages of producing the M23 that would win the 1974 and '76 World Championships, respectively driven by Fittipaldi and Hunt. Barnard carried out much of the detail design work on the M23 monocoque, but found that his perfectionist streak sat uncomfortably with the slightly free-wheeling atmosphere that the team had inherited from its founder Bruce McLaren.

Barnard felt McLaren was a little too informal for his taste. Input from the mechanics might have been all very well, he reflected, but he already believed that it was the Chief Designer who should be drawing the crucial lines in the sand. As a result he accepted an invitation to join the Vel's Parnelli Indy car team, based in California, the Barnard-designed Parnelli VPJ6B winning its first race. This led to an offer to join Jim Hall's Texas-based Chaparral team where he designed the Chaparral 2K, which would win both the Indy 500 and the CART Championship in 1980.

Yet by the time the Chaparral had achieved its great success, Barnard had split with Hall. He felt that he had reached an agreement that due credit for the design should be accorded to him, and Hall had neglected to make sufficient acknowledgement of that role. He arrived back in the UK just in time for Ron Dennis to make contact with him.

After McLaren International's formation, there followed a bumpy transitional phase as Barnard finalised the design of his new carbon-fibre composite challenger. Hercules Aerospace, in Salt Lake City, were already deeply involved in carbon-fibre technology, and McLaren forged a deal for them to supply the necessary material for the new MP4 design, which was developed over the winter of 1981/82.

When the car was launched in early 1981, much was made of the fact that it was not only stiffer, lighter and more impact-resistant than a regular aluminium honeycomb monocoque, but that also the number of components used in its construction was cut by about 90 per cent. Barnard estimated that around 50 sections of aluminium were required to build a chassis like that on the discredited M29; now there were just five main CFC panels in addition to the outer shell.

There were sceptics, of course, who worried about the impact-resistance qualities of this new material not being all they were cracked up to be. In fact, the MP4 proved to be a fine car and, driven by John Watson and the erratic young Italian Andrea de Cesaris – whose family was well connected with Marlboro – really put McLaren International on the map.

The car made its first appearance at Long Beach at the start of 1981, although it was not raced. 'I have told Marlboro that we will win at least one grand prix this year,' Ron Dennis told me. It was easy to see why he felt so confident. The MP4 was a beautifully built car, its body panel fit and attention to detail looking immaculate alongside the suddenly outdated M29.

The 1981 season marked a change in F1 regulations in that sliding aerodynamic side skirts were banned in an effort by the governing body to reduce the lap speeds of the current breed of ground-effect cars. But pre-debut testing with the MP4 raised both drivers' hopes. Eventually Watson drove the car in the Argentine Grand Prix where he ran in the top ten before retiring with a rear-end vibration.

Having been robbed of the side skirts, McLaren, in common with most British F1 teams, embarked on a programme to enable the cars to run as close to the track surface as possible in an effort to claw back lost ground-effect downforce. But the new rules stipulated a minimum ground clearance; to get round this, the team fitted a progressive double spring system, the idea of which was that the car would compress down hard on its suspension at speed, then rise sufficiently to conform with the ground clearance rule when it came into the pits. Frankly, it was a silly era of F1 endeavour, but everybody had to do it.

Whatever the rules, it was the same for everyone, and the MP4 came on strongly almost from the start. Watson finished fourth behind Gilles Villeneuve's Ferrari and Jacques Laffite's Ligier in the Spanish Grand Prix at Madrid's Jarama circuit. That was followed by second place in a controversial two-part French Grand Prix at Dijon-Prenois before Dennis's pre-season prediction finally came true at the British Grand Prix.

John and Andrea were right on the Cosworth-engined, non-turbo pace from the outset at Silverstone and qualified fifth and sixth. Unfortunately, on the fourth lap of the race Villeneuve's Ferrari clipped the kerb at the Woodcote chicane and spun wildly in a cloud of tyre smoke in front of his immediate pursuers.

Alan Jones's Williams plunged into the Ferrari and retired on the spot. Watson braked almost to a standstill, escaping unscathed, but de Cesaris – who had been riding on John's gearbox despite specific instructions immediately before the race to keep off the tail of his team-mate's MP4 – locked up his brakes and spun off into the catch fencing.

Watson resumed ninth and really piled on the pressure. Thanks to some key retirements and brilliant driving on his own part, the Ulsterman was up to third by lap 16 with only the Renault turbos of Alain Prost and René Arnoux in front. Then Prost retired and John ran second, half a minute behind the surviving Renault, for the next 30 laps. Then Arnoux's exhaust note started to sound ragged and the French car slowed perceptibly.

With seven laps to go, Watson sliced through into the lead under braking for Becketts. The MP4 now only had to keep running through to the chequered flag for Ron Dennis's early season optimism to be vindicated. It did just that, and a delighted Watson posted his second career F1 victory, a remarkably emotional success on home soil.

'I just can't get used to the idea that it is me they're cheering for,' he said as he stepped down from the rostrum. 'Sure, it's a justification and reward for all the bad years, but I'm not totally satisfied. It wasn't a win from the front. I was slightly lucky, even though I had to work pretty hard to make up the ground I'd lost. There is a difference between winning and coming first.

'The car was better in the race than it had been in the warm-up during the morning. It was good by comparison with everything except Piquet's Brabham and the Renaults, but I still couldn't pitch it into the corners and nail the throttle as I wanted to. The back end was pretty skittish. Sure, I'm over the moon, but we've still got to improve if we want to win again.'

In fact, McLaren International would not win again until the following season, by which time there had been major changes put in hand that would affect the whole way in which the McLaren empire would develop over the next few years.

Dennis had two key developments up his sleeve at the start of the 1981 season. Behind the scenes his plans to lift his team out of the Cosworth-Ford customer arena into the turbo front line were gelling. But his most publicly obvious coup was to tempt Niki Lauda out of a retirement that had lasted a few months more than two seasons.

Lauda had spearheaded Ferrari's F1 revival in the mid-1970s, although the Austrian's international celebrity status was cemented in near-tragic circumstances when his car crashed in flames on the second lap of the 1976 German Grand Prix at the old Nurburgring. Despite being given the last rites of the Roman Catholic church as his life hung by a slender thread in the immediate aftermath of this shunt, Lauda mentally galvanised himself into making the most remarkable recovery and was back in the cockpit at Monza, finishing fourth in the Italian Grand Prix, barely ten weeks later.

Niki continued defending his 1975 title right up to the final round, when he pulled out of the Japanese Grand Prix on the rain-soaked Mount Fuji circuit. Championship or no Championship, Niki rightly judged that the conditions represented an unacceptable lottery. He lost the Championship to his great friend James Hunt, and was pilloried in the Italian press for losing his nerve.

Ferrari wanted Lauda to stay on in 1977, but suggested that he retire from driving and take over the role of team manager. It was a clever ruse. Transfer your lead driver to the role of non-playing captain and you defuse the possibility of him transferring to another team and racing against you.

Not a chance, said Niki, whose buck-toothed countenance had earned him a series of good-natured soubriquets during the early 1970s. He started off being nicknamed 'Super Mouse', then 'Super Rat', and from there via 'King Rat' he finally became universally referred to in the F1 paddocks as simply 'The Rat'.

Of course, Niki being Niki, he just loved all this irreverence, particularly in the days when it was the habit for Philip Morris-backed drivers to have strips across the front of their helmet vizors carrying their names between two Marlboro cigarette logos. It didn't take him long to have his altered from 'Niki Lauda' to 'King Rat'.

Having successfully thwarted Ferrari's efforts to demote him, Lauda duly returned to the cockpit, winning three grands prix and re-taking the Championship in 1977. Then he quit Ferrari two races before the end of the season, figuratively raising two fingers aloft at those who had sought to undermine his position.

For 1978 he switched to the Bernie Ecclestone-owned Brabham team, which was using Alfa Romeo engines, but failed to rekindle his consistent winning spark. By the middle of 1979 not even a switch to Cosworth V8 power could motivate Lauda in the face of strong opposition from his youthful new team-mate Nelson Piquet.

Away from the circuits his enthusiasm for aviation was gathering momentum. Although in the early 1970s he'd admitted to me that he was 'scared witless' after taking a trip in a single-engined trainer, he soon shrugged aside that early apprehension and became increasingly absorbed by flying.

Once the bug had bitten, Niki changed his aircraft more frequently than most motorists change their road cars. After owning a couple of Cessna Golden Eagles, he switched to his first jet, a Cessna Citation, which he later sold to Piquet, followed by a Learjet, a Falcon 10, Falcon 20, then back to a Learjet again. In the summer of 1978 he founded Lauda-air, a small charter airline using a twin-turboprop Fokker F27, and hoped to expand into the charter market. With that in mind, Lauda-air placed a deposit on a DC10 jetliner.

In practice for the 1979 Canadian Grand Prix, the penny finally dropped. Niki just didn't want to race any longer. He pulled into the pits and explained his predicament to Bernie Ecclestone. 'If you really want to go, then go now,' said the Brabham team chief sympathetically. Within hours he was in California on a visit to the McDonnell-Douglas factory.

'I was no longer getting any pleasure from driving round and round in circles,' he explained. 'I feel I have better things to do with my life.'

However, even though Niki didn't know it at the time, he was merely starting an extended pause for breath as far as his motor racing career was concerned. Life is all about timing. Lauda was usually a pretty shrewd operator, but the economic downturn of the early 1980s hit the aviation world hard. Lauda-air wound up having to cancel its options on the DC10 – a costly business indeed – and also had its hand full battling its state-sponsored rival, Austrian Airlines, when it came to obtaining route licences.

So when Ron Dennis invited Lauda to test a McLaren MP4 at Donington Park late in 1981, the team chief correctly judged that the Austrian might be ready for a new challenge. But apart from the obvious suggestion that it might be a good way of replenishing his depleted personal funds, why would a pragmatist like Niki risk his glittering reputation in such a speculative fashion?

'For two years I didn't take any real interest in motor racing,' he freely admitted. 'It was a chapter in my life I believed was over. My interest was now flying, and it absorbed me totally. I could watch a grand prix start and feel not even the slightest tremble of excitement or enthusiasm.

'I would think "what's that all about?" and turn away. It wasn't until I went to the 1981 Austrian Grand Prix that I suddenly found myself thinking "I wonder . . ."

'Once I'd made the decision to come back, the rest was easy. OK, so I had a few fleeting doubts when I did that Donington test for the first time, but it was my own fault, in a way. I'd put myself in a new car, on a track I'd never seen before, on radial tyres that I'd never tried before. But the worry soon passed. By the end of the day, I reckoned I could do it.'

So Lauda, the pragmatist, was back on the grand prix scene. Always lean, bordering on the skinny, he quickly recruited the assistance of Willi Dungl, the ski-training guru who'd helped him conquer the side effects of the Nurburgring accident, to organise his revived programme of physical training.

'Getting fit is simple and straightforward,' asserts Niki. 'All you have to do is to run for ten minutes today, 30 minutes tomorrow and an hour the next day. Run, run, run. Train, train, train . . . and then you're fit. There's nothing easier in the world, once you've taken the mental decision to do it.' Oh that life was so simple for mere mortals . . .

Niki's 1982 season yielded victory in his first race at Long Beach and a second win in the British Grand Prix at Brands Hatch. By mid-season Ron Dennis was moved to describe him as 'the best driver in the car, and the best driver out of the car. That doesn't mean he's got to be winning all the time, or be the fastest man out on the track. But he has a total commitment to what he is doing and – as long as the team is behind him – that means results. We provide the ingredients, and Niki mixes the cake.'

Behind the scenes, however, there had been some clever financial negotiations with Marlboro, the team's title sponsor, in order to secure Niki's services at the start of 1982. The Philip Morris top brass were apprehensive about his competitiveness and asked him how he could be certain that he would be competitive again.

'OK, pay me nothing for the driving and three million dollars for the publicity value,' Niki retorted. 'They agreed. At the same time I had a contract with Ron that, every third race, they could cancel the deal if I didn't perform. Then I won Long Beach and they came back to me pressing me to sign a long-term contract for 1983 and '84.

'So I said, "Fine, but now I want four million dollars, but now you have to pay for the driving as well – in the past you only agreed to employ me for the publicity." So for two years I had four million dollars, but it all went wrong when we started negotiating for 1985.'

By the end of the 1982 season Teddy Mayer had sold his stake in the company and left; he and Dennis were experiencing more than a slight degree of overlap in terms of responsibilities within the company. He left on reasonably good terms, although not without a couple of parting shots as to the qualities displayed by Dennis and Barnard respectively.

As far as Ron was concerned, he remarked that 'his strongest point is that he is an excellent salesman and, in terms of a broad brush, he's a good organiser. But I sometimes feel he has a weakness over personnel. I've been told quite frequently that I've been too tough with people, but perhaps Ron is the opposite, a little too weak. Also, he has in my view less mechanical knowledge than I would have expected from somebody who trained as a mechanic.' Ouch!

On Barnard, he observed: 'Beyond question, he is an absolutely brilliant designer whose great forte is making the overall package of a design fit together very well. To be frank, I think he's got an ego that he could well trip up over and that might be his undoing. Then again, it might not.'

Then he added: 'As for myself, I think my biggest error was not taking the decision to fire Gordon Coppuck at the end of 1979 and take on John Barnard there and then. But on the credit side, I'd like to think that I've helped Ron and John by showing them how an organisation the size of McLaren should work. Neither of them had ever run a company that size before. Only time will tell how they get on with it.'

'Not badly' was the answer, as history would subsequently relate.

4

The McLaren-TAGs: Prost v Lauda, 1983–84

THE TAG – TECHNIQUES d'Avante Garde – Group is a Luxembourg-based holding company established in 1977 by the late Akram Ojjeh, a Franco-Lebanese entrepreneur who may be best known to the public for arranging the sale of the SS *France*, the biggest ocean liner in the world, from the French Line to its new Norwegian owners.

Through the enthusiasm of Akram Ojjeh's two sons, Mansour and Abdulaziz, TAG became co-sponsors of the Williams Grand Prix team in 1980 at a time when Frank's operation was closely associated with various Saudi-Arabian backers.

Yet by 1982 a new partnership between TAG and McLaren International would be established when the TAG Group agreed to finance the development of a new bespoke Porsche-made 1.5-litre turbocharged V6 F1 engine exclusively for the McLaren team. It was the start of a wide-ranging and imaginative collaboration between TAG and McLaren that is flourishing strongly to this day in a wide range of activities, as we shall see as the story progresses.

In many ways the 1982 and '83 seasons saw McLaren International marking time. The Cosworth-engined MP4s were duly developed sufficiently for Lauda and Watson to win two races apiece in 1982. John's triumphs came in the Belgian Grand Prix at Zolder – after Keke Rosberg's Williams slid wide while leading on the penultimate lap – followed by a brilliant climb through the field at Detroit, passing cars left, right and centre, in what was probably the best performance of his entire career.

In 1983 at Long Beach John would effectively duplicate this performance after an apparently dismal qualifying session for McLaren that saw him qualify 22nd, one place ahead of Niki. In race conditions the cars' Michelin tyres had more opportunity to warm up in the slightly higher ambient temperatures that prevailed, and they stormed through to finish first and second, John taking the win. Yet the worst moment of the year came at Monaco when neither car could work up sufficient tyre temperatures in the cool qualifying conditions. Both drivers failed to make the cut as a result.

While all this was going on, Barnard and Dennis were sifting through the options available to them for a turbocharged engine. After detailed consideration, neither of them could see that there was a suitable engine available from the current range of power units competing in contemporary F1.

'Too many engine-makers give absolutely no thought as to how an engine is going to be installed in a chassis,' mused Barnard. 'They get it running on a test bed, then wonder why the chassis designer isn't interested. With the TAG-Porsche project, I had the final say, and I think subsequent events proved that had been worthwhile.'

In taking the decision to develop their own engine, McLaren rejected the opportunity of using Renault's V6 or BMW's in-line four-cylinder, production-based unit. Both were regarded by Barnard as involving too much in the way of design compromise.

The eventual decision to commission Porsche to build the TAG turbo was based on a number of key considerations. The German car-maker had a huge reservoir of technical knowledge relating to turbocharged racing engines, had a customer design department and responded favourably to Dennis's approach.

Rather than ask if Porsche would consider building and supplying an engine to McLaren as a promotional tool for themselves, Dennis asked if they would do the job as McLaren's sub-contractor on a purely commercial basis, with the British company covering all the costs. It was a question that few racing engine manufacturers had been asked before – or since, come to that – and they immediately agreed.

This arrangement put John Barnard firmly in the driving seat. He set out a very specific package of requests to Hans Mezger, the leader of Porsche's engine design group, the physical dimensions of which were largely dictated by the need to fit the new engine into the best ground-effect chassis package they could achieve.

That meant making the bottom end of the new engine as narrow as possible to allow for high-mounted ground-effect 'tunnels' on either side of the car, and the packaging of the top end to incorporate a vee angle not wider than 90 degrees. Barnard preferred a V6 cylinder configuration, but asked Porsche whether they felt a V8 might be better. In the event, they both settled on a twin-turbo 80-degree V6.

Ancillary pumps were mounted at the front of the engine and, while Mezger made all the decisions as far as the internal details of the engine were concerned – that's what they were being paid for – the overall package was strictly to Barnard's requirements. Mezger hadn't encountered a situation like this before and the relationship between the two men became uneasy at times. But the customer was always right and Porsche deferred to the McLaren design chief on detail after detail.

'I wouldn't compromise,' recalled Barnard. 'We had to have the right turbos. I made them pull in bolt heads that extended outside the overall prescribed profile of the engine, re-engineer various casings and so on; the work went back and forwards between us.'

The new engine had a bore and stroke of 82mm and 47.3mm for a displacement of 1499cc, and Porsche claimed an output of 600bhp, at a stroke 75bhp more than the naturally aspirated Cosworth DFY V8 engines that McLaren had been using from the start of 1983. A single KKK turbocharger was piped into the exhaust manifolding on each cylinder bank and the engine used a Bosch electronic management system. It was officially dubbed the TTE-P01.

The commercial side of the deal was straightforward. McLaren International itself initially funded the design and prototype build, after which its production rights were the team's property exclusively. That meant that Porsche could not build the engine for another team if Dennis failed to raise the finance for further development. In the event there was nothing to worry about. The new partnership with TAG clinched it. For the new backers, of course, becoming involved with a high-profile, blue-chip company such as Porsche could only be seen as a benefit.

The first McLaren-TAG had its shake-down race towards the end of 1983, Lauda debuting the car in the Dutch Grand Prix. But in doing so, he – in his own particular vernacular – 'had screwed Ron and John Barnard' to get the car out before the start of 1984.

'Barnard said that we were not going to race the turbo engine before 1984 because I want to make the perfect car,' said Niki. 'So I went to Ron and said, "Look, if we don't start the development now, the Ferraris will win every race. We have to start to develop this car as soon as possible. Otherwise our brakes won't work, our wings won't work, all the usual problems."

'Ron just said, "I'm sorry, I cannot convince John." So I went straight to Philip Morris, to Aleardo Buzzi, with the same argument. So Philip Morris came down on them hard and said, "You want the money, then you'd better start using the turbo engine." Ron fully understood, because I told him what I was going to do. But Barnard was furious. They hated me for that.'

Dennis felt genuinely aggrieved by Lauda's intervention, feeling that the development of the test car really did waste a lot of time. There were also dark rumours that Buzzi had docked the McLaren budget around $250,000 for not having the new TAG turbo-engined car running as early as had originally been scheduled. Sources close to McLaren hint that Dennis got his revenge on this issue by making a corresponding deduction from Lauda's retainer!

As a result of Lauda's lobbying, the first TAG turbo-engined McLaren was entered for the Austrian in the Dutch Grand Prix at Zandvoort on 28 August 1983. While John Watson quietly went about his business at the wheel of one of the regular Cosworth-engined McLaren MP4/1Cs, Niki grappled with precisely the problems he had predicted to Marlboro.

For this race the engine had been installed in an old development chassis, in fact one that Andrea de Cesaris had knocked about more than a bit during the 1981 season. In John's view this was less than ideal, the car being very hastily completed, with the mechanics even adding the last few finishing touches on the cross-Channel ferry as well as in the paddock at Zandvoort.

As part of the deal with Porsche, McLaren had also funded a sophisticated new electronic engine management system manufactured by Bosch, and the car displayed remarkably few mechanical problems. Its straight line speed virtually matched the turbocharged Ferrari and Brabham-BMW opposition, but lack of downforce and poor braking meant that Lauda could only qualify 19th.

In the race Niki ran as high as 12th before retiring with boiling brake fluid. At one point a length of padding somehow became disentangled and billowed out from behind the cockpit, making it look as though Niki was wearing a Red Baron-style silk scarf. Somebody commented that, knowing the Austrian, they wouldn't have been surprised!

Watson also had a TAG turbo-engined prototype for the next race, the Italian Grand Prix at Monza, qualifying 15th two places behind Lauda. The Ulsterman reported that he was having to learn all about the new driving technique involved in handling a turbocharged engine. In the race Lauda went out with an electrical problem, but John drove impressively through to seventh place before turbo failure thwarted his efforts after only 13 laps.

There were two more races to go, the Grand Prix of Europe at Brands Hatch, then the season's finale in South Africa on Johannesburg's Kyalami circuit. At Brands Hatch Lauda retired with engine failure, while John had a frightening 150mph spin into the catch fencing at the high-speed Hawthorns right-hander when the rear wing broke. Thankfully he emerged from the car unhurt and spent the rest of his 150th grand prix outing spectating quietly from a trackside marshals' post.

At Kyalami the true potential of the McLaren-TAG was seriously unveiled. Taking full advantage of the softest Goodyear race tyre compound, Lauda simply flew and, despite losing 23 seconds with a sticking rear wheel nut during a routine tyre stop, he was running in a strong second place behind Riccardo Patrese's winning Brabham when the electrics failed with six laps to go. Watson, meanwhile, was excluded from the race for overtaking in an effort to regain his grid position on the final parade lap.

It had certainly been a promising start for the new venture, but other events were about to unfold that would substantially boost the team's competitive profile for 1984. Lauda's performance at Kyalami may have laid down a significant marker for the McLaren-TAG's future form, but elsewhere in the F1 fraternity the Renault F1 team was indulging in a painful post-mortem over its failure to win the 1983 World Championship.

After Prost moved to Renault he developed a good working relationship with René Arnoux. This was understandably a little more complex than his relationship with Watson, for Arnoux had been one of his contemporaries as a young French rising star and there was obviously some in-built rivalry that caused an extra degree of intensity.

Unfortunately, at the 1982 French Grand Prix something happened that briefly soured their relationship. 'Gerard Larrousse, our team manager, told René that as I was ahead of him in the championship order, then he should let me through if we were running in the points towards the end of the race,' he explained.

'René didn't protest and we eventually found ourselves running in 1–2 formation, René ahead and me tagging along behind, believing that he would keep to the agreement. Eventually it became clear that René had found it unable to keep to this deal and went ahead to win the race. By the time I realised that he wasn't going to ease back, there was insufficient time left to catch him. I made it very clear to the press after the race that Arnoux had reneged on the deal and the race hadn't really been a representative indication of what could have happened.

'Inevitably, in some quarters I was criticised for complaining. All I will say is that I am happy that René and I have long since forgotten that episode and get along fine now.' But it didn't help the overall picture.

In 1983 Prost was absolute number one, with Eddie Cheever recruited as his number two. Alain recalls him as a pleasant, somewhat intense professional, but one of the most fascinating relationships of his career developed in 1984 when he joined Niki Lauda in the McLaren-TAG line-up.

Alain Prost's retirement with engine trouble in the 1983 South African Grand Prix had been the crushing final straw in a season that had seen the French team steadily overhauled by Nelson Piquet's Brabham-BMW, which eventually enabled the Brazilian driver to clinch the title.

Having rather optimistically chosen to fly out to Johannesburg an army of European journalists to witness this embarrassing debacle, the Renault management cast around for a convenient fall guy. After the race they relentlessly grilled Prost and Renault competitions manager Gerard Larrousse. It was an uncomfortable experience for the two men under the circumstances, and Alain was definitely unamused.

'Every week there is a house newspaper in the Renault factories,' he recalled, 'and after Kyalami it said that I had stopped, not because there was a problem with the car, but because I was running only third and didn't want to look bad. There were also some of the French journalists who wrote the same sort of thing.

'Renault had pushed too much. If they wanted to invite journalists to the race, then OK; but journalists should always write what they truly think, which wasn't the case in the circumstances.'

Two days later in Paris, Prost was fired from the team. It was a monumental tactical blunder on the part of the Renault senior management. Over three seasons Prost had won them a total of nine grands prix. In the two years left before the team closed its doors, the yellow French machines would never triumph again.

'In fact, as it turned out, the Renault people did me a big favour,' he admitted. 'The situation had become impossible and I was very tired with the ridiculous amount of PR work I had to do for them. The guys who worked for the team were always good, but the organisation was so bad I despaired. There were too many bosses, and it was impossible to get anything done quickly because there were too many people to convince and persuade. And if you can't react quickly, you are never going to beat people like Ferrari or Brabham.

'It made me sad to realise how much hypocrisy there was in Formula 1. By the time I left Renault, I was on my guard the whole time, always wondering if that hand slapping me on the back had a dagger in it.'

At the same time that Prost was becoming disentangled with Renault, a vacancy was appearing at McLaren. John Watson, who had rather over-played his hand when negotiating at the start of the 1983 season, now realised that the team had other options for 1984. Suddenly Prost was available – and Watson found himself out of work.

A few weeks earlier Alain had opened preliminary talks about the possibility of switching from Renault to McLaren, but now the negotiations resumed with the Frenchman holding no worthwhile cards. Dennis could now virtually dictate the terms. 'I had nothing else, and Ron knew it,' smiled Prost ironically. 'It embarrasses me now that I signed for so little, but at the time I didn't care. I was away from Renault, and that was all that mattered.'

Watson was philosophical about the sequence of events that ended his grand prix career. 'I think that Ron had always had an on-going conversation with Alain,' he recalled. 'I know that at the end of 1980, when Alain decided to leave McLaren, Ron was very, very disappointed, because he knew what was coming in terms of new technology and he couldn't convince Alain of it at that particular time.

'I also think Ron was talking to everyone in 1983, because he was looking forwards, long-term, not just for the following year, but three, five years down the road. I would have expected him to have spoken to most of the top drivers available. I would have expected him to want the best, just as in 1998 I would expect him to be working equally hard to find a way of securing Michael Schumacher's services for the following season.

'As far as I was concerned, there were no negotiations with McLaren for 1984. I had a one-year contract for 1983 and, when I got to Kyalami for the last race of the season, the first signs of any discussions came from Marlboro's Paddy McNally. He said, "I suppose we're going to have to talk to you for '84", and I said, "Sure, any time you like." But that was all there was.

'What then happened was that Alain lost the Renault drive. He then contacted Marlboro, told them he'd been fired and asked if there was any chance of getting in at Ferrari. They said, "No, we can't – we've just confirmed and signed both the Ferrari drivers, but there is a seat available at McLaren."

'Alain then said, "Surely you've got Niki and John?" The response was, "We've got Niki under contract – John's contract is up." So they then decided that the right thing for the team as a whole was to look at Alain as the long-term prospect, which was the smart thing to do. The concern that Marlboro had was that at the end of 1984 they could be faced with the prospect of Lauda and Watson stopping, with the result that they would have to go out into the market place and buy somebody for top dollar. This way, they could get Prost at the bottom of the market.

'So in terms of my position, there were no firm negotiations for 1984. I wish there had been. I was always intrigued to wonder, if the situation had been reversed – had it been me with the two-year contract and Niki with the one-year contract – would they have dropped Niki and taken Alain? Or would they have tried to buy me out of my contract?

'As it was, for me it was a hard fact that I had to come to terms with and get on with the rest of my life.'

Certainly Prost's arrival was not initially perceived as good news for Niki Lauda. Dammit, thought the Austrian to himself. Watson was a bit of a push-over. This wasn't really the case, of course. John just appeared a little mild out of the cockpit, but there wasn't much wrong with his driving from 1981 to '83. But Prost certainly looked as though he might be a handful. Niki was to be proved right on the button as far as that line of thinking was concerned.

His initial reaction was characteristically clipped and to the point. 'It's not my team, I'm just a driver,' he remarked. 'So now comes Mr Prost to McLaren. Sure, I work with him. Of course. He seems like a sensible guy.'

For Alain, the prospect of working with Lauda was like something out of a dream. By the end of their first year together, he would be reflecting, 'In my karting days Niki was my idol. I used to model myself on him, dream of achieving success like him. And now I was in the same team, with the same equipment, the same chances. It was something fantastic for me, particularly as I was now free of all the tension and responsibility at Renault.

'I did not know Niki very well when I came to McLaren. In fact, it wasn't easy to know him well. But I believed he was completely honest – the most important thing – and after a year racing with him I knew this was the fact for sure.

'I was very glad to hear that he would be staying in the team for 1985. OK, so he won the '84 World Championship, but it was the mutual trust between us that was the important thing. When we agreed a joint strategy together for an individual race, we both kept to it and there was never a cross word.'

The definitive new McLaren-TAG MP4/2 was ready rather late in the day, in line with John Barnard's philosophy that one should maximise the thinking and development time involved in producing a Formula 1 machine. Inevitably such a strategy puts enormous strain on any racing team's workforce, but McLaren was well up to the challenge.

However, the original concept was seriously undermined by the governing body's decision to insist on flat underbodies for all F1 cars from the start of the 1983 season. The decision was announced on 3 November 1982, and left Barnard spitting razor blades in frustration as he was, by that stage, well advanced in the engine development process.

'The engine specification would have been different if we had been running flat-bottomed rules from the start,' he fumed. But the engine was small, light and compact. It would still prove to be outstandingly successful, even though Barnard's original concept had now been seriously compromised, in his view at least.

The 1984 season started at Rio de Janeiro's Autodromo Riocentro for the Brazilian Grand Prix. Elio de Angelis's Lotus-Renault qualified on pole ahead of Michele Alboreto's Ferrari 126C4, Derek Warwick's Renault RE50 and the McLaren-TAGs of Prost and Lauda sandwiching Nigel Mansell's Lotus in fourth and sixth places.

Ron Dennis was quietly confident. On the night before the race he told me: 'People are always saying that I look smug, but I don't think that's fair. That's how I look and I can't do anything about it. But I'll tell you one thing; tomorrow all the speculation stops and we'll see what sort of progress people have *really* been making over the winter.

'Our cars? Well, I'd be guessing, but if everybody really has been telling the truth about their performance during winter testing, then I'd say we were going to be in good shape.' Did he know something the rest of us didn't?

Prost might have felt inwardly that he was in a strong position, but by the end of the opening lap Lauda had barnstormed his way into fourth place behind Alboreto, Warwick and Mansell. He was soon up to third, then took second off Warwick's Renault after a wheel-banging moment at the end of the long back straight. Two laps later the Austrian was presented with the lead on a plate when Alboreto's Ferrari spun with a brake calliper malfunction, and, when Warwick made a routine tyre stop at the end of lap 29, Lauda and Prost were left in a McLaren 1–2 at the head of the field.

Prost made his routine stop with 38 of the race's 61 laps completed, but as the mechanics fell on the Frenchman's car they were horrified to see that Lauda had followed him into the pit lane. But as Alain resumed in second place, Niki undid his belts and stepped out, his work done for the afternoon. His car had succumbed to a frustrating electrical fault.

Prost sailed back into the race in second place, but Warwick looked set for victory until ten laps from the finish. Then the long-term legacy of his earlier brush with Lauda emerged to scupper his chances of a maiden victory for the French team. A front suspension wishbone broke, he spun gently to a halt – and it was Alain Prost who was allowed a free run through to an emotional debut triumph for the new McLaren-TAG.

Prost raised both hands to punch the air as he accelerated out of the final right-hander to take the chequered flag, the poignant symbolism of his success almost flowing from his finger-tips like static electricity.

'That win was very special for me,' he recalls with great feeling. 'Psychologically it was important, because it stopped all the shit between Renault and me and the French press. I won the race, but if Renault had won, and I hadn't finished, the press would have put pressure on me. They are like that, some of them. If I'm honest, too, I have to admit there was an element of revenge in that day for me.

'The really incredible thing, though, was that the French public changed its attitude towards me after that race. Now I was with a foreign team, and suddenly they were for me. It was the same with Michel Platini. When he transferred to an Italian club, he became much more popular than when he was playing in France.

'It's strange, you know, but the French don't really like winners. They prefer the second, the man who loses gloriously. The all-time favourite on the Tour de France was Raymond Poulidor – who never won it. But they never liked Jacques Anquetil, who won it five times.'

So Prost now had nine points, Lauda none. Yet the Austrian would exact his revenge in the second round of the title battle, the South African Grand Prix at Kyalami. Despite the TAG turbo engines proving reluctant to run cleanly at the circuit's 5,300-foot altitude during qualifying, leaving Prost fifth on the grid and Lauda eighth, Niki soon took the race by the throat.

However, he was helped immeasurably when Alain's sister car steadfastly refused to start prior to setting out on the final parade lap. In the pit lane the spare car was already fuelled and waiting –

just in case – but kitted out with Lauda's seats and pedals. The McLaren mechanics worked furiously to change the settings for Alain. But even then it nearly went wrong.

One of the local track marshals, perhaps understandably unfamiliar with the international rules, waved Prost out of the pits and on to the circuit, allowing him to chase off after the field. But there was to be no repeat of the Watson fiasco that had blighted the McLaren team's challenge in the previous South African GP.

The Clerk of the Course immediately ordered the start to be delayed and the McLaren management, correctly realising that there had been a mistake, immediately told Prost over the radio to come straight back into the pit lane. He duly started the race from there once the rest of the pack had been unleashed.

Nelson Piquet's Brabham-BMW set the pace in the opening stages, displacing Keke Rosberg's Williams-Honda from the lead going into the start of the second lap. But Lauda was chasing hard in second place by lap 12 and eventually wore the new World Champion down, surging ahead into the lead on lap 21 of the 75-lap race as Piquet made an early pit stop to change badly worn tyres.

Thereafter Niki galloped away to score his first victory of the season, but by the finish Prost had climbed right through the field into second place and the two McLaren-TAGs were a lap clear of Derek Warwick's third-place Renault. The die was now effectively cast as far as the outcome of the Constructors' Championship was concerned. It only remained to see which of the two McLaren men would take the drivers' crown.

Yet just as everybody was beginning to think that there was no beating the two McLarens, the third round of the Championship, the Belgian GP, proved absolutely calamitous for the TAG turbo-engined machines. Practice and qualifying produced a succession of fuel system problems with both cars, and fresh supplies of fuel brought in from Germany on the Friday night failed to cure the detonation problem.

Prost qualified eighth, Lauda 14th. Come the race, Michele Alboreto's Ferrari led from start to finish, with Warwick's Renault holding on gamely to post a strong second place. Prost was out after five laps with a distributor problem, Lauda lasting only until lap 35 when the water pump failed and he pulled off in a cloud of steam. Neither car had ever featured near the front of the pack.

The McLarens happily resumed their winning ways at Imola for the San Marino Grand Prix, Prost making the front row for the first time of the season alongside Nelson Piquet's pole-winning Brabham-BMW. It looked as though Alain might have to fight hard for any success that came his way, but when the starting lights blinked to green, the Frenchman accelerated cleanly into a lead he never relinquished.

Yet there was one heart-stopping moment. Coming down the hill under hard braking for the tricky Rivazza left-hander on lap 23, Alain had just touched the brakes when the McLaren snapped into a 360-degree spin, almost in its own length. But Prost was master of the situation, keeping the engine running, selecting a lower gear and accelerating away almost before the wheels had stopped turning.

By the end of the afternoon only René Arnoux's Ferrari remained on the same lap as the winning McLaren, with Elio de Angelis's Lotus classified third after running out of fuel on the very last lap. Lauda, having qualified fifth, dropped to tenth on the opening lap when he got boxed in by Keke Rosberg's Williams, which almost stalled on the grid. Nevertheless, the Austrian got his head down and had carved his way through to hold fourth place after 15 laps when the engine expired.

With four rounds of the Championship gone, Prost led the contest with 14 points ahead of Warwick (13 points), Arnoux and de Angelis (10 points apiece), with Lauda equal fifth with Alboreto and Rosberg on nine points. Niki really now needed to get his skates on if he was going to reverse the situation.

Lauda got things back under control with a finely judged victory in the French Grand Prix at Dijon-Prenois where he progressively wore down Patrick Tambay's Renault, which eventually finished second. The French driver had been pretty much the class of the field all weekend, qualifying the yellow machine on pole position and leading until Lauda displaced him only 17 laps from the end of the 79-lap contest.

Yet it had been Prost who again set the McLaren pace, out-qualifying Lauda to take fifth place on the grid, then leading the attack on Tambay before a loose left front wheel-nut sent him into the pits for an unscheduled stop. He resumed to finish seventh, ending the day still in the lead of the World Championship but with Niki now only seven points behind in second place.

From the touchlines, a remarkable situation could now be seen to be developing. For the balance of the season the McLaren teamsters would race against each other for the title, but there would be no unpleasant edge to their rivalry, none of the grinding tension that would be seen four years later between Prost and Ayrton Senna. Yet, paradoxically, both Niki and Alain were ferociously competitive in their own way.

In an effort to match Prost's sheer speed, Lauda also developed into a pretty uncompromising performer. Keke Rosberg noticed on a couple of occasions just how Niki had raised his game. 'I've been with Niki in a few corners and been given a very clear picture,' said the Finn. 'Either I move, or something's going to happen. He has been clean, but absolutely uncompromising.'

Moreover, the McLaren team management did not take long to

realise that their two remarkable star drivers could absolutely be relied upon to bring the cars home in one piece. Their confidence on this aspect became so high that they never bothered to insure the chassis.

From an engineering standpoint, John Barnard found it a fascinating exercise. 'Niki was certainly a good development driver,' he remembers, 'but sometimes he definitely wasn't as good as Alain. The problem could be that he was such a strong-minded person. If you clicked with him in the same direction, he could be an immovable force. But sometimes I felt that he was too quick to reach a conclusion during testing, whereas Alain took longer, to be absolutely sure. With Niki, there was no misunderstanding; it was either this, or it was that.

'On the other hand, his unshakeable confidence could be a big help. It would help push through programmes, particularly with Porsche on the TAG turbo project. Porsche always listened to Niki, and believed him. He had their ear, no question about it.'

Meanwhile, Alain's only controversial victory of the year came at Monaco, where the race was flagged to a halt at half distance when torrential rain virtually flooded the track. When the chequered flag fell, Prost was in the lead, but on the very point of being overtaken by Ayrton Senna's Toleman-Hart.

In the aftermath of this race, the half-baked brigade began speculating that Clerk of the Course Jacky Ickx, a Porsche works sports car driver, had deliberately called a halt to the race so that Prost – whose McLaren was powered by a Porsche-built engine – could win. It really is unbelievable how convoluted the thinking of motor racing folk can become. But some did voice that view.

Prost was scathing. 'I couldn't believe people would suggest something like that,' he said, 'but I'll tell you one thing – if racing drivers were intelligent, and if less money was involved in Formula 1, for sure we would never have started that race.

'I was on the pole, and if I'd spun on the first lap going up the hill to Casino Square, like Mansell did later, maybe 20 cars would have crashed. At first it was just slippery and unpleasant, but later, when the rain had really come down again, the visibility was ridiculous, a joke.'

Well, perhaps. In fact, Mansell didn't actually spin his Lotus, he merely got into a 'tank slapper' and grazed the guard rail. And there had been Monaco Grands Prix run in appalling weather in the past, most notably in 1972 when Jean-Pierre Beltoise surfed away from the opposition to score a surprise win for BRM. But you could see Prost's point.

As a result of the race being flagged to a halt early, Prost received only 4.5 points for his win rather than the regular nine. That half point would eventually be the margin by which he lost the Championship.

Had Senna overtaken him and Prost finished second at Monaco over the full distance, he would have taken six points. It might have been enough to give him the Championship instead of Lauda. All other things being equal. Ten years further down the line, he might have thus retired from racing having equalled Fangio's record of five World Championship titles. All things again being equal. Which, of course, in Formula 1 they usually are not.

The bottom line was that Prost came away from Monaco with 28.5 points, leading the title chase by 10.5 points from Lauda, who'd managed to spin out of the race in Casino Square.

The next race took place in Canada where Nelson Piquet's Brabham-BMW not only started from pole position, but also won convincingly. Prost's McLaren qualified second, Lauda's eighth, and while Alain ran hard behind Piquet in the opening stages, it was soon clear that he was hampered by a down-on-power engine.

Gradually Prost was caught by his team-mate, but when the Austrian pulled on to his tail, Alain played everything cleanly and by the book. Blocking Niki would have gone against the grain, so the McLarens reversed position on lap 44 and Lauda stormed away to finish second, less than 3 seconds behind Piquet. Prost 32.5 points, Lauda 24 points.

Prost's speed in qualifying was now consistently worrying Lauda, who was heard to mouth 'How the hell does he do it?' on more than one occasion during the summer of 1984. It was just the same in the Detroit Grand Prix a week after Montreal. Prost qualified second alongside Piquet, Niki was tenth.

It was certainly a fraught weekend for Lauda, as his Friday qualifying times were disallowed after a rear aerofoil dimensional infringement was uncovered by the scrutineers. 'If we have a thunderstorm at the start of Saturday qualifying, he'll be in trouble,' mouthed one doom-laden hack. Thankfully the weather was fine and the spectre of 'The Rat' not qualifying was removed.

Prost survived a start-line shunt triggered by Nigel Mansell trying to barge his Lotus into the lead from the second row through a gap between the McLaren and Piquet's Brabham that was substantially narrower than the Englishman's car. The race was stopped and restarted, but Prost found his McLaren's grip deteriorating badly almost from the word go on a track surface that had been washed clean of any rubber deposits by an overnight storm. He had to make an early stop to switch on to harder-compound rubber and later came in again for fresh tyres after picking up a puncture.

The net result of all this was that the Frenchman finished fifth, but those two points he earned at least enabled him to open out a title advantage ever so slightly, for Lauda came into the pits to report that his engine was running raggedly.

After a plug change he returned to the circuit, but came in again after only one more lap. 'I'll continue, if you like,' he told Ron Dennis, 'but it's going to cost you a lot of money when that engine lets go.' So the McLaren was retired on the spot.

The third F1 race to be held in North America was a one-off event on a street circuit in Dallas, held in broiling conditions. Both McLarens managed to end the day parked firmly against a concrete barrier with suspension damage, leaving Keke Rosberg's Williams-Honda to post an unchallenged victory.

The McLaren team headed back to Europe more than 20 points ahead at the top of the Constructors' table, but Lauda's second place in the driver's Championship was now under assault from both Elio de Angelis and René Arnoux, who tied for third place only half a point behind the Austrian.

The next race on the schedule was the British Grand Prix at Brands Hatch where Lauda had won so gratifyingly two years earlier. Again Piquet took pole position, this time with Prost second and Lauda third on the grid in their McLarens.

Even before the race was over, Prost found himself at the centre of some political controversy, and not for the first time in his career. After leading the early stages, Piquet's Brabham suddenly lost grip and he dived into the pits at the end of lap 11, just as Jonathan Palmer's RAM crashed heavily into the barrier and officials decided to red-flag the race to the stop.

However, the fact that the red flag was displayed at the end of the 12th lap meant that the grid order for the restart was determined by the race order on the previous lap – when Piquet was still ahead. So instead of Prost and Lauda taking the restart from an all-McLaren front row, the first three positions on the grid were effectively identical to the original starting order.

Prost was extremely frustrated by this, communicating his opinion to FISA President Jean-Marie Balestre that the whole thing was a fix, presumably in favour of F1 Constructors' Association chief Bernie Ecclestone, who owned the Brabham team. As a result of speaking before thinking it through, Alain found himself having to make a public apology to the sport's governing body when the F1 circus arrived at Hockenheim for the German Grand Prix, the next race on the Championship schedule.

Despite this, Prost jumped into an immediate lead when the race was restarted with Lauda taking 17 laps to find a way ahead of Piquet's Brabham before he could take second place. But when he did, he really began to apply the pressure to Prost and spectators were treated to the rare sight of the normally immaculate Frenchman dropping wheels in the dirt and cranking on the opposite lock as he battled to stabilise his advantage.

However, those fans who thought that they were at last in for a treat in the form of an eyeball-to-eyeball confrontation between the two McLaren-TAG teamsters were soon disappointed. The clutch in Prost's car wilted under the strain of two starts and he cruised into the pits after 37 laps, allowing Lauda to sweep through into the lead.

He won by over 40 seconds from Derek Warwick's Renault, with Ayrton Senna's Toleman a storming third. Niki had come to Brands Hatch saying, 'This could be my last shot for the Championship. I've just got to stop messing about like I was in North America. A win is what I need more than anything, or it's probably goodbye to any chances of the title.' As things transpired, he jetted away from Britain only 1.5 points behind Prost in the points table. Lauda had been as good as his word.

A fortnight later, Prost and Lauda sat in the Marlboro motorhome before the German Grand Prix. 'I'm the oldest,' said Niki. 'You should let me win this year, then I'll let you become Champion next year.'

Prost grinned. 'You won at Brands 'atch,' he replied. 'It's my turn to win today.'

Niki grinned knowingly.

In the event they finished first and second, Prost having started from pole even though he had to jump into the spare MP4/2 after his race machine had developed a fuel pump problem. Lauda again paid the price for his poor qualifying performance, lining up on the fourth row of the grid and having to battle through from eighth at the end of the opening lap.

Not that Prost led all the way, mind you. For the first seven laps the debonair Elio de Angelis kept his mathematical Championship hopes alive with a great performance in his Lotus-Renault. But then he retired with turbo failure.

At the chequered flag Alain was only 3.1 seconds ahead of his team-mate. But it was enough to raise his total to 43.5 points, to Niki's 39. It could still go either way.

Next on the list was Austria, a race on the super-fast Osterreichring amidst the splendour of the Styrian mountains. Niki was understandably keen to win on his home turf, but the grid had a relentlessly familiar look to it. Piquet on pole, then Prost, de Angelis and Lauda lining up behind.

Then the start and another well-practised routine. Piquet went away from Prost in the opening stages with Niki completing the opening lap sixth after another indifferent start. But within half a dozen laps it looked as though Nelson's Brabham had already broken the McLaren-TAG challenge. What we couldn't have known was that Alain's gearbox was already playing up, that the Frenchman was having to drive at least part of each lap with only one hand on the wheel while holding fourth gear in place.

On lap 29 there were oil flags waving at the downhill *Rindtkurve* just before the start/finish line, Elio de Angelis's expiring Lotus having dumped most of its lubricant on the tarmac at this point. Piquet – with both hands on the wheel – just managed to get through unscathed in the lead, despite a huge slide, but Prost, driving one-handed at this point on the circuit, never had a chance.

McLaren No 7 spun off the circuit before Alain even had a chance to apply a touch of opposite lock. Now Niki moved up into second place and worked away to wear down Piquet, successfully squeezing past into the lead on lap 39.

For a few laps Lauda pulled away. Then he seemed to ease up. Piquet, thinking that he was simply conserving the McLaren, did not rise to the bait. It was certainly a big mistake on the Brazilian's part.

Suddenly Niki flung up his arm. The crowd groaned as a Brabham flashed past his McLaren. But it was Teo Fabi, running well down, and not Piquet. Then Lauda began to pick up speed again. What on earth was going on?

'I was hard on the throttle in fourth gear when there was an enormous bang as the gear broke,' explained Niki. 'I thought that was the end of that, and I began to slow, looking for somewhere to park. Then I began to fish around to see if there were any other gears working. I got third, then I found fifth . . . so I thought "Let's go on and see how far we get."'

Niki lost the best part of 7 seconds in a single lap, but recovered to nurse the car the remaining ten laps to the chequered flag. Had Piquet appreciated his dilemma, he might have counter-attacked and the result could have turned out very differently. As it was, Lauda now led the Championship for the first time all year with 48 points to Prost's 43.5. But Alain wasn't finished yet, not by a long chalk.

The Dutch Grand Prix at Zandvoort produced another McLaren 1–2, but this time with Prost leading past the chequered flag. It was the usual story; Prost on the front row of the grid, this time taking pole, with Lauda back in sixth place on the outside of row three.

If Niki had managed to make a better start it might have been different, but he was ninth at the end of the opening lap. He had to squeeze every ounce of advantage out of his mixed hard/soft set of tyres to get within striking distance of the Frenchman. And by the time he'd done that, his grip level had deteriorated very badly. Alain simply pulled away to win by 10 seconds. Lauda 54 points, Prost 52.5 points.

Three races to go now, and the Italian Grand Prix at Monza would provide one of those remarkable twists of fortune that go to make motor racing such a tantalisingly fascinating and unpredictable sport. On the night before the race, the McLaren team went through its customary even-handed ritual when it came to selecting freshly prepared TAG turbo engines for the race. The two engines were lined up against the wall of the pit garage, their identifying index numbers facing away from the chief mechanics who made their random choices.

Just over 12 hours later, during the race morning warm-up, there were scenes of agitated debate in the McLaren pit. Both cars had suffered from loss of power, fluctuating turbo boost pressure and water leaks. Dennis and Barnard suggested that Lauda might like to run the spare MP4/2 as work had already started in changing the engine on Prost's car.

But for some reason Lauda was insistent. 'Honestly,' he said, 'if Alain doesn't mind running the spare, I would really like my race car with a fresh engine.' Prost obliged – and retired on lap four when the engine failed. Lauda watched, waited for his other key rivals to fall by the wayside, then stroked it home to an easy win. What made it all the more remarkable was that at one point it seemed as though Niki wouldn't be taking part in the race at all. The previous morning he had slipped a disc in his back and only a bout of intensive overnight therapy from Willi Dungl, his trainer, relieved the agony and enabled him to take part. So now it was Lauda 63 points, Prost 52.5 points. And two races to go.

The penultimate round of the title chase marked a return to the Nurburgring. Not the original 14-mile circuit through the Eifel mountains on which Lauda had come so close to death eight years earlier at the wheel of his Ferrari, but a brand new, bland and featureless autodrome built adjacent on the site of the start/finish complex of the old track.

If there was any sense of poignant nostalgia suffusing Lauda's mind, he certainly didn't show it. All he knew was that he would be World Champion for the third time in his career if he won this particular race, irrespective of what Prost might or might not achieve. For Alain's part, he just had to win in Germany to keep his own title hopes alive.

Prost qualified second – you've guessed it, behind Piquet's Brabham – but Niki had an absolutely dismal time in practice and qualifying. As things transpired, Saturday qualifying was ruined by rain. Prost took advantage of a mad scramble in the last 15 minutes of Friday qualifying to cut a decent time, but Niki managed his tyre choice badly after suffering car problems on the first day and had to be content with 15th.

Despite spinning into a Volkswagen course car parked precariously close to the edge of the circuit during the race morning warm-up, Prost's car was repaired and re-fettled in time for him to lead from start to finish. In the race Niki locked his rear wheels and spun trying to lap Mauro Baldi's Spirit and was unlucky not to finish second as Michele Alboreto's Ferrari and Piquet's Brabham – both spluttering low on fuel – limped across the line ahead of him almost at a walking pace.

Frustrated with his fourth place, Lauda sought out Baldi once the race was over and verbally tore into the hapless Italian. Baldi, however, was unrepentant. 'It was your bloody fault, not mine,' he snapped back at the McLaren driver before turning on his heel and walking away. Just for once, Niki was left virtually speechless.

Prost gained a welcome bonus from an unexpected source only two days after the European Grand Prix. The sport's governing body FISA had excluded the Tyrrell team from the 1984 World Championship for a technical infringement and now decided to adjust the Championship points' table in the light of this edict.

Amongst other things, this meant disallowing the six points for Martin Brundle's second place at Detroit. Prost finished fifth in that race, gaining two points. Now he was re-classified fourth and an extra point accrued to his personal tally. Going into the final race he was now just 3.5 points behind Lauda.

The McLaren team went out of its way to ensure parity of equipment for that final race, as indeed was its customary procedure. But neither Ron Dennis nor John Barnard wanted anybody to have an excuse to point accusing fingers in the event of a technical failure on one or other of the cars.

The title shoot-out was scheduled to take place at a brand new venue on the F1 calendar, Estoril, just along the coast from Lisbon. It would be the first Portuguese Grand Prix to be staged for 24 years, and the bumpy little track, just inland of the resort made fashionable by the Duke and Duchess of Windsor before the war, was generally regarded in a favourable light.

Front row? That's right. Piquet's Brabham flanked by Prost's McLaren. Lauda? Way back in 11th place on the grid and not very amused about it.

'I told the team that the engine was making worrying noises [in qualifying],' he explained, 'but the Porsche people told me that it was nothing to worry about, just the gears at the front of the camshaft clattering away. So I went out on my second run and the engine just lost about 300rpm at the top end. There was no way I could turn a decent time.' He paused for a moment, then added, 'I'm going to need a *lot* of luck tomorrow, no question of that.'

On Sunday morning his wife Marlene jetted in from their home in Ibiza to give Niki a bit of moral support. It was, he said, a characteristically wild and impulsive gesture on her part. Marlene Lauda didn't really have a great deal of time for motor racing, but this was a day when she felt she really ought to be on hand.

Meanwhile, Lauda's technical problems in qualifying resulted in some sections of the Austrian popular press getting very stoked up, hinting that perhaps Niki's car had somehow been 'sabotaged'. It was all nonsense, of course, just the ebb and flow of technical fortunes in this most complex of sports, and Lauda just reacted to the stories by rolling his eyes in mildly amused exasperation.

The tension continued to build on race morning. Lauda was

quickest in the warm-up, but his newly installed TAG turbo developed a water leak. Another fresh engine was installed for the race. On the grid, my fellow journalist Nigel Roebuck noted that 'It was Niki who told Alain to relax. The man would make one hell of a poker player . . .'

Then it was down to business. Keke Rosberg burst his Williams-Honda through into the lead at the first corner to end the opening lap ahead of Nigel Mansell's Lotus-Renault. Prost was third ahead of Ayrton Senna's Toleman, Michele Alboreto's Ferrari, Elio de Angelis's Lotus, the Renaults of Patrick Tambay and Derek Warwick, Stefan Johansson's Toleman, and Eddie Cheever's Alfa Romeo. And Lauda.

Piquet had dropped from contention by spinning on the opening lap. 'Damn!' thought Niki. 'One person out who could have taken points off Prost. What the hell did he think he was doing?'

Mid-way round the second lap, Prost neatly took second place from Mansell. Then, after carefully sizing up Rosberg's Williams for several laps, the Frenchman neatly outbraked the Finn to take the lead going into lap nine. From then on Alain tore away to win the race. Only if Niki finished second could Prost be stopped from winning the title.

By lap 26 Lauda had moved up to seventh place and was mentally debating how to handle new boy Johansson immediately ahead of him. 'I simply couldn't believe the speed of that Toleman on the straight,' said Niki afterwards. 'I eventually had to wind my boost up to well beyond qualifying level and go down the outside of him into a tricky left-hander. As I came across the front of him, I tagged his nose, which was a bit unfortunate.' The highly indignant Johansson lost the best part of two laps in the pits changing his Toleman's nose section as a result of this contact.

Lauda kept the boost pressure high to get past Alboreto into third place. Now only Mansell stood between Niki and the title. Niki had only the best part of half a minute to catch the Englishman. It looked a lost cause.

Then suddenly Mansell's Lotus could be seen skittering up an escape road. A piston had popped out of one of the front brake callipers and the fluid had leaked away. Nigel was out, heart-broken over his misfortune.

Yet Mansell's dejection was as nothing compared to the thoughts going through Prost's mind. The Frenchman's nightmare had come true. Lauda was second and the two McLarens crossed the line 14 seconds apart. It was Prost's seventh win of the season, but he had lost the Championship to Lauda by the wafer-thin margin of half a point.

'Forget it, next year the Championship is yours,' Niki told the disconsolate Alain as they mounted the rostrum. Yet one could understand Prost's feeling of desolation. He had won two more races than Niki, had stamped his mastery on F1. Yet Lauda took the title with only five wins. It was a measure of their genuinely good relationship that there was never any personal aggravation between the two men.

However, if things had been going well out on the circuit, by the end of the 1984 season Lauda and Ron Dennis were finding their professional relationship hard going. At the start of the 1983 season McLaren had re-signed Lauda on the two-year contract for $4 million a year, and this expired at the end of Niki's title season with the team.

Long before then, Dennis had made it clear that he wouldn't be paying top dollar again in 1985. And Niki, as newly crowned World Champion, wasn't about to acquiesce to a draconian pay cut.

In Niki's autobiography, *To Hell and Back* (Stanley Paul, 1986), the Austrian was uncomfortably candid about the state of his relationship with Dennis. He did not shy away from painting the McLaren boss as one of the most awkward customers he'd ever dealt with. He accused him of being jealous of his, Niki's, achievements and media profile as a driver, or complaining that Dennis and McLaren designer John Barnard never got any credit for the team's success. It was a scathing critique, reflecting an environment that almost saw Lauda walk away from the team and join Renault at the end of 1984.

Although this deal was agreed in principle with the French national team, its competitions manager Gerard Larrousse had to back-track and withdraw from the proposed arrangement. The board, he claimed, would not sanction Niki's huge retainer. Meanwhile, Dennis had got wind of those negotiations. He now had Lauda over the proverbial barrel if the Austrian wanted to continue his F1 career into 1985.

'Ron had basically offered me two million dollars for 1985,' he remembers. 'I replied, "Are you crazy, or what?" "No," he replied, "Keke Rosberg will drive for two million."

'What Ron didn't know was that Nelson Piquet and myself had both agreed that we'd peg our contractual value at four million dollars a year. But Rosberg – the other top driver available at the time – wouldn't agree. He offered himself to Ron in 1985 for three million dollars. So Ron came to me and said, "Tough, I only pay you three million."

'In the end I managed to squeeze 3.8 million dollars out of the deal, which was less than I'd earned in my World Championship year. But at the time Ron's attitude was right because there were cheaper guys around – even if I privately believed that I was really worth five million dollars as reigning Champion!'

5

The McLaren-TAGs: Prost triumphant, 1985–87

IT WAS CLEAR from the start of 1985 that the McLaren-TAGs would be under increased pressure in their battle to retain the World Championship. Although Renault's works team was fading fast, the French engine supplier's fortunes received a huge boost when Ayrton Senna signed to drive for Lotus, the British team now entering its third season with Renault power.

In addition, Honda was getting its act together as the Williams engine supplier and Ferrari's new 156/85 would prove formidably competitive all year, Michele Alboreto actually challenging hard for the Championship all season.

John Barnard had a long look at the McLaren package and came up with the evolutionary MP4/2B, which incorporated a new footbox extension, as required by the regulations, new front uprights, revised wheel hubs, and push-rod rear suspension. Revised F1 aerodynamic rules also called for the outlawing of the additional 'winglets' on the outer extremities of the rear wings, so re-designed wings were called for together with new flaps fitted to the front wings.

Barnard also wanted to improve the overall serviceability of the McLaren-TAG package, and there were several changes under the skin to this effect. 'What I wanted was a car that would be totally predictable on the servicing side,' he explained, 'so we could say this part does 500 miles, that part does 1,000 miles, enabling us accurately to life all the components, then, apart from accidents, accurately assess just how many parts we would require for a season's racing.

'I wanted a gearbox, engine and four suspension corners that we could completely ignore for two races at a time. With two pairs of races spaced only a week apart, this was vital. I have nightmares about trying to race-prepare a car away from home in circuit lock-ups.'

The other major change that was imposed on the McLaren team was a switch from Michelin to Goodyear tyres. The previous autumn Goodyear's racing boss Leo Mehl had been called up by Ron Dennis with the suggestion that McLaren might make the change, and a financially satisfactory deal was duly concluded. Then Michelin announced that it was withdrawing from Formula 1 at the end of the year, which meant that McLaren would have had no choice but to use Goodyears anyway. It would have been easy to conclude that Ron had advance warning of Michelin's withdrawal, but there was none. What looked to some observers like a slice of ruthless opportunism was in fact just a fortuitous piece of footwork.

The 1985 season was all about turbo boost pressure. Yet running great gobs of boost to produce off-the-clock power outputs was only of any use in qualifying. The fuel capacity maximum was again pegged at 220 litres, which meant that there was once again a premium on sensitive and economical driving when it came to the race. In other words, tailor-made for Alain Prost. Again.

The season opened at Rio as usual, and on the strength of qualifying it looked as though the McLaren-TAGs might have met their match. Michele Alboreto's Ferrari was on pole ahead of Keke Rosberg's new Williams-Honda FW10, while the second row was filled by the black and gold Lotus-Renault 97Ts of Ayrton Senna and Elio de Angelis. Prost was sixth, Niki Lauda ninth.

Come the race, events unfolded in the McLaren team's favour with a relentless sense of inevitability. At the first corner an exuberant Nigel Mansell, starting his first race for Williams, came bounding through from fifth place to bang wheels with Alboreto going into the first right-hander. As a result Mansell spun off and Alboreto was left with slightly deranged suspension, which meant he was battling understeer thereafter.

Rosberg thus led the opening stages from Alboreto and Prost. But the Finn's moment of glory ended prematurely with turbo failure after nine laps, leaving Prost to intensify his challenge to the leading Ferrari. On lap 18 the Italian missed a gear, and Prost was through.

Before long Michele's mirrors were filled with another McLaren, Lauda having taken full advantage of his superior straight-line speed in a race set-up to compensate for his lowly starting position. Unfortunately Niki's 1985 Brazilian Grand Prix was to have no more happy an outcome than the previous year's race. On lap 23 a warning light flickered on the dashboard to herald terminal trouble with the McLaren's electronic black box. Alain was thus left to reel off the miles to post the McLaren International team's eighth consecutive victory. Prost nine points, Lauda zero.

The second round of the title chase marked a return to Estoril where the entire grand prix grid was provided with a dramatic taste of the future as Senna speedboated to a dominant victory for Lotus. The track surface seemed every bit as flooded as it had at Monaco the previous year, even Prost falling foul of the diabolical conditions and spinning off on the straight. Lauda was unable to run with the leading bunch, worried about the response of his carbon-fibre brakes in the unseasonably cold conditions and hampered by an engine reluctant to pull over 10,000rpm. Piston failure eventually caused his retirement, his title points' score still firmly stranded on the launch pad.

The San Marino Grand Prix at Imola was next on the schedule. Revelling in the confidence produced by his domination in Portugal, Senna planted his Lotus firmly on pole ahead of Rosberg's Williams, Elio de Angelis's Lotus, Michele Alboreto's Ferrari and Thierry Boutsen's Arrows. Prost was sixth, Lauda eighth.

At the start Senna took an immediate lead and it was not until lap 23 of the 60-lap event that Prost got through into second place and began to launch a stern challenge to the Brazilian. Perhaps more than at Estoril, this was the race in which Ayrton really proved he was World Championship material. It wasn't just the fact that he proved capable of staying ahead of Prost's McLaren, but the fact that once he decided to conserve fuel he took the speed out of the car's brakes and gearbox rather than its throttle.

It wasn't enough to last the distance at such a ferocious pace, however, and lacking a cockpit fuel read-out Ayrton ground to a standstill with just over two laps to go. That left the dynamic Stefan Johansson, who'd replaced René Arnoux at Ferrari after the first race of the season, through into second place. Then he too ran out of fuel.

Prost, meanwhile, had rolled off the pace much earlier and, thanks to a final lap an amazing 14 seconds slower than his best earlier in the race, just managed to coax his McLaren across the finishing line. Then disaster! The McLaren MP4/2B weighed in 2kg below the mandatory minimum weight limit at post-race scrutineering, having consumed fractionally more brake pads and rubber than the team had calculated. Elio de Angelis took the win for Lotus with Lauda at least scoring some points with a cautious run to fourth, grappling with gearbox problems.

'I was proud of the job I did there,' Prost later reflected, 'although it was not truly a race because fuel economy played such a big part. But I fought with Senna as long as I could, until I knew I had to back off, or run out. Maybe he could run the whole race at that speed and finish. I didn't know. All I did know was that I couldn't.'

More discreetly, this was also a race in which Prost mentally made a note about Senna's driving tactics. Time and again the Brazilian took a deliberately obstructive line under braking for the uphill Tosa left-hander at the end of the 185mph straight beyond the start/finish line. He didn't make much of it at the time, but privately Prost was simmering with annoyance at what he regarded as behaviour that Ayrton should have left behind in Formula 3.

The Frenchman had already noted one episode earlier that same season that made him wary about Senna. At a media conference held just before the Brazilian Grand Prix, Prost and Lauda's place names were together in the centre of the table with Senna provisionally seated on the outer edge. Senna juggled the labels in order to end up sitting next to Lauda, the reigning World Champion. 'Senna is an *arriviste*,' noted Prost quietly to himself.

Post-race scrutineering produced another close call for Prost at Monaco, where hugely excessive fuel and oil consumption, caused by a sticking turbo wastegate on one bank of the TAG turbo engine, meant that the MP4/2B was this time just 2kg *over* the required minimum weight. Thankfully, that ensured that one of Prost's best-ever victories was assured, the McLaren having been enormously difficult to handle on this tortuous circuit as a result of this technical problem.

Senna had led the opening stages before his engine failed after 13 laps, leaving Prost and Alboreto's Ferrari to swap the lead at the head of the field. But it wasn't to be Michele's day. First he lost the lead with a slide up the Ste Devote escape road on oil dropped from a spectacular collision between Nelson Piquet's Brabham and Riccardo Patrese's Alfa Romeo. The Ferrari driver then fought back past Prost to take the lead, only to lose his advantage for a second time with a pit stop to change a punctured tyre. He got back into second place with only 14 of the race's 78 laps to run, but was still 7 seconds down on Prost at the chequered flag.

By dint of finishing third at Monaco to add to his fortunate Imola victory, Elio de Angelis now led the Championship with 20 points, leaving Prost and Alboreto tying for second on 18 apiece.

Next on the schedule should have been the Belgian Grand Prix at Spa-Francorchamps, but this was called off on the eve of the race after practice and qualifying lapsed into chaos when the newly resurfaced track surface virtually disintegrated. The race was postponed until later in the year and the F1 circus moved on to Montreal for the Canadian Grand Prix.

The McLarens had a fraught time in qualifying at the Circuit Gilles Villeneuve. Prost managed fifth on the grid, behind two Lotus-Renaults and a pair of Ferraris. Lauda wound up down in 17th place, seemingly unable to throw caution to the wind in an acrobatic scramble for qualifying times.

'I just can't break the habit of a lifetime and screw the car up for a single quick lap,' he confessed. 'I've always disciplined myself to drive neatly and that's all there is to it. Just wait for the faster circuits.'

Niki also managed to inject a little bit of light relief into the proceedings when he pulled into the pit lane and announced to Ron Dennis that 'there is a beaver on the track at the hairpin'. Dennis kept his patience as best he could, but the following morning a photograph in a Montreal newspaper vindicated Lauda's observation. Sure enough, there they were, Beaver and Rat on the track together!

Lauda would later put his critics in their place by setting fastest time in the race morning warm-up. In the race he would be running eighth when his engine began to overheat and he pulled in to retire. Prost finished third behind an Alboreto–Johansson Ferrari 1–2. Alboreto now led the Championship with 27 points, Prost and de Angelis second equal on 22. Lauda was equal ninth with just three.

The F1 circus stayed in North America for the next round of the title chase through the streets of Detroit. Both McLaren drivers were in trouble grappling with brake fade. Lauda called it a day and retired after ten laps while Prost – who sprained a wrist thanks to a brush with one of the concrete walls in practice – did the same in the race to eliminate himself after 19 laps.

Back in Europe, the French Grand Prix at Paul Ricard provided only a marginally improved outcome. In torrid conditions, the Pirelli tyres on Nelson Piquet's Brabham-BMW proved absolutely perfect and the Brazilian romped to a decisive victory. Lauda retired with gearbox troubles and Prost was pipped for second place on the last lap by Keke Rosberg's Williams-Honda. Alboreto failed to finish, but remained at the head of the points table on 31, five ahead of Prost and de Angelis.

After the French race McLaren went testing with a crucial front suspension modification that John Barnard confidently predicted would produce a worthwhile upsurge in form at the next race, the British Grand Prix at Silverstone. Both drivers had complained of an unpredictable transition from understeer to oversteer. A slight change to the suspension pick-up points did the trick and Prost found the handling much improved at Silverstone, where he qualified strongly in third place behind Rosberg and Piquet.

Come the race, Ayrton Senna's Lotus-Renault was the dominant force, but a complex electrical fault deprived him of another winning opportunity. Prost, who'd chased hard almost from the start, was thus able to slip ahead with only six laps to go, winning by over a lap from Alboreto's Ferrari. Lauda stopped with electrical troubles. Alboreto 37 points, Prost 35.

Back to the new Nurburgring for the German Grand Prix, and Alboreto came on strongly, winning cleanly after defeating Prost in a clear-cut battle. Alain, frustrated by a soft brake pedal and what he regarded as a gutless engine, spun in the closing stages as he tried to keep pace and finished a distant second. Lauda finished a troubled fifth. Alboreto 46 points, Prost 41.

The Austrian Grand Prix was a key turning point. Prost won, Lauda retired – and announced that he would be doing just that, for good, at the end of the season. Niki convened a press conference to make public that decision, but it was turned into something of an embarrassment when Ron Dennis took the microphone and delivered a lofty lecture to the effect that it was really John Barnard who should get the lion's share of the credit for the McLaren team's recent run of success.

This understandably produced a degree of tension between Lauda and his team chief. Sharp words were exchanged and Ron acknowledged that he could have chosen his words rather better. Not that Niki could have cared less by this stage. Nor Dennis, one suspects. More significantly, Prost now tied with Alboreto at the head of the Championship table. It was 50 points apiece.

The 1985 season proved to be a bitter disappointment for Lauda in terms of results, highlighted only by a single win, in the Dutch Grand Prix at Zandvoort that followed the Austrian race – beating Prost fair and square after the Frenchman had been delayed by a sticking wheel-nut at a tyre stop. From the touchlines, it was a terrific performance. Only Niki knew just how little in the way of motivation he felt before the start of that particular race.

'I had decided that I would quit at the end of 1985, so all I was interested in was staying alive,' he admitted. 'I wanted to collect all my little money at the end of the season. Herbert Volker, the journalist I collaborated with on my various books, was with me. On the starting grid I was way back, but Herbert said to me, "You're gonna win this race!"

'He was such a man of passion, a man of heart. But I said to him "Are you nuts, you fucker? I want to stay alive. I hope my fucking engine blows up after one lap." He looked at me aghast, not understanding a word I was telling him. Then he disappeared.

'So we started. At the end of my first lap I was fifth. Then I said, "Right, now I'm going to race for Herbert", because the poor guy was so demotivated after what I'd told him. So I gave it the big stick, pulled a few stunts to keep Prost behind me in the closing stages – and I won. Everybody thinks we're such great champions, winners and great guys – but if Herbert hadn't made those remarks to me on the grid, I wouldn't have cared less about that race!'

By 1997 Lauda's views on Ron Dennis's management style at McLaren had mellowed slightly, the challenges involved in running his own airline perhaps helping him to appreciate that man management skills were perhaps not as easy as he'd once thought. But he felt that his perception of Dennis was nevertheless valid at the time.

'I described the situation as it happened to me then as a fact of life,' he recalled. 'Ron treated his people at the time in the way I reported it [in my autobiography]. Today I am not employed by him. Our relationship is different. We have a good relationship with him.

'The important point is that I have changed significantly. I also think he has changed the way in which he operates. I think he has learned, as I certainly have, that you must have a degree of balance in your relationship with the people you employ. At that time Ron was very egocentric, hard and tough, wanting everything done the way he wanted it.

'I think he has learned that you get more from people if you are a little more flexible. I have the same problem today at Lauda-air. I have 1,400 employees; they sometimes drive me crazy, but I cannot run 20 aeroplanes on my own.'

But back in the 1985 season, after Zandvoort Prost was three points ahead of Alboreto and would not be headed again. He won the Italian Grand Prix at Monza after Rosberg's Williams retired with engine trouble. Alboreto failed to score, so now the Frenchman was 12 points ahead in his quest to become the first ever French World Champion.

Prost followed that up with a strong third in the re-scheduled Belgian Grand Prix and went into the European Grand Prix at Brands Hatch knowing that a strategically shrewd run could see him clinch the title with two races still left to run.

'To be honest, I drove for points at both Spa and Brands Hatch because I wanted to get the World Championship settled and out of the way,' he admitted. 'In the previous two years I lost it at the last race and did not want that to happen again. Because I had been so close so many times, it had become too important to me, both in my career and my life.'

At Brands Hatch he finished fourth and clinched the title. Mission accomplished. He rounded off the year with a third place in South Africa and a retirement in the inaugural Australian Grand Prix at Melbourne. Lauda led in Australia, but his farewell F1 outing ended when he locked his brakes and slid lightly into a wall. He walked away coolly but without regret, never to race an F1 car again.

For the 1986 season Lauda's place alongside Prost would be taken by Rosberg who moved across from Williams. Alain admits that he soon came to like the confident, cocky Finn. 'I must say I was taken aback with his confidence at the first test at Rio,' he laughed. 'Keke wasn't any old driver arriving at McLaren grateful for the opportunity. He just brushed aside John Barnard's advice to take things easy for the first few laps, put his foot down hard and flew off the road mid-way round his second flying lap. The car was very badly damaged and I don't think Keke and John ever quite saw eye-to-eye again.

'Keke was very skilful, motivated and hungry. Perhaps he didn't quite have the necessary finesse to get the best out of the sort of turbo, fuel-consumption racing we had at the time, but he was certainly a great competitor. And a great friend.'

Keke, for his part, admired Alain enormously and his year driving alongside him brought him to the conclusion that the pint-sized Frenchman was easily the best F1 driver in the business.

'I knew that 1986 was going to be my final year in F1,' said

Rosberg, 'and I wanted to drive for Ron and his operation. Yet I found [McLaren] was a team which was very, very difficult to penetrate. Within that single year I really didn't manage to get into it.

'I think it was more to do with the fact that John Barnard was on his way out already [Barnard left to join Ferrari mid-season] and was not taking part in the second half of the year at all. It was a confusing time.

'I took part in 16 races and scored five finishes. Call that a good experience? It was the worst time of F1, particularly for Alain and I, because we used to run out of fuel. It was something I could not accept and understand that F1 cars could not, were not *allowed* to, carry enough to go flat-out. It was against my system!

'At McLaren you couldn't grab anybody. You couldn't have "mates" at McLaren, everybody was a number. I had a good working relationship with Steve Nichols and Jo Ramirez, of course, but somehow it left me with the feeling that it was easier at Williams to be part of the team.

'But, of course, at Williams I was the leading driver and Prost had been at McLaren for ages. And I think I have to admit that I was like an old gramophone record that got stuck in the same groove saying "the car understeers, understeers, understeers". I suppose after six months of this, nobody bothered to listen.

'But it *did* understeer. It bloody well did! The best thing I remember was that I went to Alain once, when I was getting really mad about this, because there were one or two occasions that it didn't, and then I was very, very quick.

'So in August, I think it was, I went to Alain and said, "Listen. Just admit one thing to me. If it understeered less, would you be quicker?" He said, "Yes." And that was the end of the discussion. So I said, "Well, for God's sake why don't we change it?" But nothing was done.

'I still think I was fundamentally the fastest driver out there in 1986 and I'm sure I could have given Alain a good run for his money in a different car. The TAG turbo engine didn't have the top end power of the Honda, but the real problem was that understeer. I found it so bad that I was only really able to harness about 70 per cent of my potential. On the other hand, it was difficult to come into the pits and say "Look, this car is undriveable" when Alain was producing the results.'

'I always got on very well with Alain. I've never had a problem with a team-mate, really. Not when I was racing in F1 anyway.'

Keke also admits that he had a really good relationship with Ron Dennis, which endures to this day in Rosberg's role as Mika Hakkinen's manager. 'Ron has always been easy to deal with,' he insists. 'He has one great quality – he is straight and honest. There has never been a hitch.'

However, Keke does reflect that, during his year with McLaren, he managed to score an embarrassing commercial 'own goal' that was financially very painful. Prior to joining the team, the Finn had gained a reputation for securing lucrative personal sponsorship deals – during his time with Williams, his driving suit was literally dripping with badges identifying his diverse personal backers.

When he arrived at McLaren, Dennis offered the standard driver package. No personal sponsors, just the negotiated driving fee. 'I can't live with that,' responded Rosberg. 'I had a personal sponsor whose identification I really wanted to carry. So Ron said, "How much do you get for that?"

'I replied that it was a significant amount of money, around $250,000. So he said, "OK, you can buy the space on your overalls for that sum." So I did. And they never paid!' It must have been one of the very few occasions on which Rosberg, the businessman, managed to outfox himself.

For the 1986 season the permissible fuel load was reduced from 220 to 195 litres, a factor that heightened Rosberg's discomfiture. But although the McLaren-TAGs found themselves outclassed in pure performance terms by the rival Williams-Hondas and lost the Constructors' Championship as a result of not having two drivers who could win regularly, there was to be no trace of post-Championship blues for Alain Prost.

Prost did not get his Championship score off the ground until the second race of the series, finishing third in the first Spanish Grand Prix to be staged on the new circuit at Jerez de la Frontera. He won again at Imola, then repeated this success at Monaco, where Rosberg chased him home in second place. But the McLaren-TAGs would not win again until Prost triumphed in the Austrian Grand Prix in August, although his Championship hopes had been kept alive by the fact that Williams team-mates Nigel Mansell and Nelson Piquet spent much of the season effectively taking points off each other.

Prost had an unfortunate skirmish with authority in the Italian Grand Prix at Monza, a race that – perhaps uniquely – started with neither of its front row qualifiers in position. Both pole position man Teo Fabi's Benetton-BMW and Prost's McLaren-TAG encountered technical problems. Fabi stalled prior to the final parade lap and the McLaren had alternator problems, Alain switching to the spare car and starting from the pit lane.

While Mansell, Piquet and Alboreto all took turns at challenging for the lead, Prost came hurtling through from dead last to sixth place by the time 18 laps had been completed. But by this stage, half an hour into the race, the stewards had decided that Alain had switched to the spare McLaren a scant 5 seconds too late after the green flag had been shown to send the field on its parade lap. Out came the black flag and Prost was disqualified.

Taken at face value, it was remarkable that Alain had been permitted to risk his neck for nothing for such a long time – even making a quick pit stop to change his car's collapsed nose section – but Ron Dennis had spent much of that interval attempting to prevail on the stewards to let his driver run to the finish and debate the matter later. It was no consolation that Prost's TAG turbo V6 expired expensively on lap 28 just as he was about to return to the pits. Feisty as ever, Alain directed another broadside towards the governing body – and was rewarded with a $6,000 fine for his trouble.

Unlike his performance at Spa in the Belgian Grand Prix, where a stupendous charge through the field with a bent chassis after a first corner collision with Berger yielded a single Championship point for sixth place, this similar example of Prost's commitment at Monza produced nothing. But he was still in with a chance of retaining his title, trailing pace-setter Mansell by only eight points in the title chase.

Prost followed this up with second places in Portugal and Mexico, the latter performance reflecting great merit as he coaxed his sick TAG turbo engine through a gruelling race with only a single pit stop for fresh tyres. Alain abandoned any idea of stopping a second time as he was worried that, if the engine stalled, it might not restart.

The final round of the title battle was enacted through the streets of Adelaide, where Mansell and Piquet monopolised the front row for Williams, Frank's team having long since clinched the Constructors' Championship. It seemed as though the battle for victory might be resolved between the two Williams drivers, but although Piquet led first time round, the remarkable Rosberg soon went surging ahead on the final F1 outing of his career.

Almost magically, Keke found that his McLaren was devoid of its customary understeer – for only the second time that year. Despite the fact that he'd privately pledged to help Alain's title bid, he quickly pulled away from the pack.

Cynics suspected that he was running the turbo boost pressure off the clock. But Keke denied that. 'I swear to you, I was using only 2.8-bar boost and everything ran perfectly,' he insisted. 'I only had to snap my fingers to open out an advantage. I remember wondering to myself, "Well, if it's this easy, why the hell am I retiring?"'

Yet Prost quickly, if unobtrusively, began to assert himself as a potential threat. By lap 12 he had moved up to third ahead of Mansell; by lap 21 he was second in front of Piquet. Nelson then had a quick spin, his Williams dropping back to fourth. Then on lap 32 came one of those unpredictable, out-of-the-blue episodes by which Championships can so easily be won or lost.

As he lapped Gerhard Berger's Benetton, Prost clipped the Austrian's car and the McLaren sustained a puncture. Prost came in to have it changed, dropping to fourth. Rosberg, meanwhile, led through to lap 63 when his F1 swansong went the same way as Niki Lauda's had done 12 months before.

After hearing an ominous rumbling from the rear of the McLaren, he switched off the engine and coasted to a halt, certain that the bearings were about to fail. Once he climbed from the cockpit he immediately saw that the problem was with a rear tyre; what he'd heard had been wayward chunks of rubber battering against the McLaren's bodywork.

So was there a tyre problem that could affect the other competitors? The set of Goodyears that Prost had discarded when he came in with the puncture certainly looked in good enough shape, but from the pit wall those on the Williams-Honda, now running 1–2 in the order Piquet–Mansell, seemed to be wearing badly.

Before anybody could make a decisive judgement on the matter, Mansell's title hopes were destroyed in a 200mph rear blow-out on the fastest section of the circuit. The car skittered to a spectacular halt in a shower of sparks, Mansell displaying great dexterity – and benefiting from enormous good fortune – as he kept it away from the retaining wall.

Now it would take Piquet and Prost to retire if Mansell was to grasp the Championship. Goodyear now advised that it would be a good idea to bring Piquet in for fresh tyres. Ironically, on close examination, there was nothing wrong with his present ones. Now he could only resume second behind Prost and hope to pressure the Frenchman into a mistake.

Yet, by the same token Prost knew that he didn't have a hope in hell of finishing. The fuel consumption computer on his McLaren's dashboard told him that he was out of fuel three laps before the end. Yet the McLaren just kept going. Just as his tanks had run dry in the German Grand Prix at Hockenheim when the computer told him he had fuel to spare, now the situation was reversed.

Unbeknown, Alain had more than enough fuel available and cruised home to win his second straight World Championship. Not since 1960, when Jack Brabham retained his title crown, had the Championship remained with the same driver for consecutive seasons. It was a remarkable achievement.

For the 1987 season the technical regulations retained the 195-litre fuel capacity maximum, but power was further restricted by the introduction of a 4-bar boost pressure limit on the turbocharged engines. This was achieved by the installation of a pop-off valve, provided by the governing body, which was designed to vent the system when the prescribed level of four times ambient barometric pressure was reached.

The valves were manufactured in the USA, retained by FISA between races and distributed at each event on what increasingly seemed like a 'pot luck' basis prior to the first qualifying session. Perhaps shrewdly, the governing body was not going to risk handing out valves for the entire year just in case a touch of personal customising should be initiated to the advantage of individual, enterprising F1 operators.

As things transpired, one of the biggest talking points of the season centred round which teams had found a means of running in excess of the 4-bar boost limit – and therefore harnessed an unfair advantage in terms of extra power. There was a danger that continuous 'over-boosting' would weaken the springs in the valve to the point where they began operating at around 3.8-bar, which was something definitely to be avoided.

In qualifying, however, while chasing front-row grid positions, it became the practice for some teams to use big turbos with massive doses of boost being forced through the engines – the key factor then being how the power units themselves stood up to the back pressure developed under such circumstances.

Meanwhile, as McLaren settled down to use the trusty TAG turbo engines into their fourth consecutive full season, there had been quite a major shake-up on the design staff. During 1985 John Barnard and Ron Dennis had become increasingly at odds with each other over various aspects of the McLaren corporate structure and began to drift apart.

'In 1985 I had sold my shareholding to Mansour, because I quite liked the idea of having a nice house and a bit of money,' reflected Barnard. 'That left Ron with a 40 per cent shareholding, and although I was still Technical Director, our relationship changed subtly because I was now effectively an employee.'

The situation eventually came to a head in August 1986 when Dennis felt that negotiations – notably with BMW Motorsport over the possible design of an F1 car for the German company – had gone a bit too far. Barnard, who had in 1985 sold his shareholding in the company to TAG, agreed that it was time for him to seek pastures new. In the event, the BMW deal came to nought, but John soon found a berth in charge of Ferrari's UK-based design studio, which he was commissioned to establish near Guildford.

'We had achieved together everything that we had set out to do, and there was a variety of choices available to myself and John,' explained Dennis. 'The easy route for both of us, and certainly the easy route for me, would be to have no change. But when faced with all the things that affected that decision to either continue together or not, we decided to split.

'Each other's contribution was inaccurately perceived by the other, and I think there was more of an inaccuracy on his side as to what I was contributing in generating finances and all that sort of thing.'

Barnard agrees, at least partly. 'I think that Ron changed the situation in his own mind,' he said. 'A funny intangible element entered our relationship. I don't think he wanted the situation to change, but it did.

'But I do think, in retrospect, that we both underestimated our partnership. My mistake was thinking that everybody else was doing the same as we were at McLaren. When I eventually went out to other teams, my mouth literally hit the floor. They were not even close in terms of technology. I was dead naive in that respect and sometimes look back with regret over my break with McLaren. Where would we be now if we had stayed together?'

In 1985 TAG had also moved into the consumer goods market when it acquired Heuer, makers of high-quality watches and chronometers, which had been established 125 years earlier and had a long-established record for the manufacture of high-precision timing instruments.

One of the keys to Heuer's success had been its determination to dominate the world of sports timing, and as early as 1916 the company filed a patent for its 'Micrograph', which was the first device capable of measuring one-hundredths of a second. The TAG Heuer brand became a natural choice to sponsor the McLaren grand prix team, and since 1992 has been the official timekeeper for the FIA Formula 1 World Championship.

In Barnard's place, his protégé Steve Nichols picked up the gauntlet as design project leader. It was a busy time for the American engineer as he shouldered responsibility not only for sustaining the McLaren technical effort in the second half of 1986, but also for formulating the way forward through 1987.

The resultant McLaren MP4/3 represented yet another logical development of what had gone before, although this time the monocoque was revised to accommodate a reduced-capacity 195-litre fuel cell, replacing the 1986 MP4/2C's original 220-litre outer moulding.

The chassis configuration of the MP4/3 was largely unchanged, but Porsche had expended much time and effort matching the TAG turbo engine's development programme to the requirements of the 4-bar/195-litre regulations.

The engine's two separate cylinder banks, which were not interlinked, required a pop-off valve apiece. This offered potential for more leaks in the system, but the German-built V6 thrived on operating at around 3.7 bar, at which point it was developing a healthy 900bhp at 13,000rpm. However, over-boosting was to be avoided as this showed a tendency to send the latest induction sensing equipment in the Bosch engine management system haywire, and also had an adverse effect on throttle response.

The inclusion of the pleasant Swedish driver Stefan Johansson in the team as Prost's partner raised certain questions that were only answered later in the season. Stefan was no slouch, but was not in the same class as Lauda or Rosberg.

For Prost, the season opened on a somewhat controversial note. The sport's governing body announced that it would be charging the F1 drivers for their licences on a sliding scale based on the Championship points they had scored during the previous season. The basic fee was set at £512, plus £102 per point. On that basis Prost's bill added up to £7,800 – which equated at that time to just over $12,000.

On the face of it one was bound to wonder what on earth all the fuss was about. In real terms we were talking nickels and dimes compared with F1 driver incomes, but Prost made it clear that the drivers objected to the arbitrary manner in which the new charges had been imposed. Needless to say, Bernie Ecclestone, who had recently taken over the role as FISA Vice President of Public Affairs, did not hesitate to make it clear what he felt about the drivers' attitude.

'Some of these people are earning millions of dollars a year and they are not prepared to pay for the tools of their trade,' he insisted. 'Who the hell do they think pays Professor Watkins [the highly respected F1 medical delegate who travelled to all the races] to look after them and the emergency helicopters to stand by all weekend?

'With some of them, it's all take and no give. They wouldn't even buy you a cup of coffee. As a result of their actions, the race was close to being cancelled and I, for one, wouldn't have been sorry if it had been.

'We would have gone back to Europe, signed up a new set of drivers and, within three races, who would have remembered Alain Prost?' Ecclestone seemed to be labouring under the impression that the public came to see the cars rather than the drivers. It was not a view shared by the majority of the paddock.

Prost would be competitive in 1987, but not really a serious World Championship challenger. Sure enough, he opened the season with his third victory in four years at Rio, but then Mansell won at Imola and took the Championship points lead. Prost went back ahead after he and Johansson scored a fortuitous 1–2 in the Belgian Grand Prix at Spa-Francorchamps, and he hung on ahead until Senna had posted two consecutive victories at Monaco and Detroit in the Lotus-Honda 99T.

Thereafter Prost never headed the points table again that season, thanks in part to a succession of alternator drive belt failures on the TAG turbo engine that cost him at least a couple of likely wins. Despite this, he managed to post his third victory of the season at Estoril – an historic milestone as it was his 28th career victory, beating Jackie Stewart's all-time record of 27 wins that had endured since 1973.

'Alain produced a faultless performance to win that race,' said Stewart. 'I think he is absolutely in a class of his own among today's grand prix drivers. I honestly cannot think of anybody I would have preferred to take my record.'

Prost was also getting on very well with the McLaren management at this stage in the game. Ron Dennis freely admitted that he could not wish for a better relationship with a driver.

'We are close friends, we socialise together, we spend weekends together,' he reflected at the end of the '87 season. 'I think a good friendship consists of not only the ambience between you in the social sense, but also mutual respect from the business point of view.

'I also happen to think he is the best; he became more complete when he won his first World Championship and I think that success is something a driver needs to become a complete driver. That hunger then gets turned into a more calculating approach, as opposed to the desperation that sometimes comes to the fore. It's a slightly different form of motivation and slightly more professional.

'The only negative is, as with all friends, it's extremely uncomfortable talking about money for both us. It is true that it took three months to agree Alain's retainer for 1988 and '89, and in all that period of time we successfully avoided naming figures and shook hands and concluded the agreement.

'And when we each wrote the figures down, his was different from mine. So we had both reached a situation where we had both thought we were thinking of the same figure, but we were not. It caused some embarrassment and some great amusement. [But] we came to an amicable solution, which for me reflected the nicer part of our relationship.'

Yet for all this, Dennis had been watching the progress of the young Ayrton Senna ever since the Brazilian driver had raced in Formula Ford 2000 back in 1982. The McLaren chief even offered to fund his 1983 British Formula 3 Championship season. It was then that he first had a taste of just what an independent young man he was dealing with.

'I wanted a situation where I simply had the option on whether or not to use his services,' recalled Ron. 'I didn't want to get into a situation where I was obliged to give him a Formula 1 drive in 1984.' But Senna was having none of this. He would generate his own F1 budget, thank you very much, as he had no intention of being beholden to anybody. 'What I underestimated was how strong a position he was actually in to come up with his own F3 budget,' added the McLaren chief thoughtfully.

Senna instead went to Toleman in 1984, then drove for Lotus throughout the next three seasons, winning six grands prix by the end of the 1987 season. By then McLaren's priorities were changing. Dennis correctly judged that the tempo of F1 competition was hotting up to fresh levels of intensity. It was no longer good enough to go racing with the TAG turbo, an engine that was funded by the team itself. What McLaren required for the future was a partnership with a leading car-maker.

The road accident in which Frank Williams had been paralysed in 1986 had left his own team's engine partner – Honda – anxious about the future. At the same time Honda was very keen to secure Prost's services, whether or not that meant the Frenchman joining Williams – or Honda switching to McLaren. By the start of 1987, Frank Williams began to drop hints that it looked as though McLaren would become the third Honda-powered team in 1988, alongside Lotus and his own. In fact, things would turn out worse than that.

After working with Senna at Lotus in 1987, Honda became keen to retain its links with the dynamic Brazilian driver. This coincided with Dennis lining Ayrton up in his sights. Honda also wanted to retain Nelson Piquet, who'd won the '87 title but was feeling somewhat unsettled with the deal he'd got out of the Williams team.

Consequently it all seemed supremely logical when Honda took its engines away from Williams and gave them to McLaren, while retaining Lotus as its second team. Senna could thus join Prost in a McLaren-Honda line-up, with Piquet moving across to replace him at Lotus. That meant that Williams lost out, having its Honda engine supply contract terminated with one year still to run.

Former McLaren driver John Watson would later recall sitting next to Senna at a dinner party in Germany towards the end of the 1987 F1 season. By this time it was clear that Ayrton would be joining McLaren for the following season and the chat, perhaps inevitably, moved round to how the Brazilian newcomer would handle his new team-mate Alain Prost in 1988.

Watson, offering his own experience of going head-to-head with Niki Lauda, suggested that the best way to deal with Prost would be by stealth rather than a head-on confrontation. The young driver listened politely, then surprised Watson by telling him that he was planning a different tack altogether.

'He told me that he would beat Prost by being fitter, more motivated and more dedicated,' recalled John. 'He said he would make sure that he was in a position to drive faster, more consistently, for longer than Prost could do. He meant to beat him convincingly from the front. I remember thinking to myself that this seemed just a little optimistic.'

The 1988 season would be the second transitional year after which 1.5-litre turbocharged F1 engines would be outlawed for good and replaced by a new generation of 3.5-litre naturally aspirated power units.

Moreover, for this final season's racing, the turbos would have their performance further limited by a reduction in boost pressure to 2.5 bar and a contraction of their fuel capacity from 195 to 150 litres. On the face of it, the FIA wanted to make certain that there would be no way in the world a turbocharged machine could compete. But they had clearly reckoned without the remarkable technical ingenuity of Honda.

For Dennis's part, the new alliance could be said to represent another new beginning for McLaren. In late 1987 the team moved into a spacious new factory on Albert Road, Woking, equipped with all the latest state-of-the-art machinery required for an F1 team looking to sustain its position well into the following decade.

Yet there was more to it than that. Dennis would also concentrate ceaselessly on ensuring that his company's human relationship with Honda was conducted in a manner that their new Japanese colleagues would find comfortable and reassuring.

For months the McLaren chief read as many books as he could find on Japanese culture and business methods. Not only was he determined that the McLaren-Honda alliance would be competitive from the start, he was aiming to ensure that it was long-lived as well.

It was absolutely characteristic of Ron Dennis's attention to detail that he should go to such exhaustive lengths to ensure that the new alliance went smoothly. He was also very proud that he had managed to field a team with Senna and Prost as its two star drivers.

Objectively, this was one of the strongest driving partnerships in the history of grand prix motor racing. It was also set to be fraught with ferocious competitive tension the like of which nobody in the F1 pit lane could ever previously recall witnessing. Eventually, it would spiral wildly out of control, thwarting the team's best efforts to keep it together beyond its second season.

6

McLaren-Honda glory days: Prost v Senna, 1988–89

RECRUITING AYRTON SENNA into the McLaren team alongside Alain Prost gave Ron Dennis and his colleagues a great deal of professional satisfaction. With due respect to Nelson Piquet and Nigel Mansell, most insiders regarded the new partnership as the strongest seen in F1, possibly since Scheckter and Villeneuve at Ferrari in 1979, certainly since Prost and Lauda in 1984.

Ironically, for Prost at least, the goalposts had now subtly shifted. In 1984 he was the man who had amazed Lauda by his pace in practice and qualifying. Now he was about to be subjected to the same discomfiture at the hands of the young Brazilian incomer.

For Dennis, the pleasure at what his F1 team was about to achieve in terms of hard results would have a flip-side in terms of the rivalry that would develop in the team. Senna was unyielding and relentless in his determination to undermine Prost's position. It developed into a wearing two seasons for everybody at McLaren, although the intoxicating mood of sustained success was satisfying compensation for the bumpy ride.

It was clear from Senna's first turn at the wheel of a grand prix car that he was something special. Frank Williams was the man who gave him his big chance with a test at Donington Park in the summer of 1983. He was, unsurprisingly, instantly quick. But it was when he arrived at Silverstone at the end of that same season to try a McLaren MP4/1C as his prize for winning the Marlboro British F3 Championship that he really began to demonstrate the ultra-confident edge that would become his hallmark.

Of course, the crucial key to McLaren's success in 1988 was the remarkable 80-degree V6 Honda RA168E twin-turbo engine and its ability to perform competitively on 23 per cent less fuel than was permitted the previous year. It should also be mentioned that the naturally aspirated opposition was permitted to run at a 500kg minimum weight limit, 40kg below that permitted for the turbocars. On the other hand, the naturally aspirated cars would probably need to carry around 200 litres of fuel for a full race distance – 50 litres *more* than the turbos – which would negate any theoretical advantage.

Of course, having drivers of the calibre of Senna and Prost, there were seldom any problems with cockpit management of the crucial controls that were such a key factor behind the success of the McLaren MP4/4. In addition to the business of racing the opposition, they also had to select the correct balance of boost pressure, intake air temperature, fuel temperature and air/fuel mix to keep the engine functioning at its optimum over a race distance.

The Honda V6 would develop a remarkable maximum of 685bhp and, even in conditions of marginal fuel consumption, produced around 625bhp. With Ferrari never getting on top of its turbo fuel consumption problems and the best naturally aspirated Cosworth DFR V8 producing around 585bhp, the McLaren-Hondas understandably looked strong from the start.

The MP4/4, the development of which was now under the guiding hand of newly appointed McLaren Technical Director Gordon Murray, still bore a strong generic likeness to the TAG-propelled cars originally designed by John Barnard, although Murray's influence could be seen in the sharply reclined driving position, which he had originally pioneered for the Brabham BT55.

McLaren kept the opposition guessing until the last possible moment prior to unveiling its new car. The first MP4/4 was not tested at Imola until ten days before the opening race in Brazil, but it instantly caused a sensation. The official lap record at Imola had been established by Nelson Piquet at 1m 28.667s at the wheel of a Williams-Honda turbo running unlimited boost in 1986.

Now, with a 2.5-bar boost restriction, but admittedly more aerodynamic development, the MP4/4 was lapping in the low 1m 28s bracket straight out of the box, much to the delight of both Prost and Senna. Then they went out at Rio and blitzed the opposition at the first race of the season.

Senna qualified on pole with Prost third, the two McLaren-Hondas split by Nigel Mansell's naturally aspirated Williams-Judd. It was a performance from the Englishman that convinced some observers that a non-turbo challenger might have at least a sporting chance in F1, 1988-style. This was an optimistic illusion.

Ayrton had a disappointing first outing for the McLaren team. His MP4/4 suffered gear-change troubles on the parade lap, but instead of driving straight into the pits, he duly took up his place on pole position, then waved his arms furiously, indicating that he was in trouble. The strategy worked perfectly as the 'Delayed Start' board was displayed.

The stricken McLaren MP4/4 was pushed into the pit lane and by the time Senna joined in at the wheel of the team's spare car, Prost was already leading majestically midway round the opening lap.

Alain led from start to finish to take the flag 10 seconds ahead of Gerhard Berger's Ferrari.

For the Austrian, the race proved a salutary experience. On lap 45 he posted the fastest lap of the race, but it served simply to confirm his worst suspicions. His fine-handling Ferrari just didn't have an engine to hold a candle to the Honda turbo. Prost nine points; Senna zero.

Gerhard later recalled that feeling of abject frustration: 'Alain was about 12 seconds ahead with 15 laps to go when I started to make my counter-attack. I reckoned I was in a slightly stronger position because I'd made my second stop and had fresher rubber than he did. I set the fastest lap of the race. But Alain just speeded up. That's when I realised just what a difficult job we were facing.'

The second round of the title chase, at Imola, delivered more of the same. Senna on pole ahead of Prost, with Ayrton leading from start to finish as Alain's engine all but died on the grid and the Frenchman could only complete the opening lap in sixth place. No matter. By lap eight he was through to second place and eventually finished just over 2 seconds adrift after Ayrton rolled off the pace over the final few laps. All this on a circuit where the 150-litre fuel capacity was expected to leave the turbo brigade dangerously vulnerable. Prost 15 points, Senna nine.

At Monaco Senna simply rocked everybody on their heels. Although the two McLaren-Honda teamsters monopolised the front row, Ayrton ended up an amazing 1.5 seconds faster than Prost. By his own admission, it was almost as if he had managed to hype himself up into some transcendental state. It was almost unbelievable, even to Ayrton, as he later graphically recounted to the late Denis Jenkinson – one of the Brazilian's greatest fans – in *Autocourse*.

'In 1988 at Monaco we had race tyres, not qualifying tyres, so it was lap after lap, not just one lap,' he remembered. 'I got to the stage when I was over 2 seconds a lap faster than anybody, including my team-mate who was using the same car, same engine, everything.

'That was the direct comparison – and over 2 seconds. It wasn't because he was going slow, but that I was going too fast. I felt at one stage that the circuit was no longer a circuit, just a tunnel of armco. But in such a way that I suddenly realised I was over the level that I considered reasonable. There was no margin whatsoever, in anything.

'When I had that feeling, I immediately lifted. Then I felt that I was on a different level. I didn't fully understand that level and still don't. I understand it a bit better, but I'm still far away from understanding how it works in that [mental] band. So I backed off and came into the pits. I said to myself, "Today that is special. Don't go out any more. You are vulnerable."'

In the opening stages of the race, Ayrton simply ran away from the opposition. Prost spent many laps bottled up behind Berger's Ferrari in third place, then got clear and set a series of blisteringly quick laps, even though he was almost half a minute behind the Brazilian. Then Ayrton momentarily lost his concentration, clipped the inside wall at the Portier right-hander, slid wide and took his left-hand front wheel off against the barrier on the opposite side of the circuit.

'I'd driven almost the perfect race,' he reflected, 'probably the best I'd ever done in terms of qualifying, race performance and car set-up. Earlier, I had a moment in Casino Square when the car jumped out of gear as I began to relax. I nearly hit the barrier. I got myself back into a rhythm, but then the same process happened again and it caught me out.'

Senna walked away and immediately returned to his nearby apartment, leaving the McLaren team in the dark for over three hours as to what precisely had caused the shunt. Alain was left to win by half a minute from Berger. Prost 24 points, Senna 9. For the moment.

On to Mexico City and the bumpy Autodromo Hermanos Rodriguez. Senna qualified on pole ahead of Prost by half a second, but Alain led from start to finish. He beat Senna by 8 seconds, the Brazilian particularly worried by tyre wear on this abrasive circuit as well as unaccountably high fuel consumption from his Honda engine. Prost 33 points, Berger 18, Senna 15.

Then to Montreal's Circuit Gilles Villeneuve for the Canadian Grand Prix, where the naturally aspirated brigade again felt that they might be in with a chance on a track where fuel consumption was again traditionally very tight over the race distance. Senna again took pole from Prost, and the two McLarens again made mincemeat of the opposition.

In the closing stages the McLaren pit put out the 'Easy' signal and both men responded, but not before Senna had the final say by turning the fastest lap of the race with only 16 of the race's 69 laps left to run. The Brazilian emerged triumphant to post his second win of the season by 6 seconds. Prost 39 points, Senna 24.

A week later, the F1 circus decamped to the streets of Detroit where Senna again displayed his magical touch when it came to shaving barriers, qualifying on pole 0.8 seconds faster than Berger's Ferrari, and 1.4 seconds ahead of Prost in the second McLaren, which started in fourth place on the grid alongside the other Ferrari of Michele Alboreto.

The Frenchman complained that his engine seemed to be suffering from rather brutal throttle response, something he could well do without on such a confined circuit where there was not an inch to spare for error. But it was Ron Dennis who hit the headlines after attending the post-race media alongside Senna, who had won the race commandingly, but had failed to turn up for the press briefing immediately following qualifying.

Dennis had turned up to explain why he had not allowed Senna to attend after qualifying, but after the McLaren boss had his say there were many who wondered whether he might not have been better staying away as well. Broadly, it was six out of ten for content, zero for presentation.

'It is just not realistic to expect us to allow the drivers to be snatched away for more than half an hour at a time when we need their thought-train to be concentrated totally on the technical debrief,' he said.

'We have found that even an interruption of half an hour can take their mind off the job to the point where crucial pieces of technical input can be forgotten. This is all part of the enormous effort to be consistently competitive in this business, and we feel unwilling to compromise any area that may cause us to lose our sharp edge.'

There was a stony silence from the media. Yet his remarks dramatically highlighted the great gulf of understanding that existed between the two sides. The media may have found some difficulty getting to grips with the intensity of F1 competition, but Dennis had surely overlooked the reality that grand prix racing was, increasingly, a media-driven sport.

What he said next amounted to a stinging rebuff. 'We are trying to make history – you are only reporting it.' We were stunned. There was a brutal accuracy in what he was saying, yet it was starkly direct to the point that we felt as though we'd been mugged. But Dennis was also effectively putting his head on the block; those words might have had validity while McLaren was flying high at the front of the field, but they would echo across the years to haunt him when the team was struggling six seasons later.

The incident also threw into focus a wider issue of the McLaren team's image and behaviour, something that Dennis touched on later in that same season. It was, he reflected, extremely difficult to strike the right balance in the pit lane.

'No matter what you do, it's wrong,' he remarked wryly. 'If you smile, you are gloating. If you frown, you are arrogant. You can't win. I've told the mechanics not to wander about the pit lane, just to walk from the pit wall from the garage and back, keep their heads down and simply go about their business. I don't wander along the pit lanes any more, and that's a pity, because I liked to look at the other cars and see what's going on, and I miss that. Still, it's a small price to pay.'

The team returned from North America with Prost on 45 points, Senna on 33. Back on his home turf at Paul Ricard for the French Grand Prix, Prost seemed revitalised. He beat Ayrton to pole position, and although the Brazilian led from the start, Prost caught his rival and passed him with a brilliant move into a fast double right-hander as Senna was momentarily wrong-footed coming up to lap a Minardi.

To be fair, Senna struggled slightly with gearbox trouble, but it was the aggressive manner in which Prost handled his whole race weekend that was so fascinating. The Frenchman came away from his home track with 54 points, 15 more than Senna, but his advantage at the head of the points table would be abruptly slashed by nine points after he pulled out of a rain-soaked British Grand Prix at Silverstone. And Senna won, majestically.

Now Senna was just six points behind in the title chase. But what was worse for Prost was the way in which the French media tore him apart for withdrawing from the race. It was one of those days when the die-hards lined up on one side of the divide, tut-tutting that any racing driver might have the temerity to throw in the towel. On the other side were the Prost supporters who believed that Alain had done enough, achieved enough, to earn the right to his own opinion.

Back in 1982, during wet practice for the German Grand Prix at Hockenheim, Didier Pironi's Ferrari had somersaulted to destruction when it ran straight over the rear wheel of another car hidden from the driver's view in the impenetrable murk. That other car was Prost's Renault. In the ensuing accident, Pironi sustained leg injuries that ended his professional racing career.

That episode left a profound effect on Alain. Racing in the rain, he reasoned, was one thing. Racing when there was standing water on the circuit and questionable visibility was quite another. He didn't feel he had to make any apologies after Silverstone in 1988.

'When there's a lot of standing water on the track, I don't like it,' he explained. 'I have never pretended I do. I can be quick in the rain, especially if I'm on my own.

'At the start at Silverstone, for example, I was simply swamped in the middle of the field. OK, it's the same for everybody, but when you are flat-out on the straight, you see absolutely nothing at all. Nothing! I'm not worried about driving on a slippery track surface. That's all part of the business we're in. But when you're driving blind, that's not motor racing in my book.

'My view is that motor racing should be run in the dry. Look at the British Open Golf last week. They cancelled the third day because the weather was so bad. And in America, of course, they don't race Indycars in the rain [on ovals]. Of course, this is purely my personal opinion and I fully understand that others may disagree. But at the end of the day it's my judgement and my life. If people won't accept that view, it's their problem, not mine. I can live with that.'

That Prost could drive in the rain was demonstrated to good effect in the German Grand Prix at Hockenheim. True enough, Senna surfed to his fifth win of the season, but Prost, who'd qualified second and made a poor start, put on a polished performance to keep the Brazilian more or less in sight before a quick spin over a kerb over one of the chicanes dropped him from contention. Now it was Prost 60 points, Senna 57.

Senna was again on pole position for the Hungarian Grand Prix at Budapest, but Prost was pushed down to an uncharacteristic seventh place on the grid. He took the spare MP4/4 for qualifying after detecting a slight engine vibration on his race chassis during the morning. But he just couldn't find a gap in the traffic. A fourth-row start was certainly not going to help matters on this circuit where overtaking was damn near impossible.

Prior to the start, Ron Dennis discreetly offered Prost some moral support. While all the media attention surrounded Senna's car on pole position – and Nigel Mansell's Williams-Judd alongside it on the front row – the McLaren boss quietly walked back down the pits and stood on the wall immediately level with Alain's car. He didn't have to say a word. It was a small gesture, but a sensitive one.

In the early stages of the race, Senna set as gentle a pace as he dared in what promised to be a long and gruelling contest. Prost, meanwhile, also played himself in gently, concentrating on conserving as much fuel as possible in the hope that this might enable him to push hard later on.

By lap 47 of the 76-lap race Alain was up to second place and, two laps later, thought he saw his chance going into the first right-hander after the pits. Senna momentarily hesitated as he came up to lap a group of slower cars and, in a trice, Prost was down the inside making it three abreast.

It didn't quite come off. Prost was going just a tad too quickly; on the exit of the corner he ran slightly wide and Senna re-passed almost immediately. He wouldn't give Alain another opportunity and kept control to post his sixth win of the year. Prost briefly eased off, worried by tyre vibration, then came back strongly once he'd convinced himself that all was well. But he was still half a second down at the chequered flag. Prost and Senna, 66 points apiece.

It all seemed to be slipping away from Prost, and the Frenchman knew it. When, a fortnight after the Hungarian defeat, Senna ran away with the Belgian Grand Prix at Spa, he put into words what many of his detractors had been thinking. 'The championship is lost,' shrugged the Frenchman. At Spa, one of Alain's favourite circuits, he had never come close to his McLaren team-mate, an ill-judged last-minute change to his rear wing setting just before the start and incorrect tyre pressures merely serving to heighten his sense of frustration in defeat. Senna 75 points, Prost 72.

At Monza Ron Dennis's ambitions of winning 16 out of 16 races went out of the window. Senna led from the start, but Prost pressed as hard as he could, even when his engine began to overheat slightly, a portent of piston failure to come. On lap 35 out of 51 Alain was in the pits and out of the race.

Ironically, his early pace, hounding Senna mercilessly, may have contributed to Ayrton's downfall. In the closing stages the Brazilian was becoming extremely anxious about his own fuel consumption and Gerhard Berger's Ferrari piling on the pressure in second place.

With just over two laps to go, Senna came up behind F1 novice Jean-Louis Schlesser who was subbing for an unwell Nigel Mansell in the Williams-Judd. Under braking for the first chicane, despite Schlesser's best efforts at keeping out of the way, Senna tripped over his inexperienced rival and was out of the race on the spot. Berger was thus left to head Alboreto home to an emotional Maranello 1–2, less than a month after the death of Enzo Ferrari.

Senna was certainly exasperated by the outcome, but Schlesser was certainly unapologetic. In his view, Ayrton should have taken more care about where he was going. The two men faced each other after the race in the McLaren motorhome. Senna just shrugged after a brief debate. No matter, he still led the Championship.

Yet just as it seemed as though the title advantage would rest with Senna for the balance of the season, Prost came back at the Brazilian with a vengeance in the Portuguese Grand Prix at Estoril. This time Prost was on pole from Senna, and although the Brazilian got the jump into the first corner, it was not before Alain squeezed him to the outside edge of the tarmac and made him work for his advantage.

Then out came the red flag as a group of tail-enders tangled at the first turn, blocking the track. The McLaren lads would have to go through it all again. At the restart again Prost squeezed Senna – unyieldingly but legitimately – to the outside of the circuit on the run to the first turn. Again, Senna took the lead.

Yet Prost hadn't finished with him. At the end of the opening lap he came swooping alongside the Brazilian as they approached the start/finish, only for Ayrton to squeeze him ruthlessly towards the pit wall. If this was intimidation, it certainly wasn't working. Prost kept his foot down and mechanics hastily pulled in their signalling boards for fear of having them ripped from their hands.

Prost kept his foot hard on it, his McLaren lurching precariously as it hit a bump at 180mph, and Ayrton never saw him again. Prost won, while Senna, troubled by excessively high fuel consumption, trailed home sixth.

After the race Prost tore him off a strip behind closed doors in the McLaren motorhome. 'If he wants the World Championship that badly, then he can have it,' fumed the Frenchman. Prost 81 points, Senna 76.

The Spanish Grand Prix at Jerez saw more of the same. Senna may have qualified on pole, but Prost ran away with yet another race, seemingly revitalised now that he was armed with a brand new McLaren MP4/4 chassis, which performed to perfection throughout the 14th round of the Championship battle. Again Senna was frustrated, this time by misleadingly pessimistic warnings from his fuel consumption read-out. He finished fourth. Prost now had scored 90 points to Senna's 79.

However, the World Championship points-scoring rules for 1988 meant that competitors could only count their best 11 scores out of 16. After Jerez, Prost had to drop six points for one of his second places, reducing his effective total to 84. More worryingly, he would have to drop another six in the event of finishing first or second in the Japanese Grand Prix at Suzuka. So if Senna won that race, the World Championship would be his.

Qualifying at Suzuka was the usual story, Senna pipping Prost for pole, yet their battle was played out against the backdrop of an extraordinary exchange of letters between FISA President Jean-Marie Balestre and Honda President Tadashi Kume.

Balestre had got it into his head that there might be some inconsistent variations in the performance of the Honda engines supplied to the McLaren drivers during the course of the season, and wrote asking that no stone be left unturned to ensure absolute parity of equipment for Senna and Prost.

Mr Kume replied to this impertinent missive with great restraint and formality. He concluded by saying that 'the Honda Motor Company sees fairness as the highest requirement of its philosophy for conducting business and sets this quality as an ideology in its corporate dealings.' They were clearly as astonished as most outsiders at the FISA President's intervention.

Come the race, Alain Prost thought Christmas had arrived seven weeks early. Senna almost stalled his pole-position McLaren and was engulfed by the pack. As Prost sprinted away, Ayrton dropped to 14th at the first corner, and although up to eighth at the end of the opening lap, it looked as though his chances of the Championship had vanished.

Yet Senna drove like a man on a mission. By lap 20 he had scythed through the field into second place and the battle was on. Ayrton had no concerns about fuel consumption; hundreds of development miles carried out at Suzuka by McLaren test driver Emannuele Pirro resulted in a perfectly tuned Honda engine specification. Both drivers could go for broke.

On lap 27 Prost seemed to miss a gear as he came up to lap Andrea de Cesaris's Rial going into the right-hander beyond the pits. In a flash Senna was there alongside the Frenchman, powering through a gap only inches wider than his own car to grab the lead. Now all he had to do was to stay out in front for the remaining 23 laps.

The only hazard that intervened was a light rain shower with five laps left. Ayrton, worried that he might lose out, was pointing furiously to the heavens each time he passed the pits. Surely he didn't want the race stopped? Who knows?

Either way, Prost, by now 6 seconds behind, didn't like the conditions either. He dropped away steadily over the last few miles. Senna was World Champion and the ecstatic babble coming across the airwaves from McLaren No 12 as it completed its final lap was such that the McLaren pit crew had to remove its headsets to prevent themselves from being deafened.

It was Senna's eighth win of the season and a thoroughly deserving note on which to round off the Brazilian's dynamic first World Championship title season. Yet it was perhaps appropriate that, two weeks later in Adelaide, Prost rounded off F1's turbo era with a canny performance to finish the season where he started. With a win.

In addition to grappling with gearbox problems, Prost also had to battle understeer caused by the loss of a skirt from one front wing end plate. For Senna's part, he had to take the Honda engine's fuel consumption well into deficit to break Nelson Piquet's second place challenge in the similarly powered Lotus. Once that had been achieved, he leaned off the fuel mixture and got everything back under control in time to finish second.

'It was probably the best 1–2 result we have ever achieved, if you take into account just what we had to do to make sure Ayrton held on to second place,' said Ron Dennis. Yet at the end of the day Ayrton had won the Championship with 94 points gross, 90 net. Prost was second on 105 points gross, 87 net. A bit of an anomaly perhaps, although none would claim that Ayrton was anything but a thoroughly worthy Champion.

Just before retiring at the end of the 1993 season, reflecting on his distinguished F1 career, Prost would admit that it had sometimes been difficult to sustain his motivation. That he managed to do so reflected the fact that he took an enormous amount of interest in the physical and technical operation of the F1 cars he was driving.

'Looking back, I really loved the turbo era,' reflected Prost nostalgically. 'I think my most satisfying season was 1986 when Piquet and Mansell had the Williams-Hondas, which were much faster than our McLaren-TAGs. I think I drove at my best for the whole season that year, but it was a matter of hanging on and not making any mistakes.

'It was really something to have over 1,000bhp available, but what appealed to me also was that the strategy of the races was much more open. There were so many more variables for a driver to play with. We had to balance boost with fuel consumption, because there was no refuelling and if you ran too much boost for too long you ran the risk of running out of fuel.

'You had to be more disciplined, to think it out. And there were other things like choosing the right tyres from three available compounds. The driver's individual style was so much more important. And, of course, we had to change gear ourselves, and judging the changes by a rev counter rather than just a warning light as there is today. There was no traction control, so you had to be delicate with the throttle.

'There was really nothing more satisfying than winning a World Championship grand prix at that time – with just enough fuel to make it to the chequered flag!'

Of course, if anybody thought that the McLaren-Honda partnership was ignoring the development of a new generation of 3.5-litre naturally aspirated engines during its dominant run throughout 1988, they were to be sadly disillusioned. The first 3.5-litre Honda V10 engine had made its public debut as long ago as the 1987 Tokyo Motor Show, by which time it was producing a modest 500bhp on the dynamometer.

This was clearly only a conservative starting point, for Osamu Goto and his engineering team had boosted the V10's output over 20 per cent by the spring of 1988. In August of that year, Senna, Prost and test driver Pirro began a development programme that involved over 2,000 miles of testing using a couple of specially adapted MP4/4B chassis. The only obvious snag was a lubrication problem, which would come back to haunt the team during the course of the 1989 season.

The plan was for Honda to supply a total float of eight such RA109E engines to McLaren for each grand prix. Meanwhile, McLaren chief designer Neil Oatley executed a new chassis – the MP4/5 – to accommodate the new engine. Its development was well advanced when Honda raised the possibility of changing the camshaft operation from belt to gear drive.

It was Honda's view that this alteration would offer more accurate valve timing control, but asked whether McLaren could come to terms with the weight handicap and additional installation problems that this would inevitably involve. McLaren, anxious to capitalise on any possible performance increment, quickly agreed, although the effect of the change was to delay the overall MP4/5 development schedule by a couple of weeks. Not much to the outsider watching from the touchlines, but in the split-second world of F1 it was a significant, if manageable, setback.

It was originally planned to race a brand new transverse gearbox on the new car, but the challenge of building such a transmission with sufficient margins of strength and durability was considerable. As a result, the MP4/5 began the 1989 season using the three-shaft longitudinal box, which had been used on the previous year's machine.

On a personal level, the rivalry between Ayrton Senna and Alain Prost was still containable. Ron Dennis would later concede that the team had, perhaps, leaned over backwards to make Ayrton feel at home during 1988. This didn't impress Alain who, quite rightly, judged that if the Brazilian was given an inch he would take a mile. But they rubbed by as they went into the first race of the 1989 season at Rio.

The McLaren MP4/5s demonstrated a worrying high-speed handling imbalance from the start of practice, and although Senna wound up qualifying on pole, Prost dropped to fifth, complaining of too much understeer. At the start Senna was slow away, and as they sprinted for the first corner he found himself being sucked into a pincer movement between Gerhard Berger's Ferrari on the right, and Riccardo Patrese's Williams on the left.

Ayrton being Ayrton, he steadfastly refused to give ground. His reward was a shredded nose section and a slow crawl back to the pits for repairs. He finished the race 11th, two laps down on Nigel Mansell's winning Ferrari 640, leaving Prost to coax his McLaren-Honda home in second place.

The Frenchman was hampered by an inoperative clutch during the latter part of the race, a glitch that prevented him from making a crucial second scheduled tyre stop. But his gentle touch was enough to ensure that he ended the day with six Championship points. Senna had none.

The second round of the '89 title chase was the San Marino Grand Prix at Imola, the race at which the tenuous alliance between Prost and Senna finally fell apart. The two men qualified on the front row and reached a private agreement, suggested by Prost, whereby they would not fight for the first corner. Whichever of them made the best start would lead the other through the tricky uphill left-hander at Tosa, at the end of the long straight after the pits complex.

At the start Senna accelerated cleanly away into the lead and was already pulling away from Prost at the end of the opening lap. Then on the fourth lap Berger's Ferrari crashed in flames at Tamburello and the race was immediately red-flagged to a halt. Thankfully the Austrian driver would escape from this holocaust with only superficial injuries.

After a delay the race was duly restarted. This time Prost made the best start but, on the straight before Tosa, Senna slipstreamed past in apparent breach of their private agreement. He won the race by more than 20 seconds from a frustrated Prost, whose progress was punctuated by a harmless spin on the tight corner before the pits.

After the race Prost confronted Senna and told him his fortune. He was not, he said, a man whose word could be relied upon. Ron Dennis, understandably keen to nip this confrontation in the bud, got his two drivers together at a test session the following week and asked them to bury the hatchet. Senna was prevailed upon to apologise. But he was reluctant to do so, feeling that he had not overtaken Prost under braking, but on the straight before the corner. Nevertheless, he said 'sorry' at the request of his team chief. But it was not peace in our time, nor even an uneasy truce. At best, it was a temporary ceasefire.

The situation spiralled out of control at Monaco where, once again, Senna beat Prost commandingly for another McLaren-Honda 1–2. In the interval since Imola, Prost had given an interview to *L'Equipe* in which he had said, 'McLaren has always been loyal to me. At a level of technical discussion [with Senna], I shall not close the door completely, but for the rest I no longer wish to have any business with him. I appreciate honesty and he is not honest.'

Prost's frustrations at Monaco were compounded by the fact that he was balked shamefully by René Arnoux's Ligier when he came up to lap his former Renault team-mate. By any standards Arnoux's behaviour was scandalous and scuppered any chance Prost may have had of keeping pace with the winner. Prost and Senna, 18 points each.

Next on the schedule came the Mexican Grand Prix, another race that fuelled Prost's mounting paranoia that the McLaren-Honda technical package was not being equally shared between the team's two drivers. Senna qualified ahead on pole, but Prost pressured him strongly in the opening stages.

Unfortunately, Alain had pressed too hard and, indeed, both McLarens began to be caught by Nigel Mansell's Ferrari as the McLarens battled with deteriorating grip. Prost made his first stop on lap 20, but a misunderstanding with the team meant that he didn't get the tyre compounds fitted that he had requested over the radio. Barely 15 laps later he would be back in the pits for a second tyre change, this time having blistered his left rear Goodyear.

The net result of all this drama was to allow Senna a comfortable victory, with Prost trailing home fifth. Ayrton now led the title chase by seven points, but Alain was still concerned about the technical aspects of the team's performance.

In Mexico there had also been a perceptible disparity in the fuel consumption between the two McLarens, Senna's using more. The Honda engineers spent two days before the next race, through the streets of Phoenix, Arizona, examining all the available data. They eventually concluded that Senna was using more fuel because he was working the engine harder, spent more time at higher revs, and developed more power for longer.

However, Prost was now set to find the advantage swinging back in his favour. After winning three races out of four, it all went wrong for Senna at Phoenix, Canada, Paul Ricard and Silverstone. In fact, the McLaren-Honda technical package began to wobble ominously.

At Phoenix Senna was well in the lead when a serious misfire intervened. In an effort to get precisely to the bottom of the problem, the engine was flown back to Honda's Research & Development department in Japan where its electrical system was examined in minute detail. No obvious problem was found. Similarly, McLaren also stripped down the chassis's electrical harness. Nothing there. Subsequent tests gave reason to believe that the pits-to-car radio communication system, operating in an environment at Phoenix where it was hemmed in by high buildings, had somehow adversely influenced the engine management sensors.

Prost survived to win that race, moving back into a two-point Championship lead. It made up for a slight slip during practice that saw the Frenchman write off his first chassis in five and a half years of driving for the McLaren team.

Then came the rain-soaked Canadian race, and a disaster for both McLaren drivers. Alain qualified on pole ahead of Ayrton, but the Frenchman came hurtling into the pits at the end of the second lap, certain in his own mind that he had a puncture. A quick check found nothing obviously amiss. Prost rejoined only to stop less than a lap later after the MP4/5's top left front suspension pick-up point pulled out of the monocoque. A rare failure indeed, and one that stunned the entire team.

Senna, meanwhile, was in his absolute element, surfing to an apparently dominant victory in the torrential conditions. Except that he didn't win. Three laps short of the chequered flag, he pulled off with a Honda engine failure.

This was the first time the Honda RA109E engine had been raced in wet conditions. Afterwards the Honda engineers concluded that the oil consumption of Senna's engine had been greater than expected due to the intermittent application of the throttle, which was necessary in such conditions. This caused piston ring 'flutter', which led to the higher than expected consumption. At the same time, the fact that water entered the engine aggravated the situation, the resultant drop in the oil tank level causing the hydraulic pressure to drop and a bearing to seize.

This seemed trifling compared with what was to follow on the morning of first practice for the French Grand Prix at Paul Ricard. In front of the stony-faced Ron Dennis and Mansour Ojjeh, Alain Prost announced his decision not to continue driving for the team beyond the end of the 1989 season. Now it was official. The McLaren-Honda dream team had come apart at the seams.

'I must stress that this decision is genuinely the product of joint discussions between myself, Ron and Mansour,' said Prost in a prepared statement. 'As friends, we have debated a range of options open to me for the future and have all kept each other fully informed.

'I have always understood that McLaren would need to reach an early decision as to whether it would be mutually beneficial to renew our contract beyond its current term, which expires at the end of this season.

'However, I want to make it clear that I have not made any alternative plans and certainly do not discount the possibility of a continued collaboration with the McLaren team.' The last paragraph seemed contradictory. Surely, either Prost was staying or going. In fact, both parties to the agreement were simply attempting to extricate themselves with the maximum of dignity and good grace from what had become a sticky situation.

Prost then went out to win the French Grand Prix in unchallenged fashion after Senna suffered a spur gear breakage accelerating away from the grid, retiring after completing only a few hundred yards.

Qualifying at Silverstone saw both Senna and Prost first and second on the grid at a race that marked the debut of the new transverse gearbox, but both cars fell victim to major oil tank problems.

These were eventually traced to incomplete welding within the tanks themselves, pinpointed by the use of Honda's telemetry system to monitor pressure variations within the tanks. This information was then passed to the McLaren factory, where three revised tanks were prepared for the race, the lubrication system now also incorporating a catch tank through which the oil was circulated by means of a cockpit-activated valve operated by means of a button in response to pit signals.

Senna led from the start, but was soon grappling with slight gear selection problems that eventually caught him out, resulting in a spin into the gravel trap at Becketts. That left Prost to cruise home to victory by 19 seconds from Nigel Mansell's Ferrari, expanding his Championship advantage to 20 points.

The two McLaren drivers then staged a spectacular high-speed chase at Hockenheim in the German Grand Prix, Senna leading from the start only for Prost to take the advantage after both men were delayed at their routine tyre stops. With three laps to go it looked as though Ayrton would, for once, have to settle for second place, but then sixth gear broke in Prost's machine and the Brazilian surged past to win by nearly half a minute. Prost 53 points, Senna 36.

The Hungarian Grand Prix followed next, producing a rare outcome with Mansell's Ferrari beating Senna in a straight fight. Once he'd been wrong-footed by the determined English driver as they came up to lap Stefan Johansson's Onyx-Ford, Senna eased off, worried by vibrations from his front tyres and concern that he might run out of fuel. But second was still two places better than Prost could manage, the Frenchman making a late stop to change tyres. Senna thus reduced his points deficit to 14.

He narrowed the gap by a further three points with another brilliant wet-weather victory in the Belgian Grand Prix at Spa, Prost just squeezing home second from a determined Mansell. Then came

Right *Bruce McLaren, the gifted New Zealand driver who started the story.* (Phipps Photographic)

Below *Bruce drove for Cooper from 1958 through to 1965 before setting up his own Formula 1 operation. Here he is on the way to victory at Monaco, 1962.* (Phipps Photographic)

Bottom *Owner driver: Bruce winning the 1968 Brands Hatch Race of Champions in the Cosworth DFV-engined M7. The distinctive orange livery would be revived in 1997 and 1998 for the technical previews of the latest McLaren-Mercedes challengers.* (Phipps Photographic)

McLarens in action

Peter Revson (left) and Denny Hulme. Both won grands prix for McLaren in the early years. Revson died testing a Shadow DN3 at Kyalami early in 1974 while Hulme, having retired from front-line racing that same year, succumbed to a heart attack while driving a BMW at Bathurst in 1992. (Phipps Photographic)

McLaren director Teddy Mayer (centre) between McLaren's 1974 World Champion Emerson Fittipaldi (left) and the man who took his crown for Ferrari the following year, Niki Lauda. (Phipps Photographic)

Historic moment: James Hunt clinches the 1976 World Championship at a rain-soaked Mount Fuji circuit. Eight years would pass before McLaren took another world crown. (Phipps Photographic)

Horror show: John Watson at the wheel of the ungainly McLaren M28 in the 1979 Argentine Grand Prix at Buenos Aires. The subsequent failure of this car triggered the sequence of events that led to the formation of McLaren International. (Phipps Photographic)

The start of something big: Alain Prost on his way to sixth place in the 1980 Argentine Grand Prix in the McLaren M29. It was the Frenchman's F1 debut. (Phipps Photographic)

Left *Teddy Mayer with Ron Dennis (right), joint Managing Directors of McLaren International from 1980.* (Phipps Photographic)

Above *John Watson partnered Prost in 1980. The Frenchman has pleasant memories of Watson's open-handedness and dignity during their year together.* (Phipps Photographic)

Below *Tyler Alexander and Cosworth founder Keith Duckworth (right) examine one of the first carbon-fibre composite monocoques for the John Barnard-designed McLaren MP4.* (Phipps Photographic)

Turning point: John Watson heads for the first ever McLaren International grand prix victory at Silverstone in 1981, in the Cosworth Ford-engined MP4. (Phipps Photographic)

Niki Lauda on his way to victory in the 1982 United States Grand Prix at Long Beach, the Austrian driver's first win in a McLaren. (Phipps Photographic)

Ron Dennis with TAG's Mansour Ojjeh (right) whose family's company bankrolled the Porsche-built F1 engine that powered McLaren to three World Championships – and much more. (Phipps Photographic)

Niki Lauda in animated discussion with Ron Dennis. This wasn't always the easiest of professional partnerships, but it was one of the most successful. (Phipps Photographic)

Left *Little jewel: the Porsche-built TAG turbo 1.5-litre twin-turbo V6, which was specifically produced to John Barnard's stringently outlined design brief.* (Phipps Photographic)

Above *Last win for Lauda: Niki's McLaren-TAG at speed during the 1985 Dutch Grand Prix at Zandvoort.* (Phipps Photographic)

Below *Vain chase: Keke Rosberg's McLaren-TAG sweeps through the Massenet left-hander into Casino Square during the 1986 Monaco Grand Prix. His team-mate Alain Prost won.* (Phipps Photographic)

*Prost and Rosberg on the
rostrum at Monaco with
Prince Rainier and other
members of the Royal
Family. Ayrton Senna, who
finished third for Lotus,
stands between the two
McLaren drivers. (Phipps
Photographic)*

*The McLaren crew on the
pit wall, Rio, 1988. It was
the start of a record-
breaking season. From left,
Neil Oatley, Gordon
Murray, Ayrton Senna,
Ron Dennis and Steve
Nichols. (Formula One
Pictures)*

Ayrton Senna's McLaren-Honda MP4/4 heading for a decisive victory in the rain-soaked 1988 British Grand Prix at Silverstone. Prost pulled out of the race, unwilling to compete in conditions of zero visibility. (Formula One Pictures)

Senna leads Prost in the 1988 Hungarian Grand Prix. Although the Frenchman briefly got ahead, Ayrton immediately re-passed to post yet another win. (Formula One Pictures)

Above *Senna takes his place on pole position for the 1988 Italian Grand Prix at Monza – the only race that season, as it turned out, not to be won by the McLaren-Hondas.* (Author)

Below *Miracle worker: Honda's 1.5-litre twin-turbo V6 developed sufficient power under the 2.5-bar boost, 150-litre fuel capacity regulations to dominate the 1988 season.* (Formula One Pictures)

Right *The insuperable McLaren-Honda MP4/4s of Prost and Senna in the pit lane at Jerez during the 1988 Spanish Grand Prix weekend.* (Formula One Pictures)

In 1988 McLaren won 15 of the 16 races – Alain Prost won seven, and Senna eight. (Formula One Pictures)

Ayrton Senna celebrates his first World Championship on the rostrum at Suzuka, 1988. (Formula One Pictures)

Family trouble: Prost and Senna with Ron Dennis. The team boss spent much of his time calming the volatile relationship between his two drivers. (Formula One Pictures)

Alain Prost takes the chequered flag to win the 1988 Australian Grand Prix at Adelaide, the last-ever F1 win for a turbocharged car. (Formula One Pictures)

Honda's powerful new V10 would power McLaren into the 3.5-litre naturally aspirated era from the start of 1989. (Formula One Pictures)

The start of the 1989 Brazilian Grand Prix with Ayrton Senna's McLaren (No 1) about to lose its nose after being pincered by Gerhard Berger's Ferrari (left) and the Williams of Riccardo Patrese. (Formula One Pictures)

The first corner of the 1989 San Marino Grand Prix, and Senna takes the lead. Did he renege on a no-passing deal? Or had he really overtaken Prost on the straight, well before the corner? (Formula One Pictures)

Nice won: Prost celebrates victory in the 1989 British Grand Prix at Silverstone on a day when Senna spun into a gravel trap quite early in the race. (Formula One Pictures)

Prost takes the lead from Senna and Gerhard Berger's Ferrari at the start of the 1989 Japanese Grand Prix. It would end in tears for the McLaren duo. (Formula One Pictures)

Senna homes in. Within another couple of laps, the two McLarens would collide at this same point while battling for the lead. (Formula One Pictures)

Senna dominated the rain-soaked 1989 Australian Grand Prix – until he slammed into the back of Martin Brundle's Brabham, which was hidden in the murk. (Formula One Pictures)

Ayrton had his work cut out in the opening stages of the 1990 US Grand Prix at Phoenix, his McLaren MP4/5B seen here headed by Tyrrell star Jean Alesi. (Formula One Pictures)

*Time out: Ron Dennis (left),
Ayrton Senna and Jean
Alesi don their best bibs and
tuckers for a gathering at
Monaco's Sporting Club.
(Formula One Pictures)*

*Then it was business as
usual: Senna accelerates
out on to the quay en route
to victory in the 1990
Monaco Grand Prix. He
blitzed the opposition.
(Formula One Pictures)*

*Right Sorry Ron! Gerhard
Berger starts the long walk
home after a trip into the
gravel trap at the 1990
Spanish Grand Prix.
(Formula One Pictures)*

Attention to detail: The Brazilian checks out the cockpit adjustments of his McLaren MP4/5B, at the 1990 Japanese Grand Prix . . . (Formula One Pictures)

. . . Senna's McLaren about to hit the rear of Prost's Ferrari as the pack sprints for the first corner . . . (Formula One Pictures)

. . . Job done. Senna walks back after the shunt, his second World Championship title in the bag. (Formula One Pictures)

Ayrton Senna and Gerhard Berger, team-mates at McLaren from 1990 to 1992. They would become close friends, and given to playing practical jokes against each other. (Formula One Pictures)

Senna's McLaren MP4/6 heads for the first corner of the 1991 Brazilian Grand Prix ahead of the two Williams-Renaults. (Formula One Pictures)

Senna lets team-mate Gerhard Berger's McLaren take the initiative at the start of the 1991 Japanese Grand Prix, while Nigel Mansell's Williams (behind Berger) tries vainly to split his two rivals. (Formula One Pictures)

Ron Dennis congratulates Berger on his first win for McLaren . . . (Formula One Pictures)

. . . And Senna, who finished second, arrives back in the parc fermé having clinched his third World Championship. (Formula One Pictures)

The season after winning his third crown Senna managed only three victories in 1992. Here he is at Mexico City where he retired with transmission problems. (Formula One Pictures)

Ayrton Senna's McLaren MP4/7A just gets the jump on Nigel Mansell's Williams as the pack sprint for the first corner of the 1992 Canadian Grand Prix at Montreal. Not that it did either of them much good. (Formula One Pictures)

Another disaster on the way. Senna's McLaren battles wheel-to-wheel with Mansell's Williams in the 1992 Australian Grand Prix, shortly before the two cars collided. (Formula One Pictures)

Most satisfying victory of all? Ayrton Senna's triumph with the Ford-engined McLaren MP4/8 in the 1993 European Grand Prix at Donington Park was possibly the best win of his entire career. (Formula One Pictures)

Commentator James Allen
interviews Michael Andretti
at Imola, 1993. The
American Indycar ace had
an unhappy time partnering
Senna at McLaren that
season. (Formula One
Pictures)

In 1993 Ayrton Senna
posts a superb, all-time
record sixth win at Monaco
(five of them in a row),
beating Damon Hill's
Williams into second place.
(Formula One Pictures)

The start of the 1993
Portuguese Grand Prix at
Estoril with Mika
Hakkinen briefly leading
for McLaren with Senna
right on his tail and Jean
Alesi's Ferrari about to
accelerate ahead (right).
Alain Prost (left) later
accused Hakkinen of
squeezing his Williams in
an unsporting manner.
(Formula One Pictures)

Returning to some semblance of normality after the horror of Imola just a fortnight before, Martin Brundle drove superbly to finish second at the 1994 Monaco Grand Prix with the troublesome McLaren-Peugeot MP4/9. (Formula One Pictures)

Brundle (centre) celebrates on the Monaco rostrum together with winner Michael Schumacher (right) and third place Gerhard Berger. (ICN UK Bureau)

Left Martin Brundle abandons his McLaren-Peugeot after its attempt at self-ignition at the start of the 1994 British Grand Prix. (Formula One Pictures)

Above Battling for fourth place, Mika Hakkinen's McLaren-Peugeot takes a detour after touching Rubens Barrichello's Jordan on the final corner at Silverstone. (ICN UK Bureau)

Below New order: Nigel Mansell tests the first of the new McLaren-Mercedes MP4/10s at Estoril, March 1995. (Formula One Pictures)

Left *Mansell seals his deal with a visit to the McLaren factory.* (Formula One Pictures)

The 1995 McLaren-Mercedes MP4/10 is unveiled at London's Science Museum. (Mercedes-Benz/ Wilhelm)

Mika Hakkinen, Nigel Mansell and test driver Jan Magnussen at the launch. (Mercedes-Benz/ Wilhelm)

Above *Mark Blundell took over Nigel Mansell's seat in the team after the 1995 Spanish Grand Prix and stayed until the end of the season.* (Formula One Pictures)

Below *Jan Magnussen made his F1 race debut in the 1995 Pacific Grand Prix at Aida while Mika Hakkinen was recovering from an appendix operation.* (ICN UK Bureau)

Right *Mika Hakkinen drove brilliantly to take second place in the 1995 Japanese Grand Prix, a bright spot in a difficult season.* (ICN UK Bureau)

Above *Friends in high places: Ron Dennis may be more political than even his rivals in F1 have imagined.* (Formula One Pictures)

Below *Kart racing legend Martin Hines, boss of the ZipKart company, became a close friend of Ron Dennis and helped with the organisation of the McLaren-Mercedes Champions of the Future kart series. He was also invited to do some straight-line tests with the 1995 McLaren MP4/10B on the Lurcy-Levis aerodrome in central France.* (Author)

Right *Less successful was an outing the following year at the Idi-Ada test facility in Spain. This was all that was left of a brand new McLaren MP4/11 chassis after Martin had rolled it into a hidden ditch. He describes the ensuing telephone call to Ron Dennis as 'the worst day of my racing career.'* (Author)

Above *Ilmor's Technical Director Mario Illien (right) watches over the assembly of one of the Mercedes F1 engines . . .* (Mercedes-Benz/Wilhelm)

Below *. . . And by one of the Merc V10s on an Ilmor dynamometer.* (Mercedes-Benz/Wilhelm)

Right *The home of Ilmor Racing Engines, at Brixworth, Northamptonshire.* (Mercedes-Benz/Wilhelm)

Mika Hakkinen's McLaren-Mercedes MP4/11 runs third ahead of Jacques Villeneuve's Williams in the opening stages of the 1996 French Grand Prix. The Finn eventually finished fifth. (ICN UK Bureau)

The future is orange. The 1997 McLaren-Mercedes MP4/12 is unveiled for the technical inspection at the team's Woking factory.(McLaren)

Return of the 'Silver Arrows', with due ceremony: Mika Hakkinen and David Coulthard take the wraps off the MP4/12 at London's Alexandra Palace. (Mercedes-Benz/Wilhelm)

Scary: Coulthard and Hakkinen are joined by the Spice Girls. (Mercedes-Benz /Sutton)

Mika Hakkinen practising for the 1997 British Grand Prix at Silverstone. (Nick Henry)

Getting the job done: After winning the opening race of the season at Melbourne and ending McLaren's 50-race drought, Coulthard heads for a second victory, at the 1997 Italian Grand Prix. (ICN UK Bureau)

Above *Jurgen Hubbert, the Daimler Benz board member responsible for the passenger car division, Norbert Haug, Mercedes-Benz head of motorsport, Ron Dennis, and Jurgen Schrempp, Chief Executive Officer of Daimler Benz, at the controversial 1997 European Grand Prix* . . . (Mercedes-Benz/Wilhelm)

Below . . . *And with the newly recruited former Williams Chief Designer Adrian Newey (second from the right) who was already making such a difference at McLaren.* (Mercedes-Benz/Wilhelm)

Right *David Coulthard and Norbert Haug look cheerful, perhaps feeling confident of some good times ahead.* (Mercedes-Benz/Wilhelm)

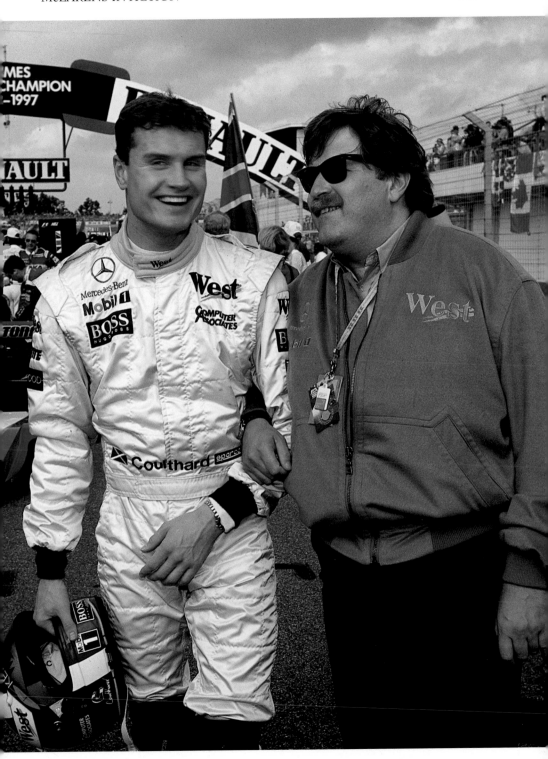

Left *In that last race of the season Hakkinen posted his first win, gifted by the Scot. McLaren's one-two finish caused some raised eyebrows, but it was nothing compared with the Schumacher/Villeneuve row brewing – or with the race-fixing accusations that would dog the team at the start of 1998.* (Formula One Pictures)

Above and below *1998 opened with heady examples of McLaren-Mercedes superiority, and considerable anxiety among the other teams. The one–two result at Melbourne again favoured Hakkinen, but at the following race in Brazil it was settled the racers' way, and tasted all the sweeter for the Finn.* (ICN UK Bureau)

Preparing for the fray, Hakkinen in Brazil. (Formula One Pictures)

Mika Hakkinen, now with the punch to battle through to the crown, or will Coulthard (left) beat him to it? (Formula One Pictures)

the Italian Grand Prix at Monza where it was announced that Prost would be driving for Ferrari in 1990.

Senna again dominated the race, but suffered another rare engine failure in the closing stages, which handed the win to Prost. Honda, thinking that it had successfully solved its lubrication problem after the Canadian Grand Prix, was shocked when the problem was apparently repeated.

Senna's engine oil level began to increase with a corresponding loss of pressure, eventually producing bearing seizure. Post-race examination revealed that the cause of the failure was different from that found in Canada, being traced to poor quality control in the manufacture of the pistons. Subsequent examination of Prost's engine showed that it too was starting to suffer from the same problem.

Prost's victory secured the McLaren-Honda alliance its second Constructors' Championship, but what should have been a joyous moment was soured when Prost dropped his trophy from the rostrum into the crowd. Ron Dennis, who was on the podium to accept the Constructors' trophy, responded to this indiscretion by dropping that trophy at Prost's feet. It was all rather pointed.

Dennis was aghast, not simply because the trophies are not the drivers' to give away, but, more than that, he felt that Alain had cynically attempted to cement his image as a future Ferrari driver by pulling such a stunt at Monza. Critics brushed this view aside, suggesting that the McLaren boss had over-reacted. It might have looked that way, but I was inside the McLaren motorhome with Dennis immediately after the race and his ashen expression left me convinced that, quite genuinely, he felt as though he had been wronged by an old friend. Perhaps on this occasion Prost had gone one step too far with his emotional gesture.

After this race there was also more criticism by Prost concerning Honda's even-handedness. Behind the scenes this caused enormous strife. I understand that Honda was so annoyed by the Frenchman's remarks that the Japanese company threatened to withdraw his supply of engines unless a retraction was forthcoming.

Alain's initial response was to tell them to go to hell, but Dennis managed to harness all the diplomatic skills available to his company to coax his driver to append his signature to a joint Honda/Prost document that was issued to the media before the start of practice for the Portuguese Grand Prix at Estoril.

At the time, and having read the document concerned, I expressed a degree of surprise that Prost was not struck by a bolt of lightning when he signed on the dotted line. Short-term expediency dictated that he do so, but it didn't prevent him from continuing to express his doubts off the record about the whole situation.

The statement read as follows: 'As a result of the consequences of press statements and incidents at the Italian Grand Prix, Alain Prost, Honda and McLaren have had extensive discussions and wish, via this joint statement, to put on record their intentions for creating the best possible working environment for the driver and the team for the remainder of the season. Honda and McLaren have again assured Alain, to his satisfaction, of their commitment to equality and will continue this policy regardless of Alain's move to another team for the 1990 season.

'Alain deeply regrets the adverse publicity and the resulting embarrassment that have been caused by his actions. Honda and McLaren have accepted that these resulted from Alain's perception of his treatment by the team and were not made with malicious intent. He has agreed that in future any doubts on the subject will be discussed with the relevant engineers prior to comments being made to the press.

'The team also expresses its disdain and dissatisfaction over inaccurate, unqualified and damaging statements made by third parties subsequent to Monza.

'Honda and McLaren wish to emphasise that their partnership is founded not only on their desire to strive for technical excellence and continuous success, but, more importantly, on achieving these objectives with the values of fairness and honesty.'

Why waste a sentence, when a paragraph will do?

It was ironic that Prost would then turn out to be 2 seconds faster than Senna in first practice. But it didn't last. Ayrton qualified on pole, but with the ever-improving Ferrari 640s of Gerhard Berger and Nigel Mansell separating him from Prost's fourth placed McLaren-Honda.

Berger led from the start, but the Austrian – by now strongly tipped to fill the vacancy created by Prost's impending departure from McLaren – over-taxed his tyres by running too hard too soon. Thus Mansell breezed by into the lead until he made a routine tyre stop at the end of lap 39. Unfortunately Nigel slightly over-shot the Ferrari pit; without a second thought, he selected reverse gear and backed up.

Now Berger went back into the lead from Senna, but with Mansell now third and closing on the McLaren. However, reversing in the pit lane was a serious rule infringement and, after considering the matter in some detail, on lap 45 the black flag, together with Mansell's race number 27, was shown at the start/finish line.

Mansell by now was running in close company with Senna and went past the black flag three times. Neither he nor the Brazilian, locked in combat and running directly into the setting sun as they came down the start/finish straight, claimed to have seen the signal.

The McLaren management on the pit wall had appreciated the situation, however, and as Senna came down the pit straight to complete his 48th lap, Ron Dennis told him over the radio to ignore Mansell as no longer being a factor in the race. Senna, unable to understand the message, asked for it to be repeated. It was too late.

Going into the braking area for the fast right-hander beyond the pits, Mansell dived inside the McLaren just as Senna turned in. The impact broke both the Ferrari's left front suspension and the McLaren's right rear. Both cars spun madly out of control into the gravel trap, which, fortunately, was wide enough to accommodate their high-speed excursions at this point. Both men were shaken, angry and frustrated. But thankfully unhurt. That left Berger to win commandingly from Prost, who was now 24 points (net) ahead of Senna.

A week later Senna won the Spanish Grand Prix at Jerez at the end of a much calmer weekend. Berger was second, Prost third. Mansell was nowhere, suspended from taking part as a result of his rule infringement at Estoril.

Yet away from the cockpit, Senna seemed increasingly uneasy about the fact that Prost was moving to Ferrari. He got it into his mind that he would be taking Honda secrets with him. At that Jerez meeting, I accidentally overheard him shouting at the Honda engineers that Prost should be fired immediately, before the end of the season. 'Otherwise we will be haemorrhaging information to Ferrari,' he railed. A man feeling the pressure, perhaps?

Now Senna was 16 points behind Prost with only two races to go. The mathematics were such that Ayrton would now have to go for broke, winning both the remaining rounds of the title chase to retain his crown. Even then it depended on where Prost finished. No matter, Ayrton would go for broke. It was just the sort of challenge he relished.

The complexities of Senna's character seemed to surface dramatically when he found himself painted into such a corner. Throughout his career he would refer to the inspiration he received from God, yet his beliefs seemed more tangled, more deep-rooted than simply a conventional faith in religion. Somehow Ayrton seemed to derive this inner strength from a home-crafted set of values, partly religious, but partly a self-generated, almost Messianic belief in his own invulnerability. This enabled him to dig deep into his personal resources more spectacularly and to greater effect than any of his rivals.

Qualifying at Suzuka for the 1989 Japanese Grand Prix was one such occasion. Granted, Prost could, more than ever, continue to play the tactical card. Sure, the Suzuka circuit had a longer lap than most grand prix tracks, therefore accentuating any performance advantage over a longer period of time. Nevertheless, Senna's pole position lap, a full 1.7 seconds faster than Alain, was quite an achievement.

Thus they lined up for the start, the two red and white McLaren MP4/5s with their distinctive 'powered by Honda' decals positioned menacingly on their engine covers, out to give the capacity crowd just the result they wanted on the Japanese engine-maker's home turf. Yet almost at the last minute, out on the grid, Prost took a gamble. He decided to remove the tail flap from his car's rear aerofoil in the interests of straight-line speed. It was a move that wrong-footed Ayrton and, indirectly, would lead to disaster.

At the green light Prost made a brilliant getaway. At the end of the opening lap he was 1.4 seconds ahead. By lap five his advantage had stretched to 3.8 seconds, and Senna quite clearly had a problem. The two McLarens were flying on the wings of the wind, both drivers punching in super-quick laps way faster than the opposition. But it was Prost who was the quicker on this day.

Both men had a single scheduled tyre stop on the agenda, each offering spine-tingling potential for an unscheduled delay. But there were no unplanned setbacks. Prost stopped at the end of lap 21, his car remaining stationary for 7.8 seconds. Senna came in two laps later and was at rest for 9.8 seconds. Now everybody braced themselves for the sprint to the chequered flag.

There were 30 laps to go as Ayrton went on to the attack. In ten laps he reduced Prost's advantage from 4.6 to 1.8 seconds. By lap 47 – with six to go – Senna had Prost firmly in his sights as the two McLaren-Hondas tore down the return straight towards the pits, slammed through the spectacular '130R' left-hander and went on to the brakes for the painfully tight chicane just before the start/finish line.

Senna went for it. Despite the fact that Prost had left him next to no room, he put his McLaren's right-hand wheels across the entrance to the pit lane and shaved the grass as he forced himself alongside the Frenchman.

He must have judged that Prost would concede. But this was a bridge too far for the Frenchman. Fed up with what he regarded as Senna's rough-house, intimidatory tactics, he turned into the corner. The two McLarens collided and shuddered to a halt, locked together in the middle of the track.

Prost undid his seat harness, jumped from the cockpit and walked away. Senna, unwilling to concede defeat, beckoned the marshals to help restart his stalled McLaren and resumed the race. But, in so doing he accelerated back into the fray *through* the chicane escape road.

Some observers believed that Prost went straight to the stewards' office and wound Balestre off the clock; the volatile president of the FIA always tended to shoot from the hip and relished being at the centre of controversy. Alain, many thought, simply loaded the revolver and then sat back to watch Balestre pull the trigger.

In Dennis's mind there was no doubt that Prost deliberately

turned into Senna. But he could live with that as one of the by-products of the intense level of competition between the two men. Even so, he knew better than most that both Senna and Prost were difficult to deal with; Ayrton was foxy in the extreme, but Alain did an equally good job attracting the sympathy vote with his Little Boy Lost routine which the press lapped up enthusiastically.

Next time round he darted into the pit lane for a replacement nose section to be fitted, resumed second and tore back to dislodge Alessandro Nannini's Benetton from first place with only two laps to go. Ayrton had won. Or had he?

Not so. After a lengthy meeting, the stewards announced that the Brazilian driver had been disqualified after opting for an illegal route by which to return to the race. McLaren lodged an appeal and the weekend finished in a swirling haze of recrimination and unpleasantness.

'I was absolutely certain that I would win the race or have an accident like this,' reflected Prost. 'One of Ayrton's problems is that he can neither accept the possibility of not winning, nor that somebody will resist his overtaking manoeuvres.'

For his part, Senna, who refused to speak to Prost after the race, later issued a lofty press statement. It read: 'That was the only place where I could overtake, and somebody who should not have been there just closed the door and that was that. The results as they stand provisionally do not the reflect the truth of the race in either the sporting sense or in the sense of the regulations. I see this result as temporary.'

On the Friday following the Japanese race, the McLaren team's lawyers duly arrived at the FISA headquarters in Paris to attend the Court of Appeal hearing. What they found took their breath away. They had expected a straightforward discussion of Senna's disqualification and the appropriate adjudication on the stewards' decision. What they were not prepared for was to be given a dossier outlining a series of what were described as 'serious errors' committed by the Brazilian driver.

The governing body concluded that, far from being excessive, the Suzuka stewards had taken a remarkably lenient view of Senna's transgression. The document went on to ask the FIA Court of Appeal to consider suspending Senna's licence for a year. The court deferred its decision and did not pronounce its judgement until the following Tuesday, when they imposed a $100,000 fine and a six-month suspended ban on the McLaren driver.

McLaren hinted at a possible legal action against the governing body. FISA President Jean-Marie Balestre warned Ron Dennis not even to waste his time thinking about it. Senna convened a press conference in Adelaide where, his eyes moist with emotion, he vowed to fight on.

'This is totally unacceptable,' he complained, 'because they are treating me like a criminal. It is both unfair and unrealistic. I never caused the accident. I am aggressive, determined and dedicated to my profession and on many occasions have worried about giving the audience a good performance.

'But the version that has been given to you about the Suzuka incidents, the logistics, the exit and everything, presented me as being an irresponsible lunatic who was breaking the rules.'

Either way, the Suzuka results would stand. Prost was World Champion for the third time in his career at the wheel of a McLaren, and the breach between he and Senna seemed irreparable. The final round of the '89 title chase was held on a near-flooded track surface at Adelaide, Senna surfing away into the lead, his McLaren almost rendered invisible within an impenetrable ball of spray.

He lasted until lap 14 when he plunged into the back of Martin Brundle's Brabham, ripping off the slower car's rear wing and the McLaren's left front wheel. He three-wheeled his way slowly back to the pits. It was all over. Prost, true to his own personal conscience, had pulled in and retired at the end of the opening lap.

For the McLaren International team, the 1989 Australian Grand Prix marked the end of one of the most bruising periods in its history. Ron Dennis had tried – heaven knows he had tried – with all the sincerity and sensitivity at his disposal to keep together one of the most volatile driving partnerships in grand prix racing history, but at the end of the day found it to be beyond his ability.

Ayrton Senna had achieved his ambition. On the face of it he had effectively crushed Prost's morale, undermining his confidence to the point where he felt there was no longer a future within the team he had regarded as home for no fewer than six World Championship seasons. Yet the story had produced a dramatic sting in the tail.

Just when Senna thought he had finally trampled the Frenchman's last vestige of resistance into the ground, Prost turned round and nipped him painfully as an almost symbolic last farewell. Yet motor racing history would, much later, throw a subtly different focus on the Senna/Prost partnership. Looking back, it now seems as though they fed off each other's competitive instincts, each driving the other on to scale greater pinnacles of achievement.

Five years later, in the last few months of Senna's life, those close to the Brazilian driver sensed that he detected something missing from the competitive world of F1 now that Prost had hung up his helmet for good. Only after Alain had stopped, they concluded, did Ayrton realise how much of his motivation had been generated by a desire to beat the little Frenchman with the crooked nose. The reality was that Senna and Prost had more in common than even they perhaps thought.

7

McLaren-Honda glory days: Senna ascendant, 1990–92

IN 1990 MCLAREN'S strongest challenge came from the Ferrari team. In a way this was only to be expected. Not only did Maranello now have Prost in its armoury, but also Steve Nichols, who had left McLaren to follow the Frenchman.

Moreover, it was possible to argue that the McLaren F1 team's design department had already been seriously weakened when, in March 1989, the TAG-McLaren Group established McLaren Cars with the objective of designing and manufacturing a unique high-performance road car.

The initial three-year programme to develop the first prototypes was led by Gordon Murray – another loss to the F1 operation – and the design responsibility for updating the MP4/5s to 'B' specification was now entrusted to Neil Oatley.

January 1989 also saw the formation of TAG Electronic Systems, a company established to provide complete electronic management and control systems in the low-to-medium automotive market, both for road and motorsport functions. It was to develop into a highly successful operation with a client base outside the TAG Group that included Alfa Romeo, Peugeot, Porsche and Toyota. By 1998 the company employed 125 people in a 27,000sq ft production and office complex adjacent to the McLaren F1 headquarters.

More worryingly, the controversy surrounding Senna and the previous year's Japanese Grand Prix disqualification refused to go away. Rather than cooling the situation, Ayrton fanned the flames by returning to Brazil at the end of the season, where he accused the governing body of manipulating the outcome of the Championship in Prost's favour.

In fact, he went further than that, accusing FISA President Jean-Marie Balestre of partiality 'whether out of patriotism, friendship or for other reasons I prefer not to mention.'

Senna was summoned to Paris for a private meeting with Balestre. He then appeared in front of the FIA World Council and refused to budge from his position. The World Council then voted to refuse

Senna's application for a 1990 F1 super licence unless he withdrew his allegations.

The deadline for team entries for the 1990 World Championship came and went. Senna had also failed to pay the $100,000 fine imposed on him by the appeal court hearing after Suzuka. McLaren had its entries for both cars returned and Balestre indicated that they would not be accepted until Senna apologised.

McLaren paid the fine. Their entry for two cars 'one to be driven by Gerhard Berger and a second by a driver who has yet to be named' was accepted. The 15 February 'final' deadline came and went; the official World Championship entry list was published showing the McLaren-Honda entries to be driven by Gerhard Berger and the team's test driver Jonathan Palmer. Within another hour, a revised list was published substituting Senna's name for Palmer's. Ayrton had made a grudging apology, of sorts.

Berger was to have one hell of a time adapting to the role of McLaren's second driver. To start with, it was almost half the season before McLaren could provide the lanky Austrian with a seating position he could work with. True enough, Berger started from pole position for the first race of the season at Phoenix, but accidentally snagged the brake pedal while running second to Jean Alesi's Tyrrell in the opening stages of the race and ended his participation firmly up against a tyre barrier.

Senna thus triumphed at Phoenix, but then Prost won for Ferrari in Ayrton's back yard at Interlagos, and Riccardo Patrese gave the Williams-Renault alliance a victory at Imola. Not until Monaco did Senna reassert himself with another victory. Then the Brazilian won again in Canada, only for Prost and Ferrari to rattle off a hat trick of wins at Mexico City, Paul Ricard and Silverstone. With eight races completed, Prost had 41 points, Senna 39.

By the middle of the year Ayrton was getting quite concerned about the performance drop-off, and used the situation ruthlessly to maximise his negotiating position when it came to renegotiating his contract for 1991. He was approaching the end of his initial three-year deal with McLaren. At the start of 1988 he had lost $1.5 million after agreeing to resolve the difference between what he wanted to earn and what Dennis wanted to pay by the toss a coin. Now it was payback time.

Senna not only pressed home his demands to the McLaren boss, but also worked Honda up into a right old lather, doing his best to convince the Japanese engine-maker that the situation with the team was critical. In truth, Senna wanted almost $12 million as his retainer for 1991 and if, in order to get it, it meant sowing the seeds of doubt about McLaren's capabilities in the mind of the Honda top brass, then that was what he was prepared to do. By any standards, Ayrton was an implacable and ruthless negotiator.

After a particularly disappointing time wrestling the MP4/5B round Silverstone to a distant third place in the British Grand Prix, Senna bounced back to win at Hockenheim after aerodynamic changes – notably to the diffuser – improved the car's behaviour considerably. He was also helped by a further revised, higher-revving version of the latest Honda V10 engine.

Second place to his old pal Thierry Boutsen's Williams in the Hungarian Grand Prix gave Senna a 10-point lead over Prost in the title chase. He then won again at Spa, expanding his advantage to 13 points over the Frenchman, who finished second. Then he paid Prost back for beating him at Interlagos by defeating the Ferrari driver by a margin of 6 seconds in the Italian Grand Prix at Monza. Senna 72 points, Prost 56.

The Portuguese Grand Prix saw Mansell and Prost qualify 1–2 with their Ferraris. By this stage the British driver had decided to retire at the end of the season after a succession of disappointments. Having negotiated his release from Ferrari, who then signed Jean Alesi as his replacement, Mansell would later reverse his retirement decision and sign to drive for Williams in 1991. But that was only part of the story.

Throughout 1990 Mansell was driven to conclude that Prost was being favoured by Ferrari. At the start of the Portuguese race, Mansell lurched across in front of Prost, allowing Senna a free run into an immediate lead. Alain was shunted back to fifth place as a result, Senna relinquishing the lead to Mansell shortly before the chequered flag.

It was a set of circumstances that, perhaps inevitably, gave rise to speculation that Mansell and Senna had conspired to 'fix' Prost at this particular race. Such wild allegations were strenuously denied, but it was still Senna 78 points, Prost 60, with only three races left to go.

The following week's Spanish Grand Prix at Jerez saw a complete reversal of the situation, which was as sudden as it was perhaps unexpected. Prost won from Mansell while Senna, like his colleagues, deeply shocked by the serious practice accident that had left British Lotus driver Martin Donnelly gravely injured, suffered an engine failure. Suddenly it was Senna 78 points, Prost 69.

Then it was back to Suzuka, where all hell let loose. Senna qualified his McLaren on pole, only to be told that he would be starting from the right-hand side of the circuit. He was furious. On the Wednesday prior to the race he had asked the organisers if they would move pole over to the left, on the cleaner racing line. Ironically, Prost agreed with that request.

However, the officials declined the invitation, saying that the grid had already been marked out with pole on the right. Prost had qualified second, giving him the cleaner outside line. That stoked up

Senna even further, the Brazilian knowing that if Prost won this race
with the ever-improving Ferrari, his World Championship chances
might be in serious danger. 'If he's ahead of me into the first corner,
he'd better not turn in, because he's not going to make it,' warned
Senna on race morning.

So they started. By my reckoning – and after consulting my
notebook from that race – it took just 9.2 seconds to resolve the
outcome of the 1990 World Championship. Prost got the jump on
Ayrton, eased into the first corner ahead – and was rammed at
ferocious speed from behind by the pole position McLaren-Honda.

The Ferrari lost its rear wing, the McLaren its left front wheel.
Both thankfully spun away from the pursuing pack on to the gravel
run-off. The race did not have to be stopped. Senna was World
Champion for the second time in his career.

After he had returned on foot to the pits, Ron Dennis threw his
arms round Senna in a gesture of congratulation. Considering that
Alain Prost had done probably more than most to put McLaren
International on the F1 map over much of the previous decade, this
was not one of Ron's more tactful moments.

In 1987 Alain enjoyed his partnership with Stefan Johansson, but
then came the huge head-to-head confrontation with Senna who
joined McLaren at the same time as the team began using works
Honda engines. Even by the end of 1993, he still found it very
difficult to speak about Ayrton, with whom he had the most
complicated of relationships.

It was clear that his feelings were dominated by that day at Suzuka
when Ayrton's McLaren plunged into the back of his Ferrari. 'And
nobody did anything about it,' he shrugged. 'Nothing! Even though
he talked about what he might do if I turned into the corner ahead of
him during the morning before the start. Unbelievable, simply
unbelievable . . .' His voice trailed away.

In that connection he was absolutely convinced that driving
standards in F1 have deteriorated. 'Yes,' he said firmly. 'I have always
said that. Can you imagine Niki Lauda behaving that way? No way,
absolutely no way. Emerson Fittipaldi, Scheckter or Rosberg? I
mean, I just ask one question – is this kind of thing [the way Senna
behaved at Suzuka] the right way to give a positive example to the
people racing in Formula Ford and so on?

'It should be the job of the international sporting federations to
defend the sport. Not the people involved. It is that which is the
most important thing, in my opinion.'

For Gerhard Berger, the 1990 Japanese Grand Prix was also a
dismal day to forget. Having accelerated into that first corner in third
place, he was presented with the lead on the plate when his two key
rivals collided. Yet going into the second lap, the pleasant Austrian
spun off at almost the self-same place. It was an unforced error and a

lapse that seemed to encapsulate the difficulties Berger had suffered in adapting to his new role.

Gerhard lacked Senna's delicacy of touch. He was harder on the tyres and, although he was an admirable team man, he simply didn't have the consistency required. McLaren failed to post a single 1–2 success during the 1990 season and that, as much as anything, told observers on the touchline all they needed to know about the comparative merits of Prost and Berger.

Yet Berger was no fool. He quickly came to terms with his position and reasoned that he could learn a great deal from Senna in terms of developing his own talent as a professional racing driver. He was honest and cheerful, with no side to his character, qualities that Ayrton came to value enormously. They would drive together in the McLaren-Honda squad for three seasons and, as time wore on, Ayrton would come to appreciate Berger as a man on whom he could absolutely rely, a man he could trust.

For his part, Gerhard helped the Brazilian become more relaxed, less intense when they were away from the business of motor racing. 'I think I showed Ayrton how to laugh,' he would later reflect on many occasions. By the time Senna died, Berger would be acknowledged as one of his real friends in the F1 business.

For the 1991 season Honda produced its third F1 engine configuration in four seasons with the introduction of the RA121E V12 with a 60-degree vee angle. The discarded V10s were now supplied to the Tyrrell team on a fixed specification basis and McLaren began to test the new V12s within weeks of final race of 1990.

Senna spent most of the winter resting in Brazil, so much of the off-season development work was carried out by Berger, together with test drivers Jonathan Palmer and Allan McNish. Yet when Senna got back behind the wheel of a V12-engined car in the run-up to the first race of 1991, he was aghast. Never a man to mince his words, he told Honda that they'd fallen behind on engine development. In words of one syllable, one gathered.

The new McLaren MP4/6 had a substantially revised aerodynamic profile, reflecting input from former Ferrari aerodynamicist Henri Durand. But the Honda RA121E V12 was heavier, longer and thirstier than its immediate predecessor and, although developing a reputed 720bhp, did not have sufficient edge over the emergent Renault V10s to offset decisively its additional weight.

The new Williams FW14, the first of the team's cars to benefit from Adrian Newey's design input, quickly developed into a formidable tool in the hands of Nigel Mansell and Riccardo Patrese. Yet during the first four races of the 1991 season the new challenger was beset by reliability problems. By contrast, McLaren's impeccable preparation contributed to Senna winning Phoenix, Interlagos, Imola and Monaco straight off the bat at the beginning of the season.

Yet Honda had taken aboard Senna's pre-season complaints. They quickly realised that they were saddled with an engine that was thirstier than they had originally anticipated, suffered from excessive internal frictional losses – and consequent heat retention – while also being prone to main bearing failures stemming from unbalanced oil distribution to the crankshaft. On the face of it, this was not promising.

Williams showed its serious promise when Patrese finished second at Interlagos and Mansell duplicated the result at Monaco. Then came Montreal, where Senna's McLaren was not only pushed off pole position for the first time in the season, but also off the front row as Mansell and Patrese posted a Williams 1–2. Both the Honda V12-engined cars were out before half distance with mechanical problems, leaving Nelson Piquet's Benetton-Ford to score a lucky win after Mansell's apparently dominant Williams rolled to a halt two corners from home, when a gear-change glitch, apparently self-inflicted, deprived the Englishman of victory.

Mexico City was next, producing an impressive grand slam for Williams, Patrese leading home Mansell on this occasion. Even before the start of practice, Senna's equilibrium seemed slightly ruffled. He'd arrived in Mexico nursing ten stitches in his head, the result of a jet-ski accident in Brazil a few days earlier. Then, in Friday qualifying, he over-drove to the point that he rolled his McLaren-Honda on the outside of the fast Peraltada banked corner just before the start/finish line.

Come the race, Senna hung on gamely to finish third, but almost a minute behind Mansell. By the end of the day Ayrton found himself uncomfortably aware that the F1 torch was poised to pass from McLaren to Williams, and he was more than usually interested in what Honda proposed to do about it. 'Unless we change our equipment pretty fast, we're going to have trouble later this season,' he noted.

Back to Europe for the French and British Grands Prix. Mansell won both for Williams, while Ayrton was third and fourth respectively in these two crucial races, his efforts having been stymied on both occasions by problems with his McLaren's fuel consumption computer.

At Magny-Cours the computer was pessimistic, at Silverstone optimistic. He should have been second in the British race, but spluttered to a halt on the final lap, allowing Berger's McLaren and Prost's Ferrari to go ahead over the final mile. Almost unbelievably, the Silverstone problem repeated itself at Hockenheim where Senna dropped from fourth to seventh on the final lap.

With Mansell winning his third race in succession, the British Williams driver was now only eight points behind Senna and could begin to sniff the possibility of a World Championship. In the Constructors' battle, Williams now edged ahead. McLaren went on red alert for a big push.

All these apparent fuel consumption problems threw into sharp perspective the difficulties involved in accurately monitoring the Honda V12's consumption rate at a time when Shell was experimenting with different fuel specifications. With collaboration from TAG Electronics, another satellite company within the TAG-McLaren Group, this complex matter was eventually resolved. Meanwhile, Honda pulled out all the stops to produce an extensively revised V12, capable of running to almost 15,000rpm, for Senna's priority use in time for the Hungarian Grand Prix.

It proved just the job. Despite some fleeting experimentation with McLaren's semi-automatic gearbox during practice, Senna put the revised MP4/6 on pole position and led every lap of the race, repulsing challenges from both Williams drivers and eventually forcing Mansell and Patrese to settle for second and third. After the race Riccardo confronted the Brazilian, accusing him of chopping him too ruthlessly on the run to the first corner. 'Oh come on,' replied Senna. 'You would have done the same to me. Of course you would!'

The weekend at Budapest also saw Prost and Senna meeting behind closed doors in another attempt to smooth out their turbulent personal relationship. The latest crisis had been sparked by a wheel-to-wheel confrontation during the previous race at Hockenheim during which Ayrton forced the Frenchman's Ferrari up the escape road at one of the chicanes.

Prost had been furious after this episode, accusing Senna of weaving repeatedly on the straight and also directing a helping of trenchant disapproval at the FISA officials for not sanctioning the Brazilian. Neither driver said much in detail when they emerged from the meeting, although it seemed clear that they wanted to get things back on to something of an even keel. This apparent attempt at a *rapprochement* was not helped when the governing body followed it up – with exquisite timing – by giving Prost a one-race suspended ban for speaking his mind in the aftermath of the Hockenheim race.

In the Belgian Grand Prix at Spa-Francorchamps, Senna won again despite gearbox troubles, heading Berger home for a lucky McLaren 1–2. Now it was Senna 71 points, Mansell 49. But the Brazilian was less than amused when Frank Williams decided to retain the Mansell/Patrese line-up for 1992 at a time when Senna reckoned he was still talking with him about a possible switch from McLaren. At a stroke, Senna's negotiating hand with Ron Dennis was measurable weakened and he was not amused.

He was even less amused at Monza where he was gradually worn down by the Williams challenge. First Patrese got past, only to suffer clutch failure almost immediately. Then Mansell re-launched a counter-attack on Senna's McLaren, and emerged with a win. Senna 77 points, Mansell 59.

Two more races followed on the Iberian peninsular, the Portuguese Grand Prix at Estoril and the Spanish race at Montmelo. Senna finished second to Patrese's Williams in the former race, but only after Mansell was disqualified for the second year running. This time the Englishman's Williams was flagged away from a routine tyre stop before its right rear wheel had been properly secured.

After only a few yards, the errant wheel parted company with the car and the team mistakenly tried to change the wheel on the spot rather than hauling it back to its allotted pit to complete the job. Out came the black flag for our Nige. Senna 83 points, Mansell 59.

A week later, on a patchy damp Spanish track surface, Mansell bounced back with one of the most steely victories of his entire career, achieved after a heart-stopping, eyeball-to-eyeball confrontation with Senna as the Williams and McLaren tore down the main straight, literally inches apart, at 180mph. In fine drizzle.

The timing of Mansell's tyre stops in this tactically complex and unpredictable race proved perfect and he won by 11 seconds from Prost's Ferrari. Senna, after a spin, trailed home a simmeringly disappointed fifth. Senna 85 points, Mansell 59. And two races still to run.

The Japanese Grand Prix at Suzuka again saw the destiny of the World Championship finally sorted out. Berger started from pole and sprinted into an immediate lead, leaving Senna to keep Mansell – who needed to win to have a shot at the title – back in third place.

Going into the tenth lap, Mansell had just radioed to his pits that all was going well when he ran wide at the first corner and spun his Williams into a gravel trap. That meant that the title was now Senna's, whatever the outcome of the race, and while Ayrton duly caught and passed Gerhard, he had no hesitation in obeying team orders to hand the win to his Austrian team-mate in the closing moments of the contest.

On the rostrum it was all smiles and back-slapping. Then Senna suddenly switched into his confrontational mode for the post-race media conference, launching a barrage of abuse at Jean-Marie Balestre, who had been defeated by Max Mosley in the FISA Presidential election only ten days before.

Rather than let sleeping dogs lie and be gracious in victory, Ayrton raked up the 1989 collision with Prost, accusing Balestre in abusive terms of partiality in his efforts to fix the outcome of the title in Prost's favour. He also effectively admitted that he had, in fact, rammed Prost's Ferrari off the road in 1989.

All this tedious nonsense meant that Ron Dennis had to apply the brakes gently before yet another Senna-orientated controversy snowballed out of control. After meeting with Senna, Mosley and Honda, the team went some way to making amends by issuing a statement that relied on the age-old chestnut that Ayrton's remarks had been 'misinterpreted'. Very tedious.

The Australian Grand Prix rounded off the season with Senna taking another victory, although it was yet another half-points affair as the Adelaide race was flagged to a halt in torrential rain after 14 laps. It was not a particularly stimulating note on which to end the title battle.

From the start of the 1992 season it was clear that the rival Williams-Renault squad had re-defined the competitive parameters of contemporary F1. The new all-active-suspension Williams FW14B in the hands of Nigel Mansell and Riccardo Patrese now assumed the position that McLaren had enjoyed for the past three seasons. It proved a painful lesson for the Honda-propelled team.

The fact of the matter is that Honda was well behind with the development of the new 75-degree RA122E/B V12 engine that would power the all-new McLaren MP4/7A. Much of this lateness was attributed to the amount of effort Honda had to expend in keeping the 1991 60-degrees V12 programme on the competitive road.

As usual, the McLaren management behaved with considerable diplomacy, continuing its discreet and tactful technique of assuming responsibility for all performance deficiencies, whether they were chassis or engine related. It was increasingly clear that Honda was scaling down its involvement and that its stated intention to withdraw from F1 at the end of the 1992 season was not negotiable.

The new Honda V12 was intended to produce more power than the 1991 engine, thanks to the use of higher revs facilitated by the introduction of pneumatic valve actuation. As things turned out, the engine was initially disappointing and it was not until after the Monaco Grand Prix, where Senna scored his first win of the season to break the Williams/Mansell run of dominant victories, that the new V12 began to make any worthwhile progress.

Senna only won at Monaco because Mansell made a precautionary late pit stop when he suspected he might have a slow puncture. That was the story of the season. Senna drove with his customary flat-out 100 per cent commitment, but the bottom line was that he only won three races when Williams dropped the ball. Berger won another two, Canada and Australia.

Some observers speculated that things might have been different had McLaren been ready with an active suspension system from the start of the year. Perhaps the team's fortunes might have been better, but the new Honda V12 demonstrated a prodigious thirst for fuel. Ayrton won again in Hungary, then Berger picked up his Australian win after Ayrton's McLaren ran into the back of Mansell's Williams while the two cars were battling for the lead.

Mansell was furious, but Senna shrugged aside his complaints and baldly stated that the Englishman had been deliberately 'brake testing' him – a technique in which a driver suddenly backs off, or lightly touches his brakes, to unsettle a competitor following closely behind. Sources close to the McLaren team later reported that Ayrton admitted that he could have avoided hitting Mansell, but was so fed up with the Williams driver's behaviour that he simply ran into him. 'I decided he wasn't going to win a race like that,' he told a colleague.

Berger's victory at least enabled the McLaren-Honda alliance to end on a victorious note, just as it had started in 1988 at Rio de Janeiro. Yet it was unclear precisely just what engine supply deal McLaren would secure for 1993. Senna was pressing Dennis quite hard on this subject, causing a degree of tension in their personal relationship. Ayrton was even considering shouldering his way into the Williams camp alongside Alain Prost, an option that was, at least on the face of it, open to him since Nigel Mansell's decision to retire after winning the '92 World Championship.

'I will not share with him, nor anybody else, including my wife, our intention on engines!' said Dennis in response to a press inquiry on the matter at Monza. He was certainly not joking.

From the start of the 1992 season I always felt that Honda's decision to withdraw from F1 at the end of the year was something that Dennis believed he could persuade the Japanese car-maker to reverse.

Even after the Williams-Renault FW14B had won the first four races of the season, Dennis told me in the paddock at Mexico City that he believed McLaren would win the Championship. To be truthful, it was couched in more forceful language than that. 'We'll win the title,' he said in a tone that almost challenged any listener to contradict his viewpoint.

Six months later the McLaren chief would be immersed in the process of analysing McLaren's performance shortcomings and focusing his strategy on how he could shape the next four years in order to guarantee a return to full competitiveness. Five wins out of the season's 16 races may have been a record most teams would have killed for, but it wasn't very satisfying by McLaren contemporary standards.

'The primary reason for the delay in introducing the MP4/7 was that in November 1991 it was very apparent that the Honda engine development programme was way behind schedule,' he reflected. 'The new V12 – the RA122E-B – did not run on the test bed until late December, so we felt together that it would be better to continue the wind tunnel development programme, using the extra time that delaying the new car's debut gave us, to optimise the design and, at the same time, to give Honda more time to develop the engine.'

Point taken, but if Ron had actually decided to start the season with uprated versions of the 1991 McLaren, why did he suddenly advance the MP4/7's planned debut from the Spanish Grand Prix at the beginning of May to the Brazilian race one month earlier?

Dennis was quite clear in his own mind why this change of plan had come about. 'The decision to accelerate the programme was a result of the performance we saw from the Williams FW14B, both in testing and immediately prior to the first race and in the South African Grand Prix itself,' he recalled.

'In that race, we thought we would be able to run a close third and fourth, but were in fact only able to run a *distant* third and fourth. As a consequence there seemed no point in delaying the debut of the MP4/7 because the question of mechanical reliability, which I thought might be a factor in the early races, just wasn't a problem with Williams.

'They clearly had a reliable package from the outset, so in order to stand a chance of winning the World Championship we just had to get the new car up and running as fast as possible.'

Yet if the V12 Honda engine was not the best in the business, Ron believed that the McLaren MP4/7 was technically the best chassis that the team had made up to that point.

'By that I am talking in terms of constructional techniques: the sophistication of the gearbox, the purity of design as regards getting down to the weight limit.

'Getting down to the weight limit with a 12-cylinder car is always difficult when you take into consideration the auxiliary systems you need to provide the engine with in terms of fuel dissipation and fuel tank capacity. These factors all make their impact on the design process, and the fact that we managed to bring the MP4/7 in under the weight limit was quite an achievement for the team.'

Dennis also predicted – correctly, as things transpired – that McLaren's development of a computer-controlled active suspension system would eventually surpass the similar set-up that Williams used as part of its dominant winning package in 1992.

'The active ride system we are currently working on is extremely sophisticated,' he predicted. 'I don't think we have really seen anybody bring in a totally new system this year at all, other than what amounts to modified earlier systems.

'What we are trying to do is take a technological leap forward with our system, because merely having the same as Williams won't make us better. And we aim to be better. The control systems and associated software are extremely complicated and it just takes time to eliminate all the bugs.'

During the course of the patchy 1992 season, Ayrton Senna had been quite outspoken in his criticism of the McLaren team's overall performance, but it was nothing that unduly rattled Dennis, who gave the impression that he was prepared to put up with a degree of grief from the brilliant Brazilian if that was part of the price of retaining the services of the best driver in the business.

'I think this year Ayrton has been exceptionally good in the car at race meetings,' he said, carefully picking his words. 'But I don't think he has had the mental commitment to our testing, which has made life no easier and, of course, he has been very distracted out of the car for a range of reasons. But that distraction has not been counter-productive in terms of moving forward.'

Berger, for his part, had enjoyed his three years at McLaren. Yet he had no interest in remaining in a team with Senna, much as he had come to like his Brazilian colleague. In Gerhard's view, the strength of Ayrton's character was so forceful that his influence on the manner in which the team was run transcended anything that he had ever experienced before. In his view, trying to be Senna's team-mate ultimately meant compromising his own professional future.

As a result, Berger accepted a lucrative offer to return to Ferrari. Yet there was to be one more final episode in his relationship with McLaren from which he would derive enormous amusement, a touch of *schadenfreude* perhaps, at the expense of Ron Dennis.

Prior to practice at Suzuka in 1993, Berger was invited to passenger Dennis in one of the McLaren F1 road cars that had been flown out to Japan to start a sales tour amongst selected Far Easter high rollers with the necessary wherewithal to meet the £600,000-plus price tag.

Dennis shunted the car at the second corner, much to Gerhard's glee. To his credit, Ron came clean and put his hand up. 'My mistake,' he shrugged ruefully. For his part, Berger went up the press room steps two at a time where he convened an impromptu media conference. He could hardly catch his breath, so obviously was he shaking with laughter.

8

Making do,
1993–94

THE 1993 F1 World Championship season produced another frustrating period for the McLaren team, although the sheer quality of its technical engineering, race strategy and driver strength saw it emerge at the end of the year with five victories, four more than the Benetton-Ford squad, which, by one of those strange F1 paradoxes, sometimes seemed to project a more successful image than the Woking-based squad.

Replacing the Honda engine supply deal was not the work of a moment. In fact, it seemed to present a major problem, for unless Ron Dennis could find a way of securing Renault's V10 units, there seemed precious little prospect of Ayrton Senna carrying the battle to the Williams team unless adverse weather conditions played into his hand.

However, Dennis duly secured the Renault engines by negotiating to purchase Ligier, the French team which already had a Renault contract in place. The idea was then to switch the Renault engines to McLaren and negotiate another engine supply deal for Ligier to use. Dennis secured the agreement of Renault that they would run the engines on Shell fuel and lubricants for one year, then review the situation. But Elf, Renault's long-time fuel partner, vetoed the deal. Dennis would not break his Shell contract and so the McLaren-Renault partnership came to nought.

As things transpired, McLaren opted to become a customer for the Ford-Cosworth HB V8 engine, a reputed £6 million investment that would be enhanced by an intensive and independent development programme incorporating technical input from TAG Electronic Systems under the direction of former Bosch electronic guru Dr Udo Zucker, who had first become acquainted with the British team during the relationship with Porsche. This programme included the development of a twin-injector configuration, which was tried in testing with inconclusive results.

McLaren usually began the design process for a new F1 car during the September prior to the season in which it was scheduled to race, but for the 1993 season its choice of engine was not finalised until October. However, McLaren's state-of-the-art computer-aided design system enabled the lost ground to be made up, and the new Cosworth-powered McLaren MP4/8 was officially unveiled on 15 February, a month before the first race of the season at Kyalami.

The MP4/8 chassis was only the second in the team's history to be built round a carbon-fibre 'female' moulded monocoque incorporating advanced materials supplied by Hercules, the US specialists who had supplied all such materials to McLaren ever since its pioneering work with the MP4 chassis in 1981.

McLaren was pinning its hopes on a combination of a light and compact fuel-efficient engine, a fine-handling chassis and such accessories as the further refined computer-controlled active suspension system, developed by MI and TAG Electronic Systems.

The new car also featured new electronic engine management, chassis control, data acquisition and telemetry systems, supplemented by a lightweight electronic cockpit instrumental panel, all of which were also designed, developed and manufactured by McLaren's associate electronic specialists.

After his 1992 season had ended on a disappointing note when he collided with outgoing Mansell's Williams in Adelaide, Senna adopted his familiar strategy of retiring to his beach house in Brazil over the winter to re-charge his batteries while the McLaren workforce toiled to ready the new car.

Meanwhile, the team's newly signed second driver, Michael Andretti, took the opportunity to keep testing the old McLaren MP4/7A, the contract with Honda ensuring that engines were made available for this purpose until the end of the year. There followed a frustrating six weeks while the new Ford-engined car was completed, during which Andretti was left twiddling his thumbs, anxious to start learning the ropes in earnest.

Senna's first impressions of the new MP4/8 were highly positive and he set the fastest off-season Silverstone test time almost the moment he got behind its wheel. His commitment to McLaren was initially presented to the world as a race-by-race deal; only later did Ron Dennis admit that this was a strategy, agreed between the two men, to coax the necessary extra funds from existing sponsors to meet Senna's financial aspirations – reputedly in the region of $1 million per race.

Whatever the deal, this looked like money well spent as Senna finished second to Prost's Williams at Kyalami, despite an active suspension malfunction that caused the rear ride height to stick in the 'up' position, then reeled off two brilliant wet-weather victories at Interlagos and Donington Park.

As Cosworth customers, footing the bill for any untoward engine breakages caused by the use of a traction control system that cut out cylinders – a technique about which the Northampton engine specialists were not totally convinced – McLaren capitalised on the use of this key accessory before Benetton's more complex 'throttle intervention' system was perfected and fitted to the rival Ford-engined cars.

Andretti, meanwhile, started the season with crashes at Kyalami and Interlagos. He then qualified sixth at Donington Park, a whisker behind Senna, only to be eliminated in a collision with Karl Wendlinger's Sauber on the opening lap. At Imola he again fell foul of the German driver during the course of a zestful drive that might possibly have resulted in a podium finish, and many people saw this as the turning point of his year.

He scored points on only three occasions, and those who believed they saw flashes of the zest he once displayed on the Indycar scene merely indulged in wishful thinking. Despite the unflinching support offered by the McLaren management, his season was a disaster. After Monza the whole deal would be quietly wrapped up and test driver Mika Hakkinen promoted to the F1 team proper. It reminded everybody just what they'd been missing.

Michael's European foray had been launched at a press conference immediately following the first qualifying session for the 1992 Italian Grand Prix at Monza. Ron Dennis had stood up looking like the cat that had stolen the cream. We all had a pretty fair idea what he was about to say.

We were right. For 1993 he was signing Andretti to drive for McLaren. The son of 1978 F1 World Champion, Michael was the scion of one of US motor racing's most prestigious dynasties. His credentials were impeccable.

His father's running mate in the pace-setting Newman/Haas Lola Indycar team for the previous three seasons, Michael had been long acknowledged as one of the naturally talented and motivated drivers to have emerged from the US Indycar series over the previous decade. Since his debut in that category in 1984 he had won 27 races and scored an equal number of pole position starts. In 1992 he'd led the Indy 500 for 161 of its 200 laps before mechanical failure intervened.

'I think he can win grands prix and become the World Champion,' said Dennis. 'It's not a question of which country you come from. It's how you demonstrate your desire to win.

'You've got to have that desire to win, and the aggression in traffic. There are probably less than five drivers in the world who have that necessary aggression.' Even for those of us who were willing these words to be true, it came over as an almost recklessly optimistic assessment.

Cynics would say that Dennis conveniently chose to overlook the inconclusive results thrown up by Andretti's two McLaren tests the previous year. On the other hand, Ron had a proven track record of absolute loyalty to those in whose talent he has chosen to invest his faith. Michael was very much His Man. Question him today on the wisdom of signing Michael, and he will offer a sincere and well-reasoned defence of his strategy.

It just couldn't go wrong and most people roundly applauded Dennis for an imaginative driver selection at the start of a week that would see newly crowned World Champion Nigel Mansell announce his retirement from F1. Mansell would duly travel across the Atlantic in the opposite direction to achieve enormous success in the sphere that Andretti had abandoned. Michael's trip to Europe, by contrast, would be distinctly less productive.

F1 is all about knowing every detail of the men you're up against. Within the Indycar fraternity, the mere sight of Michael's steely silver helmet in the rear-view mirrors had been enough to make grown men tremble – or at least clear a path. 'I tell you, Michael in traffic is just awesome,' Mario had said approvingly in the past. 'He just goes for gaps that I wouldn't even think of . . .'

Yet in F1 he inadvertently laid down a marker for himself that would initially spark an overtly aggressive stance from his new rivals. Former Indycar champion? Oh yes, well come this way. This is F1 now, a whole new ball game. Try it on me, boy!

Michael tried it – and came unstuck. From the word go. In the opening race at Kyalami he took a front wheel off against Derek Warwick's Footwork. In Brazil he was launched into a crazy cartwheel when he collided with Gerhard Berger's Ferrari almost on the start line. And at Donington Park he dived inside Karl Wendlinger's Sauber midway round the opening lap – and ended up in a sand trap.

It was clear that Andretti's whole F1 credibility was now balanced on a knife-edge. In many people's view, the crucial turning point that conspired to knock him sideways came at Imola during the San Marino Grand Prix. He was running well inside the top half-dozen, dicing with Wendlinger, when he momentarily took his eyes off the road to fiddle with the cockpit brake balance adjuster.

When he looked up again, Wendlinger was slowing for a tight chicane. Michael hit the brake pedal and pirouetted off on to the wet grass. And there he stayed.

'The problem was that he just didn't know enough about the people he was racing against,' said Mark Blundell, then driving for the Ligier team. 'In the British Grand Prix at Silverstone we were all accelerating away towards the first corner. I had one eye on Jean Alesi's Ferrari to my right, when suddenly Michael tried to go round the outside of him as we got into the braking area.

'I was thinking, "No, no, no . . . don't do that!", because anybody with any experience knows that Alesi won't be intimidated. Sure enough, Michael pulled level with him on the outside, Jean brakes really late and starts to slide. That left Michael with no choice but to get on the dust on the outside of the corner. That was it. Straight into the sand trap he went.

'There's no doubt Michael is a very good driver indeed, but he found himself in a position where he just couldn't amass sufficient experience quickly enough to become a contender.'

Yet there were practical factors that militated against Andretti being competitive during his crucial freshman year in F1. During the interval between his doing the deal with Ron Dennis and starting the 1993 season, the sport's governing body FISA imposed some crucial new regulations restricting the number of laps permitted in official grand prix practice and qualifying.

At a stroke of the pen Michael's hopes of unrestricted laps in free practice were wiped from the slate. From here on in, it was just 23 laps in the morning's untimed session, 12 laps in the afternoon's qualifying session. Now there was no room for error, even on the part of grand prix racing's established Top Guns. So what hope could there be for a novice who'd never seen any of the circuits before in his life?

Some other teams, those with a less well-defined sense of obligation than McLaren, might have been tempted to give up on their new star. But that's not the way Ron Dennis's organisation works. Fully appreciating how their new recruit had been damaged by these rule changes, they closed rank in an effort to minimise Michael's problems.

His race engineer Steve Hallam, a mild-mannered, sensitive and sympathetic guy, spent hours on trans-Atlantic phone calls preparing Michael for the challenge awaiting him at the next new circuit. Together in the motorhome, they would also study in-car videos of Michael's qualifying laps, anxious to pinpoint any area that could sharpen up his on-track performance.

Yet the technological complexity of a 1993 F1 car, with its computer-controlled suspension, traction control systems and fully automated gear-change systems, sometimes seemed beyond Andretti's grasp. Hallam spent much of the year pressing Michael for precise details of how the car was behaving, often to be rewarded with sweeping generalities.

The problem seemed to become more acute as the season progressed. Michael began over-driving in desperation. Yet the silly accidents, spins and collisions kept on coming. There seemed no way out of the dilemma.

'He's a lovely guy and very popular with the team,' said McLaren team manager Davey Ryan with a genuine air of sympathy. 'But sometimes it's very difficult to pinpoint precisely what the problem is. We're all willing him to do well and I'm certain we've not seen his true potential as a driver.'

Michael, to be sure, found the technique required to drive an F1 machine very different from any Indycar. It required more finesse, more self-control. He found this transition particularly hard to effect.

'An Indycar responds to a firm hand,' he mused early in the season. 'If you ring its neck, really throw it about, then you get a payback in terms of better lap times. But an F1 car doesn't respond in the same way. You need to be more precise, in some ways more gentle with it. It's taking me some time to get used to that.

'In addition, while an Indycar basically has the same sort of terminal speed as an F1 car, when you get on the brakes everything changes. With an F1 car the braking distances are halved. That takes some getting used to as well!'

Ayrton Senna confirmed this reality. At the end of '92 he had also toyed with a switch to Indycars and had taken the opportunity to test a Penske-Chevy on the Firebird raceway near Phoenix. It was an experience that offered him an instant insight into Andretti's potential problems.

'I believe that Michael only needed more time and more experience in an F1 car on the circuits at which we raced,' said Ayrton.

'I am sure he has the talent to become competitive, but an F1 car is very much more difficult to drive – more difficult to identify when you are close to the limit – but I think it was the limitations on laps that gave him the biggest problems. I think he probably came into F1 at the wrong moment, particularly as the handling problems we experienced with this year's McLaren exposed him to even more difficulty.'

Yet there was something more fundamental to it than even that pragmatic analysis by one of the most intelligent drivers in the business. Michael simply didn't seem to enjoy F1. By his own admission he was an all-American boy. Cheeseburgers and fries, rather than pretentious *nouvelle cuisine*, was more to his personal taste.

There is also no doubt that his refusal to relocate his family to Europe was perceived, however unintentionally, as a major question mark over his total, 100 per cent commitment. He preferred, instead, to commute by Concorde, pointing out that his Dad had always done that in the late 1970s and it hadn't done any harm to his performance.

That was a somewhat simplistic viewpoint. The pressures on a professional racing driver had multiplied tenfold since Mario's F1 heyday. There is more testing and development work to be done, more demands on a driver's time as a whole. It was the unconscious message signalled by this supersonic programme of trans-Atlantic commuting that did the damage Michael sometimes affected not to see.

The end came days after the Italian Grand Prix, ironically after

Michael's best-ever F1 finish in third place. Andretti could see that there was precious little chance of being kept on the McLaren payroll for '94 and wanted to accept the Chip Ganassi deal before all his Indycar options closed up as well. Test driver Mika Hakkinen took over his drive for the final three grands prix of the year.

'I know this isn't the end of Michael's career,' said Ron Dennis stoically. 'In any case, he owes us three races and McLaren has first option on his services if he ever wants to return to F1.'

Everybody agreed that Dennis's words represented supreme sensitivity of the highest order. They also seemed to represent a tacit acknowledgement that Andretti was certainly a world-class driver, but this little experiment just hadn't worked out. In fact, sources close to the team hinted strongly that Dennis had run out of patience with the American driver before Monza, and had only permitted him to race in that event because of what the Andretti family name still meant to the Italian fans.

For most aspiring stars, third place at Monza would have seemed the light at the end of the tunnel. Sadly, for Michael Andretti, that glimmer of hope had proved simply to be, as they say, the lights of an oncoming train. He'd gambled for high stakes and lost. He had meant it to turn out so very differently.

Meanwhile, Senna had hoped that McLaren would reach an accommodation with the rival Benetton team to make available the higher-revving pneumatic-valve Series VIII version of the Ford V8 engine in time for Imola, the original contractual arrangement stipulating that they would not get parity of equipment until the British Grand Prix.

In anticipation of the agreement of both Ford and Benetton that this upgrading could be brought forward to the San Marino race, Cosworth had delivered a couple of Series VIII engines into McLaren's custody. One was installed on Friday night, but removed and replaced with a Series VII unit before free practice on Saturday morning when McLaren and Benetton proved unable to reach an accord.

Hand in hand with all this behind-the-scenes drama, Ayrton Senna decided to indulge in one of his periodic displays of brinkmanship, staying in Brazil until the night before first practice. He then boarded an Alitalia flight to Rome, whence he was whisked to the Imola paddock by private jet, helicopter and motorcycle.

Throughout practice at this race, both McLaren drivers experienced a spate of almost identical spins when they rode the kerbs on the exit of two key corners; this was an aerodynamic problem related to the operation of the ride height control.

Manually activated by a button on the steering wheel, by means of which the drivers could lower the car on the straight for reduced aerodynamic drag, the idea was then to de-activate the system going into the corners, either manually or automatically through sensors on the throttle, in order to enhance airflow over the diffuser and thus increase downforce.

The intricacies of operating this system also contributed to Senna's violent accident at Ste Devote during the first free practice session at Monaco, the Brazilian nevertheless recovering from this setback to notch up a record sixth victory through the streets of the Principality. Later, as the World Championship battle moved to the faster European circuits, McLaren's performance deficit became more pronounced and Senna's total commitment was not always easy to discern.

Throughout the year McLaren displayed its customary high level of mechanical reliability. Failures associated with the car's hydraulic system caused Senna's retirement at Imola and Montreal, electrical problems intervened at the Hungaroring and he suffered engine failure at Estoril. In addition, McLaren's cockpit fuel consumption computer displayed its customary aversion to Silverstone – where the team used the Series VIII Ford engines for the first time – stranding Ayrton out on the last lap of the British Grand Prix for the third successive year, and the Brazilian made a rare error at Monza where he slid into Brundle's Ligier under braking.

During July and August the MP4/8 chassis lost the initiative to Benetton's B193B in the 'Ford race', but a package of revised aerodynamic modifications, introduced at Monza, went a long way to rectifying the car's high-speed handling imbalance, and the McLaren-Fords ended the European leg of the season where they had kicked off at Kyalami – best of the rest behind Williams.

As Senna progressively lost ground to Prost in the Championship battle, increasingly he vowed that he would not subject himself to another season as an also-ran. Thus by the end of the European season it was established that he would switch to Williams for 1994, turning his back on the equipe that had delivered him three World Championship titles in six years.

Yet when an off-the-record briefing with the British press went badly wrong, and one journalist breached confidentiality to attribute to Ron Dennis some remarks, Senna was extremely upset with the McLaren boss. It didn't seem to occur to him that Dennis had been a paragon of patience and discretion on the occasions when he had been critical of the McLaren MP4/8 chassis performance, particularly to the Portuguese-speaking media. But then, seeing other people's points of view has not always been one of Senna's most obvious qualities.

Ironically, the Japanese Grand Prix at Suzuka yet again saw Senna at the centre of controversy for the fourth successive year. Having won the race in magnificent style, he went down to the Jordan team's base to complain that their new driver Eddie Irvine, who had finished sixth, had messed him around and – horror of horrors – *re-passed* his McLaren while the Brazilian was in the process of lapping him.

What followed was a typical Senna outburst. 'What the fuck do you think you were doing?' he asked Irvine. The Ulsterman just shrugged. 'I was racing,' he replied.

'You were racing?' continued Senna, eyes agleam. 'Do you know the rule that you're supposed to let the leaders come by when you're a back marker?'

'If you were going fast enough, it was no problem,' said Irvine, resolutely refusing to give ground.

'I overtook you, and you went three times off in front of me, at the same place, like a fucking idiot where there was oil. You took a very big risk to put me out of the race.'

And on, and on, and on in the same vein. Eventually Senna lost his patience and took a swipe at Irvine, hitting the Jordan driver on the right side of the head, sending him to the floor.

A fortnight later Senna qualified on pole and won the Australian Grand Prix, leading from flag to flag at Adelaide. It was an emotional occasion for the whole McLaren squad, particularly team co-ordinator Jo Ramirez. Not only was it Senna's final race for McLaren, but also Prost's final race before retirement. Alain had ended a year's sabbatical to drive for Williams in 1993, winning his fourth Championship crown. Yet it had not been a particularly happy year for the Frenchman as it soon became clear that Frank Williams was hell bent on having Senna in 1994. So Prost retired.

Ramirez was one of that exclusive handful of men who got on well with both Senna and Prost on a personal level and was always working away behind the scenes to encourage a *rapprochement* between the two men. But at Adelaide in '93, the emotion was almost too much for him.

'Just before the start of the race, Ayrton called me over to do his belts up,' remembers Ramirez. 'That was strange to me as he always used to do the last pull on the belts himself with both hands. So I went down close to him in the cockpit and realised that he didn't want that, but said, "It's strange for me to do this for the last time in a McLaren."

'And I said, "If it's strange for you, then it is very strange for us. If you win this, I will love you for ever." Then he grabbed my arm and I could see tears in his eyes. I was actually quite worried.

'For me it was also emotional as the last race for Prost. It was very hard for me when they stopped talking to each other. I always tried to get them together again. At the beginning, Ayrton was very difficult, you know, to get round to it. So I said, "Look, you're going to be on the podium together a great deal, so you'd better get on with it."'

For Prost, that other celebrated McLaren Old Boy, it was also an emotional period of his life. He later admitted that he first started to think he might retire the day after finishing third in the 1993 European Grand Prix at Donington Park. 'The following day I just stayed at home in Switzerland,' he recalls. 'I didn't move. Even though I had a lot of support from the team and from Renault, I really seriously thought that I would stop. Perhaps even immediately. I didn't, of course, but the more the season went on, the more convinced I was that I would retire at the end of the year.'

Alain firmly believed that he was discriminated against by the rule-makers. 'Look at the start at Estoril,' he remembers. 'Hakkinen nearly put me off on the run to the first corner. After five or six laps he was weaving all round in front of me. You know, for them the rule is different. I didn't want to stay in that environment.

'This is all symptomatic of a basic problem in F1, which is that sport has been taken over by business. That sort of driving etiquette has gone. The sport is not going in the direction I would like. If you are a driver, it seems that the way to do things is to take more risk, to do stupid things on the track. That's what the people want to see, so for sure people like Bernie Ecclestone don't want to see a guy like me racing because I'm not stupid about my driving and every time I think something is wrong, I say it. That has not made me popular.

'The problem is, increasingly, that you cannot – you are not allowed to – speak against anything in this business. That upsets me a great deal.'

Looking back over his career, Alain admits that the most special relationship he had with any team was probably with McLaren. 'I enjoyed myself at Ferrari during my first year there,' he recalls, 'and obviously this year with Williams has been very special.

'But McLaren was something very different. For a long time I felt very much part of the family. I fitted in very, very well. Another two years with Williams might have led me to a similar judgement about them, but as I speak at the moment, McLaren was something totally different that I don't really want to compare with anything else. It wouldn't be fair.'

As far as the future was concerned, Alain's plans had been surrounded by speculation and rumour. What was the truth of it all?

'When I announced my retirement in Portugal, I knew already that there was a very small possibility that I could be involved in some way with the Ligier team,' he explained. 'But during the week after that race I made some further investigations – and remember, I know everything about their situation because, in 1992, I almost bought the team – but it became clear that everything was becoming very complex and I decided not to continue considering an involvement. So there is no way.

'Then there was another rumour that Ron Dennis called me and asked me what was my real situation. He just wanted to know whether we could do anything together, but nothing more than that. But I did not choose to leave Williams – with the best car and the best engine – to move to McLaren. That would have been stupid. But I suppose you can't blame him for asking!'

It was fashionable to paint a doom-laden portrait of the McLaren team's prospects by the end of the 1993 season, yet this was far from the case. By the end of the season the company was heavily involved with a Chrysler development programme using the Lamborghini V12, and Mika Hakkinen's third place on the grid at Estoril had put a spring back into its corporate step.

At the time Chrysler had major plans to step up the pace of its F1 involvement in 1994 with the Lamborghini-badged V12 engine that currently powered the Larrousse team.

Chrysler-owned Lamborghini Engineering – the Italian super-car-maker's high-technology division – had been linked with McLaren, which carried out installation tests with the Lamborghini F1 V12. Although McLaren sources remained discreet about the link, Chrysler would not deny that it associated with the famous British F1 team.

'We are not going to say anything at the moment,' said Chrysler spokesman Tom Kowaleski in October 1993. 'When it is definite, then we will say it.'

In fact, Senna tested a Lamborghini V12-engined McLaren test car at Silverstone in the early autumn of 1993, and it proved almost 2 seconds a lap quicker than the Ford-engined MP4/8. Ayrton was keen to drive the car in the last two races of the season, but Dennis balked at the idea. Apart from the obvious problems involved with interrupting the development of the existing car, the McLaren chief could see the possibility of a high-profile partnership with French car-makers Peugeot looming on the horizon. And that just might be sufficient to keep Senna in the team for 1994.

Nevertheless, Chrysler remained very keen to get involved with McLaren. Kowaleski revealed that Chrysler had expanded its engineering involvement in the Lamborghini F1 programme during 1993 and taken a more active role in its management. Three of the Detroit company's most senior power-train engineers formed the nucleus of the project's management team, co-ordinating development of the V12 with Lamborghini Engineering Managing Director Daniele Audetto.

The trio comprised British engineer Howard Padgeham and his US colleagues Rich Schaum and Floyd Allen. They headed development Groups within Chrysler's platform team concept, which speeds up the designs of new models. The direct involvement of top-ranking engineering executives was taken by many as a clear indication that Chrysler planned a bigger, and more visible, involvement in F1 from the start of 1994.

Previously Chrysler had stayed at arm's length from Lamborghini's F1 efforts, providing minimal funding and engineering resources. But in 1993 the Chrysler name and emblem were emblazoned on the engine covers of the Larrousse team's cars, as well as on the V12 cam covers.

Chrysler's high-profile association followed the appointment of Bob Eaton as head of the company. Eaton, former chief of General Motors Europe, had previously attempted to convince GM to bankroll an Opel F1 engine as long ago as 1987. He believed that F1 was the ideal image-maker to lead Chrysler's planned push into the European market from 1994. Spearheading its return as a volume car seller on the European market was the Neon small car. Chrysler was therefore looking for a top team to help bankroll a major upgrade of the Lamborghini V12, and McLaren was a possibility.

Allied with this activity was Chrysler's desire to sell Lamborghini Automobili, which made the low-volume Diablo super car. However, Chrysler wanted to keep Lamborghini Engineering, a profitable and prestigious operation run along the lines of Lotus Engineering. If Lamborghini's automotive division was sold, the F1 engine would wear only the Chrysler nameplate.

According to Kowaleski, engineers at the state-of-the-art Chrysler Technical Centre at Auburn Hills had been assisting Lamborghini Engineering's F1 team, running dynamometer and computer tests to improve cylinder-head gas flow and cure vibration problems. Chrysler engineers Kim Lyon and Michael Royce were based at Lamborghini Engineering, although others were rotated on six- to eight-month assignments. Lyon developed the software programme that controls the operation of Larrousse's traction control system.

Kowaleski also confirmed that Chrysler was committed to further development of the Lamborghini V12, which had provided valuable feedback to the company's road car programmes.

Chrysler came close to pulling off a deal with McLaren. In fact, it got so close that the US car-maker believed it had concluded a contract in principle to get together. Dennis later vigorously denied this, saying that he had only agreed that, if a deal was to be finalised, he would commit his company to conducting it 'in a lean management style'. But eventually he felt more secure committing McLaren to Peugeot for 1994.

The arrival of Mika Hakkinen as McLaren test driver at the start of the 1993 season had also been an occasion to be savoured. Managed by the team's former driver Keke Rosberg, the Finn had originally been on the Williams short list to partner Alain Prost in 1993. But for some reason that Rosberg doesn't understand to this day, Frank Williams changed his mind and said that he didn't want to do the deal after all.

'It wasn't the fact that Frank seemed uncomfortable with the proposed deal,' reflected Rosberg, 'but rather sheer amazement that after you've worked your butt off for months, you are told that we're not going to do it.

'As soon as the Williams case turned sour we started negotiating with Ligier, then something happened in the Ligier camp that I will never fully understand. The team manager Dany Hindenoch called me the day before we were due to sign and changed something in the contract.

'I said, "We can't live with that", so immediately picked up the phone to Ron Dennis and asked him whether he was ready to do a deal for Mika to be his test driver. This is two days before Christmas '92 and Ron says, "Right, where is Mika?"

'I tell him he is on his way from Helsinki to Geneva, and he doesn't know why. So Ron says, "I'll meet you at Courcheval airport."

'My son was quite gravely ill at the time and I'd promised that I would be back home. "You can't go, you can't go," he said to me. So I promised I would phone him from the car, only to find that the bloody car phone was broken. So here I am really questioning whether I've got my priorities upside down.

'So we met Ron at Courcheval and Mika and I eventually landed back at Salzburg at 2 minutes past 10 that evening – the airport is supposed to close at 10. We then drove to my house and stayed up all night debating it. Did he want to race a Ligier or test a McLaren?

'I said, "Mika, if you are serious, and I believe you are, then take the McLaren." He said, "No problem." I think I was using Mika as much as a sounding board as vice versa.'

It turned out to be a great partnership and, at the time of writing this volume in March 1998, Mika Hakkinen is still a member of the McLaren team.

The McLaren-Peugeot alliance had developed with almost surprising speed. It was born only at the start of October 1993, while the first of the 72-degree Peugeot V10 engines to be developed by the design team operating under the direction of former Renault engineer Jean-Pierre Boudy was delivered.

'Understandably, Jean-Pierre Jabouille and the Peugeot engineers have a cautious approach to what is a very difficult task,' said Dennis. 'It will take time to equal or surpass the level of Renault performance, but I have a very positive view of the season. Aided by the superior performance we anticipate from Peugeot, I am quite certain we will be competitive and will win races in 1994.'

Yet the whole mood of the occasion seemed strangely lacking in vitality. For some reason, unspecific and difficult to pinpoint, there had been little feeling of true synergy between the British F1 team and the French car-maker.

The team had been unquestionably weakened by Ayrton Senna's

defection to the Williams camp after six years, and although Alain
Prost tested the McLaren-Peugeot at Estoril, the Frenchman
decided he would stay retired. As a result Ron Dennis opted for the
services of Martin Brundle as partner to Mika Hakkinen, the reliable
English professional sitting on the sidelines until late in the day,
correctly judging that McLaren would eventually pick him from the
remaining available players. Early season testing was also shared by
Peugeot nominees Yannick Dalmas and Philippe Alliot, the latter
standing in for Hakkinen at Budapest after the Finn was given a one-
race suspension for triggering the first-corner multiple shunt in the
German Grand Prix. Alliot was not really grand prix material and
many observers judged that his inclusion in the team simply reflected
a lack of serious commitment on Peugeot's part.

It was 20 January 1994 when Ron Dennis and Peugeot Sport boss
Jean-Pierre Jabouille took the wraps off the first of the new
McLaren-Peugeot MP4/9s at the British team's Woking
headquarters. The chassis was broadly based round the Ford HB-
engined MP4/8 with which Ayrton Senna had won on his final outing
for McLaren in the 1993 Australian Grand Prix. However,
establishing the cooling requirements of the five-valves-per-cylinder
Peugeot A4 V10 was a problem, as the new engine had yet to run by
the time McLaren had to design the cooling package. Consequently,
much of this crucial work had to be based on McLaren's general
experience combined with Peugeot's data from the 905 endurance-
racing V10.

The MP4/9 aerodynamic package was subtly different from its
immediate predecessor, in particular the floor and side pods, and the
car was fitted with a clutch activated by paddles on the steering
column, effectively offering two-pedal control that number one
driver Mika Hakkinen particularly liked, enabling him to brake late
into the apex of a corner and contributing to the car retaining a more
balanced aerodynamic configuration during the cornering process.

'We ran it for the first time on the Ford-powered MP4/8 at a
Barcelona test after the end of the '93 season,' explained Chief
Designer Neil Oatley. 'It was something that had developed out of
general discussions between the engineers and drivers – in particular
Mika, who reckoned if there was no gap between coming off the
throttle and going on to the brakes, and vice versa, he would have
better control of the car. It was not a problem, but Martin never
really used it. He drives more conventionally and, as a consequence,
had his pedals positioned slightly differently.'

The team also got into problems with the FIA over its
interpretation of the technical regulations relating to the
transmission. The McLaren's six-speed, transverse gearbox had a
fully automatic downchange facility that was subsequently declared
illegal by the governing body. Its presence was also brought to a

wider audience after Philippe Alliot, the team's test driver, commented on the lack of such a facility when he joined the Larrousse team for the Belgian Grand Prix – one race after standing in for Hakkinen in Hungary!

After preliminary tests with the five-valve A4 engine, Peugeot switched straight to the four-valves-per-cylinder A6 engine for the start of the season, these being used exclusively with the exception of Hakkinen's preference for the A4 installed in the spare car that he used in the Pacific GP.

From then on Peugeot made steady progress throughout the season, producing the Version 1 Mk 2 for Imola with an increment of around 20bhp, then a major revamp with Version 2 for the French GP in July. This unit had revised camshafts, offered 500rpm more and gained 35bhp, and this was followed with Version 2 Mk 2 for Hungary (plus 15bhp) and Mk 3 for Jerez (plus a further 10bhp).

Unfortunately, most of the pre-season McLaren-Peugeot testing was carried out in fairly cool conditions, which masked the threshold beyond which the V10's serious overheating problems began to be a major problem – and these turned out to be disastrous in the early season races.

Alterations were made to the cooling system, in particular the radiator installations, but the FIA did the team a favour by changing the rules at Barcelona. The shorter diffusers produced resulted in reduced back pressure through the radiators and significantly reduced the engines's operating temperature from that point onwards. Not that the Peugeot V10 had a trouble-free run in other areas, however, for Brundle suffered broken flywheels at Interlagos and Barcelona, and a crankcase pressurisation problem, which caused the Englishman's car to pump out all its oil on the grid at Silverstone, was only solved by a change of piston ring specification.

The MP4/9 was fitted with power steering for the first time at the Monaco Grand Prix, two hydraulic pumps operating the system with pressure regulated by a Moog electro-valve. The drivers preferred manual steering for the faster circuits like Spa and Monza, but power steering was generally used on the tighter tracks.

The MP4/9's handling was always a little difficult on slow corners, the problem proving difficult to isolate and identify, although things were definitely improved by the adoption of a revised underbody and different rear wing for the Hungarian GP in mid-August.

Hakkinen was undeniably quick, and highly motivated, in both qualifying and the races, but Brundle seemed to have difficulty producing the requisite qualifying speed and invariably lined up too far down the grid to make a worthwhile impact when the green light came on. That said, his race lap times stood close comparison with Hakkinen's and his experience was unquestionably of value to the team as it battled its way through what was a pretty difficult season.

Brundle enjoyed his stay at McLaren, which merely served to increase his admiration of Ron Dennis's F1 operating style. Yet he was a perceptive lad with a keen eye for detail, recalling his season behind the wheel of the Peugeot-engined car with pin-sharp accuracy.

'I didn't actually get finally told that I would be driving until the Tuesday of the week before the race,' recalls Brundle, 'so it was literally little more than seven days before I was supposed to be signing on at Interlagos.

'The big thing, of course, was whether or not Prost was going to drive the Peugeot-engined car. I was on holiday in Mauritius during the January and Flavio Briatore was trying to get me to sign for Ligier, and it all seemed very confusing. But I wanted the McLaren drive. God, I wanted it, to the point that my phone bill in Mauritius was £1,500 – mainly to Ron.

'That month I got a glimmer of what I wanted to hear. You've got to remember that these were difficult times for Ron. Senna had just left and McLaren has got the new Peugeot engine. I'm sure he wanted an established World Champion, or a race winner, and in Hakkinen he didn't have a race winner.

'On the way home from holiday I just made the decision that I was prepared to risk everything in order to get the McLaren drive. That meant giving up the chance of Jordan. I went to see their factory, then I had a guided tour of the McLaren factory, which just blew my mind, all these men walking round in white coats. I just wanted it all the more, really badly.

'In fact, I left the Jordan factory in tears. Eddie wanted a decision, gave me an ultimatum. I went into another room, thought about it, then said, "Sorry Eddie, I'm going to wait for McLaren." When I got outside I was crying for about 10 minutes on the way home, because I suddenly realised that I might have turned down a wonderful opportunity, for nothing. With nothing as a reserve!'

Shrewdly, Brundle judged that Prost would not accept the drive. Then Ron Dennis decided to give Martin a test at Estoril. Hakkinen had been running round the track for days. That same morning the Finn had done 55 laps. Then Martin took over the MP4/9.

'Just as I'm coming past the pits to complete my out lap, the engine blew up so badly that the con-rod actually put a hole in the surface of the race track,' he laughed. 'My first ever lap in a McLaren-Peugeot. I mean, I should have known, shouldn't I? It wasn't my fault, obviously, but it just had to blow up when I was driving it.

'It then ended up with me constantly talking to Ron. I'd been through the mangle with him once before, in 1986 or '87, I think it was. Ron is very good at keeping several balls in the air. This has two effects: it keeps his options open, and destabilises lesser teams who are also forced to wait. But the moment I'd driven the car, I reasoned that Prost wasn't going to drive it.'

The deal was eventually sealed after an evening with Ron and Martin exchanging faxes between each other. 'I didn't have a manager, and Ron didn't want to deal with anybody else, either,' he said. 'Ron faxed me and I faxed back. We eventually struck a deal. It was actually very reasonable. Peanuts compared with what Senna was being paid, but then I hadn't got Senna's credentials.'

It was obviously a difficult time for the McLaren team in the post-Senna era, but Brundle found it to be a much warmer, friendlier team than he imagined. And very enjoyable. Apart from the results.

'I pushed myself too hard,' he reflects. 'But we were really struggling with the engine and the car. It was strange to be jumping into McLaren No 8, 11 years after I'd first tested a McLaren No 8 – Niki Lauda's number – back in 1983. But this was now Senna's McLaren No 8, and being at McLaren post-Ayrton Senna was not really a smart place to be.'

Brundle got a taste of this reality at a pre-Brazilian Grand Prix press conference when Dennis stormed out, remarking, 'I am used to addressing full press conferences.'

'It just cut the legs from under me,' says Brundle. 'I think it had just dawned on Ron just what the full implications of not having Ayrton Senna in the team really were.'

It would not be the first tactless remark to be made by Dennis in 1994. After Brundle finished a strong second to Michael Schumacher's Benetton-Ford at Monaco, he remarked to the Peugeot crew, 'Just remember, second place is the first of the losers.'

Brundle grins broadly. 'Ron and I share the same birthday, 1 June, and that makes us Geminis,' he says. 'We have two personalities. Whenever I put a crash helmet on, I become ten times more aggressive a person than I am in everyday life.

'Ron can be fairly direct and cutting, but I also know that he can be extremely kind to people who are in trouble. Extremely kind.

'During practice and qualifying at Interlagos I spent all the time flying off the road because the throttle kept sticking wide open. My eyes were popping out of my head by the end of it. Fair dos to Ron, he was the first to come up to me afterwards, and said, "Martin, I'm really sorry." I appreciated that.

'Then in the race the flywheel came off and bounced through the floor of the car. I'm trying to control that as Eddie Irvine and Jos Verstappen roll over and end up hitting me on the head. It was difficult for a while.'

The Peugeot V10s used to start the races with 15 litres of oil in their sump. 'When my engine blew up on the start line at Silverstone, which Mr Jabouille laughably tried to lay at my door, bearing in mind they'd taken an oil control ring out to reduce friction, the thing used 8 litres of oil on the start line,' said Martin.

'Basically the breather system fed back into the air box. Sure enough, when they got it back to the pits it started up, of course it did. But meanwhile it had *melted* the rear suspension and undertray. Jabouille said I should have carried on, which was ridiculous considering I very nearly barbecued my mate Mark Blundell who was right behind me on the grid in his Ligier.'

There were some good moments, of course, most notably Martin's second place at Monaco. 'How that car ever got to the end of the race, none of us knows,' he recalls. 'It had no water and no oil left in it by the finish and the whole engine was glowing. But to be beaten only by Schumacher at Monaco was pretty satisfying.

'Understandably, the Peugeot guys were quite relieved after all the disappointment, so they opened some champagne, at which point Ron came in with his "Second is the first loser" remark. The point he was trying to make was that one swallow didn't make a summer, and while it was a good day it wasn't good enough. But we all knew that and didn't need reminding of that.'

For Mika Hakkinen's part, however frustrated he may have felt about the performance of the McLaren-Peugeot, the Finn tended to keep his thoughts to himself. Through 1994 he carved a reputation as an upbeat, optimistic youngster with great confidence in his own F1 future.

'I'm very pleased to work with McLaren,' he said tactfully mid-season. 'All of us have worked very hard, the best that we can, and I'm pleased that the relationship with the team is very good. But with the results, of course, I'm not happy. It is terrible. It doesn't look very good.

'Everybody knew that we had a new engine, of course, and we just had to see how we go over the balance of the season. But horsepower is only one factor – and we needed extra power, because at Montreal the Ferraris were 20kph quicker than us.

'We needed quite a lot of extra power to make up that speed. The Peugeot engine had been improved, for sure, but there was still a long way to go. The driveability and other areas needed attention. It was unbelievable.

'You told the engineers that it was doing this and this in the corners, but when you looked at the telemetry everything looked fine. But you knew it was not right. It was very complicated, very difficult, and there was a long way to go. It annoyed you when you saw the others go away, but there was no point in jumping up and down. There's just no point in losing your temper. I tried to stay calm.'

Hakkinen admitted that he was impressed with Schumacher's winning streak, although that reality served to frustrate him. 'As I said before, I am very happy with the team, but I would like to be out front leading like him. But at McLaren there was no compromise in terms of the effort that they put into their racing. I had to be very optimistic and I was sure that we would eventually be in a situation in 1994 when we would be in a position to win a race.

'We had to admit that we didn't have the power yet to get pole position in qualifying, but at the moment we need to concentrate on reliability. To be honest, I did expect more from this season. It's strange, when you are getting ready for the season, you are always expecting that you will win. If it doesn't happen, it's always disappointment, but that doesn't mean you want to walk away from your situation.

'You just have to understand the problems, solve them and then we will win a race. But whether it's going to be the next race, or next year, I don't know. Can't tell.'

As far as the opposition was concerned, he admitted that he'd been trying to help his team-mate Martin Brundle. But he believed, quite openly, that he was significantly quicker than the Englishman.

Hakkinen believed that one key factor in his speed was his commitment to the left-foot braking technique. 'You can brake later, get on the power earlier using this technique,' he insisted. 'It could be worth a couple of tenths of a second a lap. Over a full race distance that can add up to a really worthwhile amount. But it's not only the time benefit, but also the fact that you are balancing yourself more comfortably in the car. It's basically like skiing, you feel everything that's going on with the car – cornering forces, braking. Your whole body feels in balance.'

Yet by the same token, he also made the point that there is very little sympathy between the drivers. 'When I was coming up through F3, I tried to learn as much as possible,' he said, 'and now I am feeling comfortable with my position. I feel sorry for the other drivers who have not yet made it, but I believe I belong here. I suppose it's good that the grid is mainly full of young drivers now, but I think most of them are committed to looking after their own interests. There is not always time to worry about everybody else.

'I am sure they are all doing their best. But I am in a good situation, not only in the team, but also with my advisor Keke [Rosberg] who has given me a lot of help. This is fantastic. It makes the whole system work.'

On the subject of taking over the number one McLaren drive from Senna at the end of the previous year – and Ayrton's subsequent death – he became understandably introspective.

'Senna taught me a lot,' he conceded, 'and he was the standard by which the rest of us judged our progress. But he is gone now and we all have to come to terms with that reality.'

As far as Ron Dennis and the McLaren team were concerned, they couldn't be happier with their new number one driver. 'I haven't been so excited about a new driver for years,' said Dennis. 'He has a youthful enthusiasm and serious commitment that motivates the entire team. I believe he has the potential, both from the point of view of driving ability and commitment, to become a regular grand prix winner. He is definitely somebody I enjoy working with.'

Dennis continued to say that he always makes a point of never comparing McLaren drivers of different generations. 'They are in different situations, using different engines and competing in widely different environments over the years,' he says. 'But I firmly believe that Mika has got what it takes to become a World Champion.'

In purely relative terms, by the end of the 1994 season, the Peugeot V10 hadn't really improved since its debut at Interlagos when one took into account the improvements in form displayed by its key rivals over the 16-race programme.

Ron Dennis kept a smile on the company's corporate face, reiterating his loyalty to Peugeot on many occasions throughout the season. But the bottom line was that 1994 became the first year in which his cars had failed to win a grand prix since McLaren International's first full season in 1981. The McLaren-Peugeot partnership wasn't working in the way both parties had envisaged and, with two races to go, the two companies negotiated a dissolution of the arrangement to go their own separate ways.

On 25 October – just ten months after the unveiling of the MP4/9 – Dennis was present at a press conference in Paris to explain that McLaren and Peugeot were divorcing by mutual agreement. Much had been expected from the new combination, following McLaren's decision not to use the Chrysler-Lamborghini V12. More by far than it delivered.

Peugeot took their engines off to forge a new deal with Jordan, while only 12 days after the European Grand Prix at Jerez McLaren announced a new engine supply partnership for 1995 with Mercedes-Benz.

During 1994 McLaren certainly seemed to be experiencing some growing pains and Dennis admitted that the challenges involved in running the company as it expanded seemed to be changing all the time. In that connection he admitted that he was struggling to make the transition from being something of an autocrat to more of a democrat.

With remarkable candour, Ron talked me through his feelings about how the company was developing. The occasion was the 1994 Hungarian Grand Prix and we were chatting in his hotel suite in the centre of Budapest. At the time the significance of his self-analysis was difficult to understand fully. Yet in the light of what the team would have achieved by the start of 1998, in retrospect his words can now be seen to have had an overwhelmingly prescient ring.

'I don't think that people at McLaren – and now I'm generalising across the board – are very unhappy,' he volunteered, 'but, equally, I don't think they are very happy.

'I think they are very loyal and, if something from outside threatens the company, they have a strong defence mechanism that stimulates them, bringing them together to a point where they are supportive. And then you feel it's all worth it.

'It does not come easily to say that I know people are not particularly happy. I can give lots of reasons, and those reasons will sound like excuses. As you try to move forward and grow [as a company], inevitably you look back on things and find yourself not particularly happy with the way they have been executed.

'Now that may be something you have done, or it might be something done by a manager. In those situations there is a double frustration, because inevitably one's ego says, "If I'd done that, I might have done it better." So it's quite painful, because I have removed myself into a position where I can take a more strategic role in the company.

'Some people may think I haven't done this fast enough, that I am not strong enough in terms of the functioning of the group. Other people feel I've deserted them, left them behind, and that decisions are not being taken that I should be taking.

'So I have to accept, reluctantly, that there are some people who are not as happy as I would want them to be. And I have to accept the criticism that sometimes I am not as decisive as they would like me to be. I have to accept criticism that I don't take a greater and more dominant role in administering all the group companies.

'Each person has a viewpoint and, as hard as I have tried to be what people want me to be, the reality is that you only have so much time in the day. When you try to apportion that time, I find myself asking, "Have I moved forward on all fronts or have I done purely a damage limitation exercise? What is the quality of the work I have done? Have I just dealt with a pile of paperwork, none of which has made the grand prix cars go faster?"

'I can find long periods where I haven't achieved anything because of the constant avalanche of administrative that comes on to my desk. Some people can be absolutely ruthless about handling these sorts of things. They can make an imperfect decision and can live with the consequences, whereas I always want to make the right decision, the best decision on each and every issue. So then I have to ask myself whether I have got my time management under control, whether I have balanced my strategic role within the group against my day-to-day role within the individual companies.

'It is so frustrating, because the formula by which you win grands prix is constantly changing. Subtly, but constantly. What you really need is the ability to second-guess what is going to happen – not at the next grand prix, sometimes not even next year, but what is going to happen in the longer term. You need to be constantly gearing up with that in mind, and that is where I think I need to apply my time.

'We are talking about something very hard to touch, feel, grab hold of. But I just know what McLaren can achieve; I know the formula by which the company needs to be run in the future. I know the direction that is right for the company. And to get there, I have to implement the right strategy and, at the same time, share that strategy so that everybody who has to contribute to it will do so in a positive and productive way.

'Satisfaction comes in different forms for me. Most of the people in the grand prix programme are feeling the failure, because we are losing, not winning. And they are right. But there are reasons for this. It serves no function to go over those reasons time and again. My job is to effect change in such a way that we come back as quickly as possible to a position of winning grands prix.

'That is not about getting involved in the optimisation of the car's fuel system, or whatever. I know I have the ability to grasp most areas of a grand prix car – and maybe even contribute in those areas – if I totally immerse myself in it. But the company is not going to get out of me what it should get out of me if I allow myself to slip back into that hands-on-type approach. One minute I'm accused of being too hands-on, the next that I am too removed from it. It is hard to get the balance right.

'It is almost a question of blind faith. I never say it, but I think there is a high degree of the "trust me" approach. Don't worry, there is pain before the pleasure, but it will come right. I believe you can power your way through these problems; you just have to stick together.

'To those who say it [life at McLaren] is not as they would want it, fine, I understand that. But they will believe, they will understand in the end. In the meantime, some will perhaps choose to leave the company. I hope not. We are very loyal; we try desperately at that. In principle I will do anything for anybody in the company as long as there is a fairness and balance to it.'

There are many people within the McLaren workforce to have benefited from unsung acts of kindness, both personal and professional, from Ron Dennis and who would certainly testify to the accuracy of those words.

You would also be hard pressed to find anybody who would testify that he was anything but a good and considerate employer.

9

Mercedes
and Mansell,
1995

RUMOURS OF AN impending alliance between McLaren International and Mercedes-Benz had been building steadily throughout the 1994 season. It was clear that the chemistry between the team and Peugeot, questioned by several F1 insiders when it was announced, simply failed to develop in the manner that McLaren might have hoped for.

By the same token, Mercedes's efforts to edge back into the F1 business with the Sauber team, although logical on the face of it, were meeting with a similar lack of success. Mercedes had enjoyed a successful partnership with Sauber in long-distance sports car racing and gently revived its F1 presence with the 'Concept by Mercedes-Benz' identification on the Swiss team's cars from the start of the 1993 season.

By the start of 1994 Mercedes had come out into the open as a technical partner with Sauber, carrying its identification on the Ilmor-built V10-cylinder engines. Persuading the Mercedes-Benz board that F1 would be a good idea after an absence of 35 years was a task performed with great delicacy and tact by Norbert Haug, the company's motorsport manager, who took over that position at the start of October 1990.

A former editor of the specialist magazine *Sport Auto* and deputy editor of *Auto, Motor und Sport*, Haug identified the up-side of any potential Mercedes F1 involvement. But it had to be seen to be making worthwhile progress, and when the German car-maker found itself having to step in discreetly to supplement the Sauber budget after one of the Swiss team's sponsors had problems during 1994, it became clear to Haug that an established top-line F1 operation would make a better partner for Mercedes.

McLaren clearly fitted the bill perfectly, both companies having philosophies founded on a commitment to technical excellence, even if Mercedes was perceived as a trifle staid by many younger potential car-owners. Moving into F1 with McLaren would represent the latest chapter in an effort to brighten up the image of the three-pointed star as a supplement to existing involvements in the International Touring Car Championship and Indycar scene. However, the new partnership was not finally cemented until October 1994, leaving both parties with a considerable challenge to be fully prepared for the first race of the following season.

The first technical information relating to the all-new Mercedes F0110 3-litre V10 was communicated to McLaren's design department in mid-October '94, although by that time the team, under Chief Designer Neil Oatley and aerodynamicist Henri Durand, were already well under way with other aspects of the MP4/10 chassis concept.

To maximise the opportunities provided by the new 50mm stepped-undertray regulations, McLaren boss Ron Dennis had insisted that Ilmor Engineering, the Mercedes racing engine division, adopt a completely fresh approach to the architecture of its new 3-litre V10.

The introduction of the 50mm stepped-bottom rules meant that the undertray profile would make considerable inroads into the amount of space available alongside the engine itself, complicating the challenge of packaging such ancillaries as the exhaust manifold and oil, water and hydraulic pumps.

From the outset Ilmor has been a key element within the McLaren-Mercedes equation. The company was started by Mario Illien and Paul Morgan, two engineers who had previously worked at Cosworth Engineering before striking out on their own in 1983.

Illien had been working on the Sierra Cosworth road car engine programme as well as producing the DFY variant of Cosworth's proven 3-litre DFV grand prix engine. Morgan, meanwhile, had been responsible for looking after the company's Indycar engine programme as Chief Engineer on the DFX V8 project.

At the end of 1983 the two men decided that they would go it alone and established Ilmor Engineering on an estate at nearby Brixworth, a picturesque English country village about 5 miles from Northampton – on the opposite side of town to Cosworth!

They decided that they would endeavour to take on their former employers. 'When we left Cosworth, we considered carefully which racing category to tackle and concluded that taking on Cosworth's monopoly in Indycar racing would make most success,' recalls Illien. 'So we called Roger Penske!'

Penske, the patrician multi-millionaire driving force behind Indycar's most consistently successful team, listened with interest as Illien outlined the new company's plans. He was impressed with the young engineer's confidence that he and Morgan could improve on the Cosworth DFX. The two engineers, in turn, were impressed by Penske's decisiveness.

'All he wanted to know was how much it would cost and how long it would take to complete the first engine,' said Illien.

With characteristic commercial audacity, Penske agreed the financial backing required to underwrite the project, convinced that, in turn, he could persuade a major American manufacturer to take an interest.

When he finally came up with the answer, the international motor racing world was stunned. Penske had successfully persuaded General Motors to invest in the new project, and plans were being laid for a brand new Indycar V8 engine with the name 'Chevrolet' emblazoned on its cam covers. By October 1984 GM had become a shareholder in Ilmor Engineering.

Illien and Morgan started work on the first Indycar engine in October 1983, and the first Ilmor 265A V8 burst into life on the test bed on 16 May 1985.

By 1987 the Penske-Ilmor partnership had achieved its first win, and by 1991 Ilmor/Chevy V8s totally eclipsed Cosworth on the Indycar trail, recording a remarkable 17 pole positions and 17 wins out of 17 races.

In 1989 a 3.5-litre F1 V10 engine project was initiated for the Leyton House team and commenced track testing in August 1990. That was raced by Leyton House throughout 1991, then by Tyrrell and March in 1993. Then came Ilmor's big break.

'In August 1991 we were asked by Peter Sauber whether we could supply engines for his forthcoming grand prix team,' recalls Illien. 'At the time we were still together with Leyton House, who were not paying their bills and we were effectively financing their whole operation. Mr Akagi [Japanese businessman Akira Akagi, owner of Leyton House] was already having problems at the time and we were desperately trying to buy back the rights to the engine from them.

'We obviously wanted to carry on in F1 and wanted to make use of what we had. So we decided that we had to buy the rights back in order to be in charge of our own destiny. This was not quite straightforward and it cost us quite a bit of money, but it left us free to look in the direction of Sauber and Mercedes-Benz.

'However, Mercedes-Benz then decided that they would not go into F1 with Sauber, so before Christmas 1991 we made a deal with Tyrrell and March to do the engines for them in 1992. It was a very low-budget affair, but we wanted to stay involved. But then Sauber decided to enter F1 on his own and we got a package together from the start of 1993.

'There was still a strong connection between Sauber and Mercedes-Benz, and throughout that season it became clear that was an increasing interest on Mercedes's part. Chevrolet, meanwhile, was not that keen to go on, so suddenly we had a situation where we were on our own in F1 and Indycars felt a little bit weak.

'Then Helmut Werner took over in charge at Stuttgart and, with

Roger Penske having had a close association with Mercedes over many years, they began to have an interest in Indycars and F1. But that came after we were disconnected from Chevrolet; I guess you could say we were in "free-fall" for, I guess, about two months.

'Then in November '93 Mercedes decided that they wanted to go with us, that we had the right package. This started with the new engine we had supplied to Sauber in time for the 1993 Italian GP.'

However, to start with there was the question of Indycar engine supply to be addressed. General Motors indicated that they wished to quit at the end of 1993, but even though the Mercedes deal was cemented soon after, Illien felt that it would be better to have a 'clear season' between the end of the GM Indycar involvement and the full-time Mercedes link.

With great honesty, he felt that it would be too cynical an exercise simply to switch badges on the cam covers of what was essentially the same engine for 1994, so, with the glorious exception of the one-off pushrod engine that won that year's Indy 500 carrying the Mercedes badges, the works Penske units for the rest of the Indycar Championship carried straightforward Ilmor badging throughout the season. In 1995 the Mercedes identification would be carried for a full Indycar season on what would be a heavily redesigned V8 unit.

'We kept that pushrod Indy engine in our back pocket and kept that very secret,' says Mario, 'but we did admit to Mercedes that we had it in the background. Our initial tests looked fairly positive, then we had a meeting on 6 April in Stuttgart between Penske, Mercedes, Paul and myself and put the proposition to Mr Werner that it should be used.

'He said, "If you [Penske] will take the risk of running all three cars with it, then I want to be part of it!"'

Keeping quiet about the new project was an achievement in itself, but for the cars to run competitively, one qualifying on pole, with Al Unser emerging as a commanding winner, was a quite remarkable milestone for Ilmor, which must be seen as cementing Mercedes's faith in the British engine-builder.

Indianapolis reacted favourably, reducing the boost limit for pushrod engines from 55 to 52 inches, with which Illien reckoned they could live for 1995. But then, three months later, they further restricted it to 48 inches, and at that level Mario calculated that there was no way they could continue to compete in the 500 the following year. So the Mercedes V8 was consigned to history as the engine that won its only race!

For 1995 Ilmor squared up to its biggest challenge so far, designing, building and maintaining their all-new 3-litre V10 Mercedes engines that would power the McLaren MP4/10s of Mika Hakkinen and Nigel Mansell. Although he opened out the vee-angle from 72 to 75 degrees on the new engine, Illien remained convinced that the V10 concept was the best, despite the reduction in capacity from 3.5 litres that followed on as part of the FIA's package of measures to curtail lap speeds after Ayrton Senna's death the previous year.

'Being with McLaren obviously put us under massive pressure,' he conceded. 'First of all we changed ship halfway down the road towards designing a 3-litre engine. With that change [from Sauber] came some changes in the idea of how we should best deal with the engine's "architecture" to deal with the new 50mm stepped undertray regulations.' They would do a good job.

'I believed that the V10 still left us with a little more technical freedom,' he said, hinting that the new Mercedes F1 engine would run to around 16,000rpm from the outset to develop a power output that needed to be as close to 700bhp as possible to be fully competitive.

He was not worried about weight, dimensions or packaging. 'Our current 3.5-litre V10 is the shortest, lowest and lightest F1 of the current generation,' he smiled. 'So we are not too worried!'

Illien was obviously proud that his new 3-litre V10 would start the 1995 season as the only totally new engine, apart from Hart's V8 and Peugeot's new V10. 'The pressure is certainly there – particularly if we have Mr Mansell in the equation,' he grinned, perhaps ironically.

With 173 people working in a state-of-the-art engine manufacturing facility, Illien is delighted at the degree of technical interchange that has been produced by the Mercedes partnership. 'They have an elaborate transient dynamometer, more sophisticated than our own, which can produce total track simulation, gear-changes, changes in temperature and so on,' he explains.

'At this facility we can do most things in-house, apart from the pattern-making and the castings of block and heads. The biggest bottleneck is probably deciding what to do and drawing it all, followed by the manufacture of the crankshafts. These are currently manufactured by an outside contractor, but we are installing facilities to enable us to make them ourselves.

'Pistons, connecting rods, camshafts – we make them all ourselves. We have very sophisticated robot-controlled, robot-loaded machining facilities that can work, untended, throughout the nights and weekends. The requirement to run these facilities round the clock is an absolute priority in order to keep up with the workload.'

Back in 1983 Mario, Paul Morgan and Roger Penske split the shareholding in Ilmor Engineering 25–25–50 per cent. Then Penske sold 25 per cent to GM, which was subsequently acquired by Mercedes-Benz.

'Roger was the man who took the risk originally,' says Illien. 'A telephone call, a meeting and a handshake. And off we went!'

To cater for the stepped-undertray rules, Ilmor made a

fundamental change in configuration when designing the new V10, opening out the vee angle from 72 to 75 degrees in order to position the hydraulics pump between the two banks of cylinders. This in turn demanded an exceedingly compact exhaust system, Mario Illien choosing to abandon the conventional fan-shaped manifold in favour of a tightly curved spiral, leaving room for the oil and water pumps below.

As far as the driver line-up was concerned, Mika Hakkinen was starting the second season of a three-year contract with McLaren, but pressure from the team's sponsors for a high-profile name brought Nigel Mansell into the equation once he had been passed over in favour of David Coulthard for the vacant Williams-Renault seat.

The announcement of Mansell's recruitment was made amidst outpourings of mutual admiration from both Ron Dennis and Nigel himself, but seasoned F1-watchers simply kept their fingers crossed. A time-bomb was ticking away here; it was only a question of when or how it would be detonated.

Approaching his 41st birthday, Mansell knew that he needed a competitive car from the outset if he was to make a full-time F1 return stick. The real question was whether McLaren could provide him with an instantly competitive package from the outset.

The up-side to the Mansell/McLaren equation was easy to see. If the car was good enough to enable Nigel to compete at the front of the field – effectively carrying over the form that saw him win for Williams at Melbourne – the 1992 World Champion could expect to do his bit.

Frank Williams, his former employer, knew that too well. 'We would look a right bunch of idiots if Nigel came back this season and destroyed everybody,' he reflected shortly before the start of the season. 'I do think that the cars will be very close in 1995 and I can see no reason why McLaren cannot win the first race. Nigel is highly motivated to win and is still very quick.' Was this tongue in cheek? Or was Frank simply hedging his bets?

Ron Dennis might have been reassured to hear such words from the mouth of possibly his biggest rival. Yet perhaps the McLaren boss could have been forgiven for asking 'Why?' when he heard Frank's response to the enquiry 'In that case, why did you choose David Coulthard instead of Mansell?'

Frank deftly avoided making a direct answer to this controversial question. 'Obviously, I don't want to talk about "Why David? Why not Nigel?". Whatever I say I will put my foot in it and I don't want to offend anyone.

'Obviously we felt that it was better for Williams to have David rather than Nigel, so we went down that route. We believed that over the course of the season Coulthard would be the better choice, but we could easily be wrong and Renault [the Williams team's engine-supplier] wouldn't be very happy.

'But we believe our choice to be right and there is no animosity towards Nigel. He has proved that he can win races, but we think David can win as well and that he has a good future ahead of him. He will win a race this year if our new car is a winner.'

With that in mind, did Frank have any advice to offer Ron Dennis on the question of handling Mansell? After all, Nigel drove for Frank from 1985 to '88, then again from 1991 to '92, and finally on a guest-driving basis in 1994. Williams allowed himself an enigmatic smile.

'I wouldn't dream of giving Ron any advice,' says Frank. 'He needed him [Mansell] and they will work out an accommodation. They will get on just fine.

'In his last two races for us in Japan and Australia, Nigel was a total pleasure to work with – no trouble on or off the track and a ball of fun the whole time. He was there partly because he knew he had to help Damon win, so he was not at war and arguing with his team-mate, as is the norm.

'We were straight with him. He was being well paid and had a competitive car, so he was happy, relaxed and felt good. When he is in his normal "wartime" environment, his attitude will be different, but that is what makes him good.'

Of course, what Dennis knew better than anybody was that Mika Hakkinen believed himself to be the one man who, given an equal opportunity, could mix it with Michael Schumacher in terms of pure driving talent.

The Finn wasn't the least bit interested in deferring to Mansell, an old man of 41, and was clearly quite capable of putting the English veteran under enormous pressure from the very start of the season. When Hakkinen had been promoted to the full-time McLaren race team as successor to Michael Andretti in 1993, he had out-qualified Ayrton Senna's identical Ford HB-engined MP4/8 at Estoril for the Portuguese GP. Ayrton had been highly impressed.

'Nigel is a quick driver,' acknowledged Mika. 'He's been World Champion and he's been around for a long time. I'm ready for it, though. I'm interested to see what he's like to work with and I hope we can help each other.

'Everyone has different opinions of him, I know, but for me he's a very special driver, and of course my manager, Keke Rosberg, used to be his team-mate and tells me good things about him – but that was a long time ago.'

Behind all the negotiating and mutually complimentary words, it was Marlboro – McLaren's title sponsor – who wanted Mansell the most. Perhaps they privately believed that McLaren had gone a little soft in 1994 and that Martin Brundle wasn't capable of putting

Hakkinen under sufficient pressure to force the Finn to raise the standard of his game.

Perhaps, but since Ron Dennis had previously indicated a distinct lack of interest in securing Mansell's services as a McLaren driver, this was a delicate issue.

Meanwhile, Martin Brundle was still hovering in the background. He would have liked the chance to stay with McLaren, particularly entering its Mercedes era, but he fully appreciated that Mansell's sky-high profile put him in pole position for the drive. In mid-January he asked Dennis what the situation was. Ron admitted that he was unable to give him a positive decision, so Brundle signed for the Ligier-Mugen squad. He was simply fed up with being regarded as a 'back stop' man whose presence on the reserve bench could be used to strengthen the McLaren chief's negotiating position with Mansell.

Once the pre-season hullabaloo had abated, the chill winds of reality blew into the McLaren/Mansell equation. Sometimes in F1 the truth of any particular matter is hidden beneath a layer of subtleties. But there are other occasions when it can be more sensible to trust one's first impressions.

Face value reigned on this occasion, and, from the time of Mansell's very first test at the wheel of one of the Mercedes-engined MP4/10s, the signs of impending disaster were already breaking the surface of the not-too-calm waters. From the outset the trouble with the deal was that Mansell and McLaren were approaching things from very different perspectives, wanting different things from their uneasy partnership.

From the first pre-race test it was clear that the MP4/10 was suffering from a significant handling imbalance. Despite predictions from other designers that the new '95 breed of F1 challenger would be somewhat less pitch-sensitive than its predecessors, Neil Oatley had correctly predicted that this would not necessarily be the case. But he could hardly have anticipated the problems in this area from which his new design would suffer.

Worse still, Mansell also found that the cockpit dimensions lacked sufficient elbow room for him to steer properly. Even before the season began the team thus found itself facing a major crisis and, after considerable detailed deliberation, decided that there was no alternative but to design and build a slightly wider monocoque for Nigel's use. There was no way in which the McLaren management would leave any door open for Mansell to make excuses, so they hurried through the development and manufacture of the new car.

In the meantime, Mansell had to stand down from the first two races of the season, and his place alongside Hakkinen was taken by Mark Blundell.

With characteristic McLaren commitment to detail, once the green light had been pressed on the project the re-design was completed, executed and delivered with seamless efficiency in fractionally over a month.

Front-end grip was the key problem with the MP4/10 from the outset, although the new Mercedes-engined challenger proved promising in its first two outings in Brazil and Argentina. Hakkinen took fourth place at Interlagos, Blundell sixth, the Finn running particularly strongly in the opening stages of the race, losing only fractionally to Damon Hill's Williams, Michael Schumacher's Benetton and David Coulthard's Williams.

During the Argentine Grand Prix at Buenos Aires, Hakkinen qualified on the third row, only to spin off at the first corner after his McLaren's left rear tyre was punctured against the nose of Eddie Irvine's Jordan, while Blundell stopped with an oil leak from a cracked gearbox casing. For the third round of the Championship, the San Marino Grand Prix at Imola, Mansell returned to the wheel of the revised MP4/10B, the car having been substantially redesigned from the dash bulkhead to the rear seat back. The process had taken only 33 days – just over half the 65 days that the team would normally allocate for such a major transformation.

Once Mansell fitted the car, it quickly became clear that the team had to face up to more problems. The MP4/10B's handling was still beset by understeer and Mansell made no bones about the fact that he felt uncomfortable with a car that so demonstrably lacked front-end grip.

Returning to Imola one year after the death of Ayrton Senna was not easy for anybody, least of all the Williams and McLaren teams. Ayrton had been killed at the wheel of one of Frank's cars, yet the loss for McLaren was felt perhaps even more poignantly as this was the circuit on which the great Brazilian had won three times in the red and white cars from Woking.

Mansell clearly wasn't about to perform miracles first time out in the McLaren-Mercedes. On Thursday morning an extra practice session was put on by the organisers to allow the drivers to get used to the revised circuit configuration, chicanes having been installed at the Tamburello and Villeneuve corners to slow the flow of the traffic.

Nigel had hardly taken to the circuit before he spun off at the downhill Rivazza left-hander, apparently having instinctively gone for the clutch pedal, only to remember – too late – that the McLaren-Mercedes had a hand-operated clutch mechanism. He spun into a gravel trap, but would recover to qualify ninth fastest – 0.8 seconds behind the sixth-placed Hakkinen.

'The McLaren-Mercedes team has done a sensational job building this new car,' he agreed, 'so we are now at the point where we can start developing it. I feel happy and comfortable in the cockpit. I can even apply opposite lock, which was impossible in the original car as there was just no room to move my arms.'

Mansell's race proved disappointing. To start with, both he and Hakkinen – like most of the field, to be fair – started on slicks on a cold track that had only just started to dry after heavy rain during the morning. It was a tactical error that compromised the performance of both McLarens.

He then tapped Gianni Morbidelli's Arrows on the run down to the first corner on the opening lap, thereafter running steadily, moving up to sixth place by lap 23, although he was then on the verge of being lapped by the leaders.

He made his first routine refuelling stop on lap 28, his second on lap 43 when the MP4/10B's nose cone was replaced. After this stop he rejoined only for Irvine's Jordan to touch his left-rear tyre under braking for Tosa, sending him back into the pits to replace the resultant puncture. He finished tenth. It would be the only occasion that Nigel Mansell finished a race at the wheel of a McLaren.

Just to round off his frustrating day, some Ferrari-mad photographer managed to hit Mansell on the head with a telephoto lens as he rushed past the McLaren garage after the race.

Mansell then managed to qualify within half a second of Hakkinen in Spain, but the Finn easily outclassed him in the race and Nigel opted for retirement after a couple of lurid slides across a gravel trap.

The body language radiated by the British driver as he walked through to the back of the pit garage at Barcelona without a backward glance should have told us what was coming. The Mansell/McLaren marriage was over.

Their respective paths had crossed at a moment when each was looking for something the other could not offer: Mansell, an instantly competitive car that could do battle against a Williams-Renault; McLaren, a dynamically motivated driver who could inspire and help carry the team on to greater things.

Before the next race at Monaco, Mansell and Ron Dennis had agreed to terminate the partnership with considerable dignity. It was an ill-starred episode, a rare occasion perhaps on which Dennis's grasp of driver psychology let him down. But neither man has ever voiced a word of recrimination against the other since they shook hands and walked away from the deal. Ironically, Marlboro's Monaco advertising promotions centred round Mansell in a McLaren-Mercedes.

With Blundell now restored to the full-time driver line-up, team morale bucked up considerably from the Monaco GP onwards. Mark's equable temperament and willing approach made him enormously popular with the McLaren mechanics and factory workforce, almost as a counterpoint to Hakkinen's increasingly aloof intensity.

Even so, Dennis continued to employ Blundell on a race-to-race basis for the balance of the season, a strategy that the McLaren boss clearly believed was calculated to get the best out of the Englishman.

The British GP at Silverstone saw a major step forward in power and driveability from Ilmor, a revised version of the Mercedes V10 allowing Hakkinen to set fastest time in the race morning warm-up, and at Hockenheim both cars ran in the top six before suffering engine failures.

Throughout the balance of the season Ilmor concentrated on improving the engine's mid-range torque and driveability while at the same time inching forward in terms of power output. The need to progress quicker than the opposition in an effort to catch up resulted in Dennis pushing his entire workforce to the outer limits of endurance throughout the season.

Yet it was in this area that McLaren and Mercedes demonstrated time and again the sheer depth of their commitment. After engine failures in Hungary, Ilmor stripped the troubled V10s, assessed the problem, made and installed fresh components and bench-tested the revised engines in time for a test at Silverstone a week later.

While this was going on, McLaren pulled out all the stops to produce a revised gearbox casing specially to accommodate new rear suspension geometry in time for the Belgian Grand Prix at Spa-Francorchamps, where Hakkinen qualified third, then blotted his copybook with an absurd second-lap spin at La Source, caught out in part by the engine's abrupt throttle response.

Blundell came home fifth at Spa, but the team achieved its best result of the year at Monza with second and fourth, although both Ferraris, both Williams and Schumacher's Benetton had retired while running ahead of the MP4/10Bs.

This was satisfying progress in the right direction, but McLaren kept up the pressure and pushed ahead with the development of a revised C-spec car for the Portuguese race at Estoril and the European Grand Prix at the Nurburgring, but design problems with yet another new rear geometry package left them struggling.

The Nurburgring race was about as bad as it got for the McLaren-Mercedes alliance; a combination of unpredictable weather conditions, chassis problems and abrupt throttle response made starting on slicks in cold conditions a huge challenge for both drivers.

Hakkinen soldiered home eighth, two laps behind Michael Schumacher's winning Benetton, the only consolation being that the Finn's lap times improved dramatically in the closing stages, offering a tantalising prospect of what might have happened had the tyres warmed up to their operating temperature earlier in the race.

The Nurburgring weekend also brought confirmation of the fact that Scottish driver David Coulthard would be joining McLaren at the start of 1996 as Hakkinen's team-mate, thereby leaving the Williams squad after only his first full season in F1.

Coulthard had originally signed with Ron Dennis in November 1994 as a means of attempting to get the FIA Contracts Recognition Board to adjudicate on the validity of his 1995 contract with Williams. As things transpired, the Board found that Frank had first call on Coulthard's services, but throughout the following season a cloud of ambiguity and uncertainty had continued to surround the precise nature of his commitment to McLaren, this speculation further fuelled by the fact that he had signed only a one-year contract with Williams, with no options on either side.

Coulthard had been through a difficult season in 1995. The lingering effects of tonsillitis were not finally resolved until he was briefly hospitalised for an operation after the Canadian Grand Prix, and Williams was unimpressed by his failure to get on terms with Schumacher's Benetton, which he vainly chased for the lead throughout the German Grand Prix at Hockenheim.

Williams was also under pressure from FIA Vice President Bernie Ecclestone to sign Indycar Champion Jacques Villeneuve for 1996. Eventually Frank Williams and his partner Patrick Head decided not to press for further negotiation with Coulthard, as they suspected that he already had a prior deal in place with McLaren.

'In many ways it was difficult to leave Williams after two and a half years,' said Coulthard. 'But I think that after Hockenheim the team stood back from its inner knowledge to make the decision it took. I was suffering from tonsillitis for the early part of the year and spent most of the time driving in survival mode rather than attacking.'

However, in the closing races of the 1995 Coulthard enjoyed such an upsurge in form that Frank Williams quietly admitted that 'letting him go could have been one of my greatest mistakes.' Yet David remained confident that he had taken the correct route. 'I may take a step backwards initially, but I feel that I will grow with the team,' he said. They were propitious words indeed.

Mika Hakkinen missed the Pacific Grand Prix at Aida as he was recuperating from the after-effects of an appendix operation, allowing the young Dane Jan Magnussen to be promoted to the race team for a one-off outing. He did a good job to finish tenth, one place behind Blundell, but Mika was back in harness for the Japanese Grand Prix at Suzuka the following weekend.

Hakkinen simply flew to qualify third, then finished the race a strong second, proving that the McLaren-Mercedes technical package was certainly developing in the right direction. By contrast, Blundell slammed off the road at around 170mph during Saturday free practice on the fast left 130R kink before the start/finish line.

The McLaren hit the protective tyre barrier with a sickening thud, shedding its nose box, but Mark duly staggered away from the damaged car without any lasting physical damage. Doctor's orders kept him away from second qualifying, though, so the Englishman found himself starting from last place on the grid. His race performance, which saw him pound through to finish seventh, only 1.8 seconds behind Mika Salo's sixth-place Tyrrell, went down as another of motor racing's great unsung achievements.

The 1995 season ended on a deeply worrying note for the McLaren-Mercedes squad. During first qualifying for the Australian Grand Prix at Adelaide, Mika Hakkinen lost control of his MP4/10B after its left rear tyre suddenly deflated due to running over debris on the track surface. Hakkinen was accelerating hard as he approached the 110mph fourth-gear right-hander leading out on to the long Brabham straight, and as he turned into the corner the car spun wildly over a high kerb before literally flying sideways into the tyre barrier facing the concrete wall on the outside of the corner.

Prompt action by the medical staff on the scene forestalled any risk to Hakkinen's life. His head was held straight to prevent him choking and a tracheotomy performed at the trackside to prevent any brain damage through oxygen loss. He was then immediately transferred to the Royal Adelaide Hospital where his recovery was duly monitored by Professor Sid Watkins, the FIA Medical Delegate.

Thankfully, after an initial period of nervousness about his condition, Mika emerged from any physical danger to start out on a path to recovery that would see him return to the cockpit at the start of the 1996 season. Happily, he would completely regain his prowess behind the wheel and, within six months, had shrugged aside virtually all the after-effects of this painful experience.

McLaren-Mercedes finished fourth in the 1995 Constructors' Championship, but with 30 points to Benetton's title-winning tally of 137, this was nothing in particular to shout about. However, Ron Dennis's faith in the team's ability to turn the corner, and thereby keep his partners at Mercedes and Philip Morris happy, remained as unobtrusively focused as ever.

With that in mind, the season finished in a mood more upbeat and optimistic than the results might justify at first glance. McLaren may have been down in 1995, but only the reckless would have counted them out.

Yet despite the fact that Ron Dennis and Mercedes were committed to F1's 'long game', there was a perception that McLaren were embroiled in an F1 crisis by the end of 1995. The European Grand Prix performance at Nurburgring, under the noses of the Mercedes top brass, represented an embarrassing low-point. Surely events were now at boiling point? The sponsors must be getting worried?

I put these questions to Dennis in his office suite at Woking on 6 October 1995. Surely, I suggested, there must not only be question marks hanging over the future of your key sponsors, but also over your own capacity to manage the company effectively? He fielded these inquiries in a firm and very succinct manner.

'If you are sponsored by a range of prestige companies who lead in their fields, they obviously wish to invest in other companies that have similar objectives,' he explained. 'We are more than aware of the necessity to achieve the maximum amount of exposure for the people who invest in us – and that is best achieved by leading races.

'However, there have been periods in this company's history in the past during which it has failed to perform and, following those periods, changes have been made that have restored the competitiveness of the team.

'I am not particularly young, but I am most definitely not old [Dennis was 48 at the time]. I consider that I have a clear understanding of what is required to win in grands prix. My personal commitment to the challenge of winning in grand prix racing is probably greater, if anything, than it has ever been. This is not because of pressure coming from third parties, but because of the pressures I am putting on myself with a view to achieving.

'Change for change's sake is foolhardy; it is important in my mind that, if you have a belief in a particular direction of change, then you should follow that and you should effect change. But to arbitrarily change things – which could involve people – you must be certain that you change them for the better, and not for cosmetic reasons to satisfy those people who stand on the outside of the company with opinions that are not based on fact.'

That point was easily taken. Yet how did he manage to placate his sponsors during difficult times such as he was now experiencing? 'When it comes to the perception of our sponsors such as Philip Morris,' he replied, 'it is part of my job to give them a clear understanding of what we are doing, why we are doing it, what our strategy is and how we are addressing the problems as we see them.

'If they subsequently choose to redirect their investments, then it would be as a result either of my failure to convey our strategy to their satisfaction, or my failure to lead the company back into a pattern of success. That I completely accept. It is my responsibility, and it is not a responsibility I am uncomfortable with. It is what I want, it is what I am here for, and it is what I am committed to.'

Dennis also discounted that any problems were developing with Mercedes-Benz. 'They have an even greater desire, if anything, to succeed than McLaren,' he explained, 'because of the direct relationship between their company and the performance of the car. Given the facts, they understand what we are trying to achieve and how we are trying to achieve it. McLaren and Mercedes would have liked more success [in 1995] and better results, but when we publicly fail it is through trying to take bigger steps than the opposition, because that is the only way to catch up during the course of a season.

'We believe that our engine development programme has come on in leaps and bounds from where we started. So has the car, but other people have done a better job. Where we failed was in taking a massive chance in introducing a complex set of changes into the car at Estoril – and one element of that package was incorrectly designed, and badly caught us out.

'It was a mistake that came from the pace at which we were undertaking the development programme. And we paid the price. But this doesn't mean that we are going to behave like chickens with their heads cut off. We know where we are going and we know how we are going to achieve it.'

The problem at Estoril had related to suspension geometry, and with the European Grand Prix taking place at Nurburgring only a week later, there had been precious little time to address the problem.

'The kinematics of suspension is a complex subject and is not just a matter of an individual making a simple mistake,' continued Dennis. 'It is more complex than that and, ultimately, the responsibility falls on several people's shoulders – including mine, I might add, because it is me who has been pushing harder on everybody to bring those developments through the system faster than perhaps is practically possible.

'So you could say that I am as guilty as anybody, but I have that desire to improve, a desire to go to the races in the latter part of a season in a more competitive situation than in the early part of the season.

'You have your tape running, so therefore it is very hard for me to convey the reasons why our car has not done a particularly good job this year or last [1994]. But there are other factors that come into play, and inevitably the team takes the brunt of the end performance of the entire package.

'This year we started with our eyes open, with an engine that first ran in January, raced in March, and was then developed in parallel with an intensive race programme. The achievements of everybody involved in that programme have been considerable, if you could understand what has been achieved. I cannot get into details of the developments, but what has been done is almost superhuman.'

Dennis also stressed that Mercedes-Benz had certainly proved to be a great deal more than fair-weather friends. 'After the European Grand Prix, which was less than spectacular for us with our two drivers struggling on cold slicks, there was a meeting between myself, Roger Penske and the Mercedes DTM representatives,' he recalled.

'This was a scheduled meeting to discuss the overall strategy and results within the Mercedes-Benz motorsport programme. Each representative discussed the negatives of their programmes – not the positives – and there was also an overall discussion designed to share

with each other the technical, and sometimes commercial, problems
that each of the teams encountered.

'Roger had the embarrassment of his team's poor performance at
Indianapolis to deal with, I had the embarrassment of the
performance in the grand prix, and the DTM team had the
satisfaction of having achieved [success] that season, but also being
challenged in respect of the integrity of the series as a whole.

'So nobody was sitting there with a smug grin on their face. We
were having a business discussion about the negative aspects of
those programmes. But the overwhelming point of the meeting was
the desire by Mr Helmet Werner and Mr Jurgen Hubbert of
Mercedes to convey to all of us the absolute support that Mercedes
has to its motorsport strategy.

'They radiated unswerving commitment and any questions they
had were designed to understand how they could contribute more to
achieving on-circuit success. When I left that meeting I felt that I
was not partnered by simply fair-weather friends.'

However, as far as continued support from Philip Morris was
concerned, one began to discern that the tide had changed direction
far across the sands. The cigarette company's President, Walter
Thoma, was clearly pressing for results and explanations. A
Marlboro-McLaren had not won a grand prix since Adelaide in
1993. Understandably, the team's title sponsor was signalling its
concern.

'Yes, Walter Thoma is tough,' acknowledged Dennis. 'He pushes,
demands, needs to understand. But he has never been a rug-puller. If
our performance does not justify the level of commercial support
that we receive from any of our sponsors, then the process of
withdrawal would be professional, face to face. But I believe they will
give us the time.'

Three days later I was sitting across the desk from McLaren-Merc
driver Mark Blundell, who by now knew that he would not be
included in the team for 1996. A pleasant and easy-going fellow,
Blundell confessed that, while it was satisfying to have been taken
back into the McLaren race team after Mansell had left, being
employed on a race-by-race basis had been a nerve-wracking
experience.

'As far as I am concerned, that was detrimental to me in terms of
giving me the best opportunity to go out and do the best job,' he
reflected with three races of the season still to run.

'I feel that I should have been put on a contract that was firm until
the end of the season. The team was looking for 100 per cent
commitment from me, but was not giving 100 per cent back to me in
that particular area.'

Yet for all these problems, Blundell was certainly impressed with
the sheer depth of technical resource that the team deployed in its

effort to improve the McLaren-Mercedes package throughout the 1995 season.

'There is no other F1 team capable of responding in the same way,' he insisted. 'I am sure that other teams would put up a good argument that they could, but I haven't seen it. You've got to take your hat off and say McLaren is the best at doing that.

'Yet the car is not a race winner and, at the end of it all, McLaren has been used to winning races. We need to take all the elements away from the whole package and see what is not working, but that is a long process when, at the same time, you are trying to go racing and keep up with the other side of it.

'Our biggest problem is that we have got a pitch-sensitive car. Sure, everyone else in the pit lane is in the same boat, although perhaps they've done a better job in accommodating it.'

Blundell expressed extremely strong views about what he regarded as the shortcomings of the McLaren team at the time. Blundell continued: 'Maybe they have to cut away some people or infrastructure, and even if it turns out to be the wrong thing to do, people will say at least they are trying to go forward, make changes and get back to their winning ways.

'I respect Ron's loyalty, but we are talking about a high-performance environment – and I have been put into this and now taken out again. Obviously they are not happy with my performance, because they have taken me out of the equation, so there must be other areas of the team where the same rules need to be applied.'

So does Ron try to do too much? 'I would say that there is an enormous workload that he takes on, so at some point there must be areas that become compromised over others,' said Blundell.

'Yet at the same time he seems 100 per cent in control. He is a remarkable guy in the sense that he steers that ship. If anybody sees where he's come from and what he has achieved, they wouldn't mind being a step behind in attempting to emulate him.'

Dennis was not amused by some of Blundell's observations. He did not feel that they were appropriate and judged that they infringed the confidentiality of the employer/employee relationship between team and driver. But with Mark leaving the team at the end of the season, there was nothing to be achieved by stoking up the issue into a slanging match. Dennis admonished Blundell, then kept his thoughts to himself.

10

'Winning is what our company exists for', 1996–98

MUCH WAS EXPECTED from the McLaren-Mercedes alliance in its second year, yet by the end of the 1996 season it was clear that even more work would need to be done before the technical recipe gelled to perfection.

Nor did Ron Dennis and the McLaren workforce need reminding that the third anniversary of their last grand prix win was looming large in their sights. Since Ayrton Senna's memorable final victory in the 1993 Australian GP, McLaren fortunes had fluctuated dramatically. The 1994 and '95 seasons had turned out to be periods of readjustment and reorganisation, and while 1996 proved a definite turn for the better, it certainly fell short of the team's rigorous standards and high level of expectation.

With only an estimated 7.5 per cent component 'roll-over' from the 1995 chassis, McLaren put an enormous amount of detailed effort into the MP4/11, which looked as though it would be competitive straight out of the box when Mika Hakkinen posted a 1min 19.65sec fastest lap in the final pre-season test at Estoril in Portugal.

The new car was powered by a totally new Phase 3 version of the Merc V10, which had initially burst into life on the test bed on 3 February, just over a week before the new car ran for the first time. Ilmor had set itself the target of boosting the V10's power output by 5 per cent, with the result that only the oil pumps were carried over from the engine's immediate predecessor.

The engine weighed in at a claimed 120kg and was capable of running to 16,000rpm, the key areas of improvement relating to enhanced low-speed torque, lack of which the drivers complained about with the 1995 engine.

The power was transmitted through a totally new longitudinal McLaren six-speed gearbox with semi-automatic change mechanism developed by TAG Electronics. The car also featured a highly sophisticated TAG 2000 integrated engine and chassis control data acquisition system.

The MP4/11 concept was produced by McLaren's highly

experienced design group under Neil Oatley's direction, but with an increased degree of input from fellow engineer Steve Nichols, who took a particular interest in suspension geometry and configuration. Nichols was responsible for the use of carbon hinges rather than ball joints on the front suspension, and also co-ordinated most of the chassis design, while Oatley focused more specifically on the engine installation and gearbox package. Overall, the MP4/11 monocoque was around 60 per cent stiffer than that employed for the 1995 car.

On the driver front, McLaren started the season looking extremely strong. Mika Hakkinen had continued his impressive recovery and, while initially the Finn looked strained and pale, he quickly proved that there was nothing much wrong with his ability behind the wheel.

Meanwhile Coulthard was champing at the bit, eager to add a second grand prix victory to his first scored for Williams at Estoril the previous year. In addition, Jan Magnussen remained on as test driver, while Alain Prost continued a high-profile role as technical consultant and some-time development driver, his experience helping to cross-reference input from the team's two regular drivers.

The handling balance of the new McLaren MP4/11 initially proved to be something of a problem. Neither driver felt totally confident about its behaviour on turn-in, but improvements were initiated for Nurburgring – where David finished third in the European Grand Prix – and then again in time for Imola, where the Scot led the first 20 laps of the San Marino GP in superbly confident style.

Revisions to the front wing mounting points were made after testing revealed that the point where the wing attached to its vertical supports was flexing. Some of this testing was carried out at the Idi-Ada motor industry development complex in Spain, but after karting ace Martin Hines had the mother-and-father of accidents there early in the season, the venue was wisely abandoned.

Hines, who had come to know Ron Dennis through some charitable work, admits that this was not one of his greatest days. But it did not prevent the ZipKart boss from collaborating with Dennis to launch the McLaren Mercedes Champions of the Future karting awards, which further expanded the McLaren commitment to encouraging young driving talent that had already been started by the McLaren Autosport Award scheme.

Engine response was progressively improved during the course of the season, using both Ilmor and Mercedes-Benz transient dynamometers in addition to circuit testing. Meanwhile, McLaren also developed a short-wheelbase car, which was used at Monaco for the first time, then became the team's standard configuration from Magny-Cours onward.

Coulthard scored the team's best result with second to Panis's Ligier at Monaco, the team just losing out to their French rival in the spate of refuelling stops. This was also the scene of Hakkinen's biggest error, when he wrote off a brand new MP4/11 during a 15-minute extra pre-race acclimatisation session in the pouring rain. Running 2 seconds faster than anybody else on the circuit, he lost control attempting to beat his own time. It was Mika's lowest point of the year, but thereafter he gradually asserted his superiority over Coulthard and scored strong third places in the British, Belgian and Italian Grands Prix.

It was not easy to pinpoint precisely why Coulthard made heavy weather of the second half of the year, although anybody arriving at McLaren from Williams at this point in the teams' respective histories was bound to have struggled in some measure.

At Williams he had enjoyed enough power to run sufficient downforce and produce a virtually neutral-handling car. It was a luxury the genial Scot now seemed to miss. At the wheel of the McLaren MP4/11 he could never quite develop a handling balance to suit his style, often struggling, in his own words, 'to keep the rear end under control'.

The McLaren-Mercedes were generally most at home on high-speed, low-downforce circuits, as emphasised by their performances at Spa and Monza. Coulthard looked a potential winner at one point in the Belgian race, only to spin off on his second set of tyres, while Hakkinen's dynamic performance at Monza, where he climbed back from 17th to third after an unscheduled early stop to change a damaged nose section, was one of the most impressive single driving performances of the whole season.

The general consensus from the touchlines was that McLaren squandered Jan Magnussen's potential, offering the Dane insufficient test and development work. Many observers felt he should have been considered for full-time promotion to the race team for 1997, but with Coulthard finishing the first year of a two-year deal and Hakkinen restored to better-than-ever form, there was sadly no space for the talented youngster at McLaren.

Clearly Magnussen was not interested in kicking his heels in a testing driving role any longer, and McLaren evaluated Ralf Schumacher for this valuable role in the late summer. Eventually the World Champion's younger brother decided that he was ready for the race action on an F1 grid and accepted a drive from Jordan instead.

The other big change for McLaren in 1996 came when it was announced that its 23-season partnership with the Philip Morris cigarette conglomerate would end after the Japanese GP. Rather than accept reduced funding from Marlboro – who now wished to scale up its sponsorship of the Ferrari team – Ron Dennis remained determined to negotiate the team's title sponsorship on his own terms and concluded a long-term deal with the German tobacco company Reemtsma, whose best-known brands are West, R1, Davidoff and Peter Stuyvesant.

On a completely different front, McLaren was one of three teams that declined to sign the new Concorde Agreement, which came into force at the start of 1997. Dennis claims that concern over various clauses contained in this protocol, and their implications for the future administration of the sport, persuaded him to withhold his agreement. For the moment that simply meant that McLaren, together with Tyrrell and Williams, were deprived of a lucrative share in television revenues. However, none of that would affect the McLaren-Mercedes team's determination to be regular winners in 1997, when they would go into battle carrying a distinctive new silver and black livery with title sponsorship from the West cigarette brand.

It is a sobering thought, but the distinctive Marlboro livery carried by the McLarens had been the most enduring to be seen on an F1 car throughout the 47-season history of the official World Championship. In many ways the McLaren corporate identity had perhaps been too bound up with this symphony of red and white. Anybody visiting the McLaren International headquarters in Albert Drive, Woking, might have been forgiven for thinking that this was in fact the company's corporate livery. In the foyer, red and white Marlboro McLarens seemed to extend beyond the horizon, their serried ranks bearing witness to almost two decades of F1 achievement.

Under the circumstances the switch to the new livery represented a major turning point in this F1 team's history, the severing of the umbilical cord that had linked it to Marlboro ever since the beginning of the McLaren International story.

There was also another, even more emotional dimension. The new livery raised memories of the famous Mercedes 'Silver Arrows' that dominated grand prix racing in the early 1930s and again in 1954 and '55. It was therefore no surprise when the dramatic new West McLaren Mercedes colour scheme was unveiled at a lavish party hosted at London's Alexandra Palace to the backdrop of the pulsating beat provided by top pop groups the Spice Girls and Jamiroquai.

Earlier, on 14 January 1997, the new McLaren MP4/12 had been unveiled at the McLaren factory wearing the distinctive orange livery that had been used by the first McLaren F1 cars back in 1968. This was a neat promotional device ensuring that the team got two bites of the promotional cherry, the initial launch of the new car in no way damaging the subsequent high-profile launch of its distinctive new colour scheme.

A totally new machine from the ground up, the McLaren MP4/12 was designed to incorporate the latest batch of F1 technical innovations including a rear impact zone, collapsible steering column, reduced winglet area and suspension components of restricted aspect ratio.

The further revised Mercedes F0110E 75-degree V10 represented another major evolution from what had gone before, Ilmor using a new block design for both performance and installation reasons. The inlet system was redesigned and the whole package was marginally lighter. Power output was enhanced, said Mario Illien, but how much better the engine would be in terms of driveability was not something he wanted to predict before the new car had run on a circuit for the first time. Privately, however, the Ilmor boss was optimistic.

Ron Dennis was similarly cautious when speculating on the MP4/12's competitive prospects. 'We know that we have made quantifiable gains in the wind tunnel,' he admitted, 'but I would be surprised if the other teams haven't made corresponding improvements. That said, I think attempting to evaluate the qualities of the opposition is pretty much a waste of time. We just have to concentrate on developing the best car that we can.'

On its race debut at Melbourne, the new McLaren was close to the front-running pace from the outset. The new Williams FW19 continued that team's pace-setting reputation, with Jacques Villeneuve the only driver to break the 1min 30sec mark during qualifying, this being an amazing 1.8 seconds ahead of his own team-mate Heinz-Harald Frentzen. Coulthard qualified fourth with Hakkinen sixth. It was a good enough start.

On the sprint to the first corner, Eddie Irvine obliged his key rivals by taking both Villeneuve and Johnny Herbert's Sauber-Petronas out on the spot. That allowed Frentzen to settle into an early lead ahead of Coulthard, David surging into the lead when the surviving Williams made the first of its two scheduled stops on lap 17 of the 58-lap race.

The Scot now found himself running barely half a second ahead of Michael Schumacher's Ferrari, yet far from showing any strain, Coulthard was handling the McLaren with admirable coolness and precision, refusing to be ruffled by the red car's distant presence in his mirrors.

Frentzen was on course to make a second refuelling stop on lap 40, and, given Coulthard's consistent pace, it would be touch and go whether the Williams would be able to squeeze back into the race ahead. As things transpired, a sticking rear wheel nut caused a crucial delay and David raced past into the lead with Schumacher still a couple of seconds further back.

Frentzen, now third, quickly began to make inroads into Schumacher's advantage, but when the Ferrari was called in for a precautionary second fuel stop with only eight laps to go, the Williams driver was left with a clear run at Coulthard's McLaren. Yet with three laps to go the Williams challenge finally evaporated as Heinz-Harald pirouetted out of the contest with a shattered right front brake disc.

All this drama at least allowed Coulthard a handful of straightforward laps through to the chequered flag. Up to that point he had been under pressure all afternoon and never made a single slip.

'The car was going well, but that doesn't mean we don't have a lot of work still to do,' said David with quiet satisfaction. 'At the moment we're being held back a little by having to find the confidence to push, but we're getting there and I think I proved I could withstand any of the pressure I experienced today.'

With Mika Hakkinen finishing a strong third, it had been a memorable moment of restoration for the McLaren team, its first victory since Ayrton Senna had signed off in Adelaide just over three years earlier.

Ron Dennis allowed himself a wry grin of satisfaction. 'Williams still has the best car,' he noted, 'so we must try to beat them by ensuring that we are the best team. After the morning warm-up we felt very confident. Winning is what our company exists for, and our approach has always been to try to be the best in everything we do.'

The McLaren boss was right to caution against over-optimism at this early stage. In the first few races of the year there seemed to be a frustrating inconsistency about the MP4/12's performance, and it was Hakkinen who seemed best able to adapt his driving style to accommodate any handling imbalance.

This subtle disparity between the early season performances of the two drivers was demonstrated in the Brazilian Grand Prix at Interlagos where Hakkinen battled home fourth, despite being obliged to make a premature early second refuelling stop after his tyres suddenly began to deteriorate and lose grip. By contrast, Coulthard never seemed to get into his stride all afternoon, spending much of the race bogged down in traffic to finish a disappointing tenth.

There was no better fortune awaiting David two weeks later in Buenos Aires. His McLaren lost a wheel in a first-corner collision with Ralf Schumacher's Jordan, leaving Hakkinen to climb through from an undistinguished 17th on the grid to fifth at the chequered flag. This performance reflected well on the team's resourcefulness in terms of pit-stop strategy, for the MP4/12 was not at its best in qualifying trim on the harder of Goodyear's two available compounds, so a long opening stint and a one-stop strategy was certainly the right way to go under the circumstances.

The team returned from the two South American races holding second place in the Constructors' Championship, a single point behind Williams, for whom Villeneuve had won in both Brazil and Argentina. Prior to the first race of the European season at Imola, McLaren took another significant step to enhance its technical base by confirming the news that Adrian Newey, formerly the Williams team's Chief Designer, would be joining as Technical Director as from 1 August 1997.

One of the most highly regarded aerodynamic specialists in the F1 pit lane, 38-year-old Newey had been involved in a dispute over the terms of his contract with Williams, as a result of which he had been sitting at home on full pay since November 1996. One of the key areas of contention had been whether or not Williams should have discussed its driver selection policy with him, in particular the decision to replace Damon Hill with Heinz-Harald Frentzen for the start of the 1997 season.

The matter had now been resolved by lawyers acting for the two parties, and Newey, who would reputedly attract an annual salary in excess of £1 million under his new deal with McLaren, now sat and waited until the day arrived when he could pick up the threads of his career with his new employer. Securing his services certainly was regarded as a significant coup on McLaren's part, although there was nothing he could do for the moment to influence the performance of the MP4/12.

The San Marino race saw McLaren produce only average qualifying performances, Hakkinen lining up eighth, 1.5 seconds away from Villeneuve's pole position, with Coulthard two places further back. But with both cars again running on a one-stop strategy, they duly worked their way steadily through the field once the race settled under way.

With 25 of the 62 laps covered, David was up to fourth place and made his sole refuelling stop ten laps later without losing a place. This was followed by a ripple of unexpected excitement when Mika came straight in after the Scot, having ruined his first set of tyres with an unscheduled trip across a gravel trap while attempting to lap Mika Salo's Tyrrell.

Unfortunately, soon after the pit stop David's engine began to trail a haze of smoke due to a water pump problem, which eventually led to his stopping with engine failure on lap 39. Mika was left to finish sixth, boxed in behind the obstructive Jean Alesi's Benetton-Renault during the closing stages of the race.

Of the 1997 Monaco Grand Prix, the less said the better as far as the McLaren team's fortunes were concerned. The MP4/12 would have been a strong contender had not Mika clipped a barrier during qualifying, breaking a steering arm with the result that he ploughed straight into the guard rail on the opposite side of the circuit. At the time the Finn seemed on course for third fastest time at worst, but was now reduced to taking the spare car, in which he qualified eighth. David would end up fifth on the grid, barely half a second shy of Frentzen's pole-position Williams.

Rain began to fall heavily before the start, but McLaren's professional weather forecasters advised that it was only likely to be a brief shower and, as a result, Hakkinen started on slicks, Coulthard on intermediates. On the second lap David spun and stalled under braking for the waterfront chicane, leaving Mika to bounce off the right-hand guard rail and into the back of Alesi's Benetton as the pack ahead of him braked hard to avoid the Scot's wayward machine. Both MP4/12s were out on the spot.

The Spanish Grand Prix at Barcelona saw the practice debut of the new F-spec version of the Mercedes F0110 engine, reputedly developing in excess of 740bhp at over 16,000rpm, despite a rather peaky torque curve. It helped Coulthard to qualify third at Barcelona, but both he and Hakkinen wrestled with acute tyre wear problems during the race, finishing a disappointing sixth and seventh, the Scot only losing fifth to Johnny Herbert's hard-driven Sauber on the final lap.

The F-spec engine made its race debut in the Canadian Grand Prix at Montreal, where Coulthard ran a comfortable third from the start behind Schumacher's Ferrari and the Jordan of Giancarlo Fisichella. The Scot drove a brilliantly disciplined race to keep his original set of tyres in fine condition through to his single scheduled pit stop on lap 40, well beyond half distance in a race originally scheduled to last for 69 laps.

After Schumacher came in for his second stop, David was left with such a commanding lead that the team judged there was sufficient time in hand for him to make a precautionary second stop to change a blistered tyre. The mechanics performed their tasks with characteristic efficiency, but when Coulthard was signalled back into the race a problem with the clutch actuation system cost him precious seconds.

Schumacher surged through into the lead only for the race to be red-flagged to a halt after Olivier Panis crashed heavily at high speed, the Frenchman being lifted from the wreckage of his Prost Mugen-Honda with two broken legs. The result was thus declared based on the order at the end of lap 54. It didn't take much of a mathematician to work out that if Coulthard had stayed out a single lap longer, he would have been celebrating the second McLaren-Mercedes F1 victory. As it was, he had to make do with seventh place.

Not that his mind was focused on his own misfortune. 'Clearly, Olivier had a very big accident and maybe we need to look at increasing the amount of tyres at that point on the circuit,' he mused, 'because something in the impact was enough to split the front of the chassis, something that is very unusual to see with a modern F1 car.

'This was not a particularly difficult corner; it is no more dangerous here [at Montreal] than at Monaco, and I don't class Monaco as a particularly dangerous circuit. Clearly, if you make a mistake there, you hit the wall, but we all know that an initial impact at a shallow angle is pretty safe. The worry is when you have a head-on impact. Maybe that's what split Olivier's car.'

Coulthard and the McLaren team were obviously bitterly disappointed that the race had ended on such a disastrous note, and Hakkinen had also had a bad day, being swept up in a first-corner collision to retire at the end of the opening lap with his MP4/12's rear wing ripped off. Nevertheless, the revised Mercedes engine had certainly further enhanced the overall 1997 technical package.

Yet the French Grand Prix produced another acute disappointment. A succession of niggling little mechanical problems and difficulty working out a decent chassis balance consigned both drivers to mid-grid starting positions. Mika was out early with engine failure, but David was heading for a hard-won fifth place when Alesi shunted him into a gravel trap midway round the final lap.

'It was totally unacceptable,' said the Scot. 'I would go and have a word with him, but I don't think there would be any point. He wouldn't take any notice.'

Silverstone then beckoned, with hopes high for McLaren-Mercedes prospects in the British Grand Prix. Hakkinen proved consistently quick from the outset, squeezing the maximum out of Goodyear's softer available tyre compound in the relatively cool summer conditions.

He looked on course for pole, an amazing 0.3 seconds ahead at the second timing split on his best lap, only for slower traffic to intervene. He wound up third on the grid behind the Williams-Renaults of Villeneuve and Frentzen. Coulthard lined up sixth, having spun off on Friday and never quite catching up the time he lost as a result.

Come the race, Villeneuve and Michael Schumacher sprinted away at the head of the pack with Coulthard benefiting from another terrific start to come round at the end of the opening lap in third place.

Within a few laps Coulthard began to encounter problems with locking brakes, but he still hung on ahead of an increasingly impatient crocodile of cars. Both McLarens were on one-stop strategies, as opposed to the two each favoured by Villeneuve and Schumacher, but even allowing for this, the Williams and Ferrari were simply streaking away in first and second places. By lap 19, two laps before Schumacher made his first stop, they were 27.2 seconds ahead of the Scot's McLaren.

Schumacher resumed second, but Villeneuve came in next time round, so the Ferrari went through into the lead. Villeneuve had been in trouble for the start with an apparent wheel hub problem, and his hard-won advantage now evaporated as the Williams sat stationary for over half a minute, resuming in seventh place.

Schumacher was left with a comfortable lead over the two McLarens, but many in the pit lane were wondering why the team's management were not instructing Coulthard to get out of the way and let the obviously much quicker Hakkinen through. However, as Ron Dennis would later point out in similar circumstances after the final race of the season at Jerez, long-established McLaren convention meant that no team order would be imposed if both drivers still retained a mathematical chance of winning the World Championship. They did, so he didn't.

The log-jam was finally broken when David locked a brake once too often braking for the slow entrance to Club corner and Mika was through the resultant gap in an instant. On lap 33 the Finn made his sole refuelling stop, resuming eighth ahead of Coulthard. Now the mathematical certainly of the McLaren one-stop strategy unfolded precisely to schedule, although helped by the retirement of both Ferraris during the second half of the race.

When Villeneuve made his second refuelling stop on lap 44 – with 15 laps to run – Hakkinen surged through into the lead. It could have been argued that Jacques might have still been ahead by this stage had he not been burdened with that lengthy initial stop, but by the same token Mika would have been further up had he not been boxed in behind his team-mate. Either way, it was now nip and tuck between the McLaren and Williams drivers, both of whom were relishing the prospect of a flat-out sprint to the chequered flag.

Hakkinen was 5.8 seconds ahead on lap 45, then lost a lot of time lapping Jarno Trulli's Prost, which brought Villeneuve to within 2.8 seconds of the leading McLaren. From then on there was really nothing in it, the two cars running nose-to-tail with Jacques wracking his brains as he turned over in his mind just what he might have to do to get ahead of the silver machine.

Then, abruptly, Hakkinen's engine failed with seven laps to go and he pulled off out on the circuit. It was a glorious failure, yet a failure nevertheless. I walked back into the McLaren garage and stared beseechingly at Ron Dennis. He shrugged.

My despair was not motivated by altruism. We'd both placed money on Hakkinen for a win with the bookmakers who'd set up their stall at Silverstone for the weekend. The McLaren boss may not be one to count his chickens before they've hatched, but I have to confess I thought the money was already in the bank. 'Let's send the bill to Norbert Haug,' joked Ron mischievously.

Hakkinen finished third at Hockenheim, but both cars failed to finish in Hungary, after which there was a double dose of pain delivered at the Belgian Grand Prix after Mika's car suffered a suspension structural failure on the daunting 190mph climb towards the Les Combes corner during Saturday's free practice session at Spa-Francorchamps.

The McLaren slewed wildly out of control, slamming head-on into the reinforced plastic barrier in the escape road at the top of the hill. Mika was winded but unhurt, providing yet another telling endorsement of the high degree of impact-resistance offered by today's sophisticated breed of grand prix cars.

Yet there was worse to come. After Hakkinen qualified fifth, a fuel sample taken from the McLaren's tank did not match the gas chromatograph 'finger print' of the fuel sample lodged by the team prior to the race. The team was fined $25,000 and Hakkinen's time disallowed, consigning him to a starting position at the back of the grid. McLaren appealed, and Mika raced strongly from his original grid position through to third place. McLaren subsequently lost the appeal, the fine was doubled to $50,000 – and Mika's efforts were wiped from the record book as he was disqualified from the Belgian results.

Some unworthy cynics judged that the FIA had got it in for McLaren. The team, together with Williams and Tyrrell, was still refusing to sign the new Concorde Agreement, as it felt that FIA Vice President Bernie Ecclestone – whose F1 Holdings empire controls all the television rights to the FIA World Championship – was still not offering the competitors a decent share of the takings. More than that, it believed that the seven teams that had already appended their signatures to the Agreement had failed to understand just how much in the way of their commercial rights they had signed away to Ecclestone. Either way, the three dissenting teams seemed to be having a subtly uncomfortable ride on occasion during the 1997 season.

On a completely different tack altogether, McLaren announced that it would be continuing with David Coulthard and Mika Hakkinen as the team's drivers in 1998. This was confirmed after negotiations with Damon Hill, the 1996 World Champion, failed to get far beyond the preliminary 'sounding out' stage over the previous month.

Dennis and Norbert Haug were cautiously interested in examining the possibility of Hill joining the team. Adrian Newey, who had taken up his position as Technical Director at the start of August, confirmed that Damon's input on car development might be useful. Yet Dennis moved cautiously.

He knew too well that relationships with drivers are more complicated than they sometimes look from the outside of a team. Such partnerships are built on unpredictably shifting sands, and a team chief needs to know when to be hard, and when to be sympathetic. Drivers are not automatons. They can be strangely vulnerable at times, needing tender loving care and firm cajoling in pretty well equal measure. For McLaren, Hill was an unknown quantity.

Dennis made a preliminary approach with an offer of a $1 million retainer and a bonus of $1 million per win up to a maximum of 12 victories in 1998. Hill contemptuously brushed it aside. Dennis, satisfied that he had tested Damon's seriousness of purpose – and found it wanting – was therefore more than happy to stick with the driving partnership he knew.

Hill issued a critical statement on the subject of these negotiations. 'After consideration of the terms of the offer, I felt I was left with no alternative but to reject it,' he said. 'It did not accord with what I had been previously led to believe, and I did not consider that it demonstrated a serious commitment to me as a driver for McLaren-Mercedes.'

Dennis replied, 'Our press release says it all.' He was referring to the media bulletin announcing the decision to retain Coulthard and Hakkinen.

The McLaren management's faith in its two drivers was admirably rewarded in the Italian Grand Prix at Monza. David Coulthard won superbly, while Hakkinen set fastest lap – and a new circuit record – as he tore back through the pack to finish ninth after an unscheduled stop to replace a delaminated front tyre.

Monza was a classic example of a 1997 F1 race where the outcome was resolved not by dare-devil out-braking manoeuvres on the circuit, but by slick, well-choreographed pit work by a highly drilled team of mechanics.

The Italian race offered a graphic example of such intricacies. In the opening stages of the race, Jean Alesi's Benetton B198 sprinted away from pole position to take a commanding lead, shadowed closely by Heinz-Harald Frentzen's Williams and the McLaren of David Coulthard.

Once into the rhythm of the race, Frentzen and Coulthard quickly cut back Alesi's advantage to less than a second, but the Frenchman was driving immaculately under extreme pressure and didn't seem likely to be flustered into an error of judgement.

The procession continued until lap 29 when Frentzen came in for a 10.3-second refuelling stop. This subsequently proved to have been slightly premature as, on returning to the fray, he was not in a position to get ahead of either Frentzen or Coulthard when they made their stops three laps later.

Alesi led the McLaren into the pit lane and his Benetton was stationary for just 8.7 seconds. But Coulthard was at rest for only 7.8 seconds, enabling him to squeeze back into the battle ahead of his rival. From then on, providing he made no mistakes, he was on course for victory.

In fact, the race was won due to the fact that the McLaren had a slightly bigger fuel tank than the Benetton, perhaps allowing it to carry 125 litres to its rival's 120, and this offered an obvious and crucial advantage. While both cars would be full to the brim at the start, it was clear that the McLaren would require fractionally less additional fuel than the Benetton to top up to the original figure. Thus was the race resolved.

Coulthard achieved this success despite a huge fishtailing moment when he clipped the kerb exiting the Variante Ascari a couple of laps before his refuelling stop. 'For a split second, I thought the wheel had fallen off,' he said. If the victory celebrations were slightly subdued, it was largely due to the fact that Princess Diana's funeral had taken place in London only the previous day.

From this point onwards, the McLaren-Mercedes duo were firmly established as front-runners. Yet mechanical reliability continued to desert them. At the heavily revamped A1-Ring circuit, Hakkinen qualified on the front row of the grid for the Austrian Grand Prix only to pull off with engine failure while leading at the end of the opening lap. Coulthard finished second.

A week later at the Nurburgring, Mika and David were walking away with the Luxembourg Grand Prix when, under the noses of the Mercedes-Benz top brass, both their engines failed within a lap of each other. Norbert Haug was deeply apologetic. 'We knew that our speed was there, but our reliability could be a problem. I am really sorry for Mika and David and the whole team, which did a perfect job. The engine failures prevented a double victory. I apologise to the drivers and promise that we will sort out this problem very soon.'

It was true enough that oil system aeration problems and bottom-end failures had overshadowed the season for Mercedes-Benz, but the Ilmor-built V10s steadily picked up the pace in the second half of the season to the point where many regarded them as potentially the very fastest of all. Objectively, McLaren should have won six or seven races in 1997, but eventually they wound up with three wins and, saving the best until last, their first 1–2 success in five years.

The 1997 World Championship was rounded off by the European Grand Prix at Jerez where Jacques Villeneuve clinched the title after a controversial collision with Michael Schumacher's Ferrari. That had left Villeneuve's slightly crippled Williams running at the head of the field, but with Coulthard and Hakkinen steadily making ground on the Canadian's machine. Earlier in the race McLaren had been scrupulous in keeping both their drivers out of the way of the World Championship contest and now, with Villeneuve not needing the race win to clinch the title, both McLarens closed in relentlessly, knowing full well that Jacques would not resist.

Yet, knowing that Villeneuve would move over, about 12 laps from the finish Ron Dennis asked Coulthard to move over and allow Hakkinen to overtake. It was a highly charged moment, the disappointment of which was firmly etched on David's face after the race. Sure enough, Villeneuve moved out of Hakkinen's way on the final lap and David followed the Finn through to end the season with what he regarded as a bitterly disappointing second place.

Dennis was acutely aware that this was a contentious issue, particularly as the Ferrari team adopted a holier-than-thou attitude to the whole affair, throwing up their hands in mock horror and suggesting that they'd never known they were being 'ganged up on' by both the McLaren and Williams teams. This was a convenient means of deflecting attention from the fact that, not only had Schumacher attempted to bundle Villeneuve off the road, but that the Italian team has been listening in to other teams' pit-to-car radio conversations.

McLaren and Williams were further embarrassed by being forced to appear in front of an FIA World Council meeting to explain suggestions that there had been collusion between them during the European Grand Prix. The charges were dismissed almost before the hearing started. Quite rightly, too.

Prior to the hearing, Dennis robustly denied that his team had anything to feel ashamed of. 'The evidence of the race completely supports the fact that neither McLaren was ever in the way,' he insisted. 'The timing of these allegations could be seen by some as a smoke-screen deflecting from the main issue facing Schumacher.

'At Jerez I reiterated to Frank Williams that there was no way our cars would get involved in the Championship battle – and that if we were in the way, we would get out of the way, even to the detriment of our own team's effort.'

Yet the question of Coulthard being asked to allow Hakkinen through still lingered. 'At McLaren the rule is that there are no team instructions given to a driver during the period in which he can mathematically win the World Championship,' Dennis reiterated very specifically.

'But after that point has been reached, I think the team can justifiably expect that the drivers perform for the team before themselves. [At Jerez], in our efforts not to interfere with the outcome of the World Championship, we reversed the first pit stop sequence previously agreed for Mika and David. Mika stopped first and that advantaged David, and therefore I decided, when Villeneuve was clearly not going to resist any overtaking manoeuvre, to instruct David to reverse the order again.'

Yet Dennis knew what Coulthard was thinking. Shorn of his self-respect, vulnerable and angry, the Scot wandered the paddock, a solitary, beleaguered soul in the immediate aftermath of the race. How did Ron square the apparent conflict on this deeply emotive issue?

'I don't have to justify this to anybody, and you might say that it was a hollow win for Mika,' he conceded. 'But for him not to have won a race in his career, not through the lack of his own efforts, would not have been right. So I felt completely justified in taking off his shoulders for 1998 the psychological pressure of not having won a race.

'There were lots of races he should have won, but didn't. You might argue that this was a race he shouldn't have won, but he did. But I only reversed a situation that the team had already created, and the disappointment that was clearly on David's face – and I'm being kind to myself saying "disappointment" – was due to the fact that there had been no dialogue before the race, and he couldn't understand why we were apparently being unfair to him.

'The language over the radio between our team manager Dave Ryan and David was extremely colourful. Perhaps I have even shaken David's faith in my or the team's even-handedness, but when I reflect on my years with McLaren, I feel comfortable that we have always acted with extreme fairness and balance to both drivers. I feel that, as time passes, David will understand that.

'He is not angry, not aggressive, but I clearly understand that there is now that lingering doubt in his mind that can only be addressed with the passing of time.'

Again, McLaren had finished the Constructors' Championship in fourth place, only four points behind Benetton. But in 1997 the team had been regular front-runners, carefully crafting a platform from which they intended to aim at the 1998 World Championship title.

Over the winter it was a question of working flat-out yet again at the McLaren headquarters. Yet the new MP4/13 – no superstition allowed here – was to be the very last of the new F1 generation to break cover, barely a month before the season was due to start in Melbourne.

The new season brought with it dramatic new technical regulations with a narrower track, down from 2,000mm in 1997 to 1,800mm. At the same time the minimum chassis width at the front axle centre line was increased to 350cm to give the monocoque added torsional stiffness and strength. Less grip would be afforded by tyres that now had to have three grooves at the front, four at the rear. The chassis impact test requirements were also dramatically increased, and while other teams struggled in this respect, it was a matter of great professional pride to McLaren that the new MP4/13 passed all of them with flying colours at the first attempt.

McLaren also switched to Bridgestone rubber from Goodyears for the start of the 1998 season. It was to prove a shrewd move. But it was to throw yet another variable into the design equation on which Adrian Newey, chief designer Neil Oatley, aerodynamicist Henri Durand and the whole McLaren design team had been working on since the summer of 1997.

'The new car has had a fairly compressed design cycle,' admitted McLaren's new Technical Director, 'and that, in turn, has knocked on to the manufacturing process. Everything has been done in a shorter space of time than we would have liked, but everybody has worked very hard and we will be there with four cars in Australia.

'I think that, especially when there has been a big regulation change like this, you are on a fairly steep learning curve. You have to remember that people like Benetton, Ferrari and Williams all started that learning curve in February/March last year, but we started a hell of a lot later than that. So we had a very steep ramp to climb.'

Nevertheless, the first signs were promising. Hakkinen and Coulthard set the pace in the car's first testing outing at Barcelona, and increasingly the F1 pundits were tipping McLaren for its first World Championship title since 1991.

Ron Dennis, as always, was playing things down. 'The worst thing we can do is climb willingly on to some kind of hypothetical pedestal,' he reflected. 'Even if you deserve to be there, inevitably you will be torn down. We are intent on keeping our feet on the ground.'

Yet the TAG McLaren Group was also continuing to expand in other areas. Almost unnoticed, Ron Dennis relinquished the role of Managing Director of McLaren International to his right-hand man Martin Whitmarsh, although he would continue as MD of the TAG McLaren group as a whole.

Whitmarsh, a focused, professional and highly motivated former British Aerospace executive, had joined McLaren in 1989 to be groomed for just such a high-profile position. In 1987 Dennis had admitted in an interview that he reckoned he'd got 'ten good years left'. Did that mean he was slowing down? Preparing for retirement?

Not at all, he assured his workforce. But he did want to be in a position where he could take a wider view on some issues and, if need be, draw back from the day-to-day grind.

In addition, there were other business aspects on which to concentrate. The TAG McLaren Group was taking a 99 year lease on Farnborough airfield with the intention of establishing it as the biggest, most comprehensive private jet centre in Europe. In addition, the group was purchasing Aeroleasing, the Geneva-based jet charter firm, and a similar company in the USA. There was also the small matter of a brand new, bespoke group headquarters, the construction of which was to begin in 1998, to come on line just over two years later.

So you can see that there is precious little chance of Ron Dennis and his colleagues easing their business pace, which regularly amounts to a 12-hour day. And often much more.

On one occasion I returned to my office to pick up a message on the answerphone. It was 6.30pm one weekday and Ron's voice came over the tape. 'How many times do I have to tell you, Alan?' he said. 'You will never be a great success in life, or make worthwhile sums of money, as long as you leave your office this early in the evening. I've told you about this before, so shape up; get with the programme.'

In many ways that tells you everything you need to know about Ron Dennis's commitment and single-mindedness, and the ethos he has tried to pass on to all those who work within his organisation.

One final point. The McLaren International workforce has remained remarkably stable over the past ten years or so. From time to time people grumble, as workers always do. But the low turnover amongst those on the factory floor probably tells you more about McLaren's qualities than all the glossy brochures and PR tours could ever do.

The bottom line, of course, is that grand prix racing is not primarily a business about technology, nor competition, nor, indeed, finance. It is a business founded and centred around people, and having the right people in the right places at the right time.

McLaren International knows that as well as anybody else in Formula 1 today. And probably a lot better than most.

11

Back onto
the high wire

PRE-SEASON TESTING can be a nerve-wracking affair for any Grand Prix racing team. The design calculations have been completed and the cars duly built. But how will they stack up against the opposition? Will a key rival have gained a crucial performance edge in an unexpected area? And how much store can really be put by their testing times?

From the first time the McLaren-Mercedes MP4/13 rolled out onto the circuit, the signs were promising. Lap times appeared suitably competitive – particularly as McLaren traditionally tested their cars carrying a reasonable amount of fuel. Gratifyingly, both Mika Hakkinen and David Coulthard reported that the performance of the new Bridgestone tyres was dependably consistent, with none of the sudden deterioration of grip which several rival Goodyear users had complained about.

There was, of course, one great unanswered question. How good would the new Ferrari F300 turn out to be in the hands of Michael Schumacher? While McLaren had been able to gauge the comparative strength of several rival teams during tests at Barcelona, Ferrari Sporting Director Jean Todt had shrewdly kept his team's new car away from any such pre-season head-to-head scrutiny.

The famous Italian team had effectively pledged itself to win the 1998 World Championship come what may, and was therefore keeping its powder dry for its first confrontation with the opposition at the opening race of the season in Melbourne. With that in mind, Ferrari concentrated on testing at its own private circuits, Fiorano and Mugello, far from the attention of prying eyes.

Elsewhere on the horizon, Williams could obviously never be discounted as a potential threat, while Benetton, now under the vigorous stewardship of David Richards, needed to be kept in mind, not least because they had also made the switch from Goodyear to Bridgestone tyres over the winter. Richards, whose Banbury-based Prodrive company had fielded the World Rally Championship winning Subarus, was certainly keen to reproduce this mastery on the F1 scene.

Yet McLaren was hopeful, even confident. All the indications pointed towards the MP4/13s having an early season performance advantage and, with characteristic organisation, the team's management produced a contingency plan to ensure that any such edge would not be squandered.

Basically, they went to Melbourne with a strategy in place to ensure that Hakkinen and Coulthard did not race each other needlessly. The new McLaren-Mercedes might have the pace, but the first race of a season inevitably posed all manner of potential reliability problems. Racing each other into retirement would not be a sensible option for the drivers.

Consequently, Ron Dennis asked them to race for the team in the first two grands prix, after which the gloves would come off and they would be free to battle as they pleased. You might be forgiven for thinking that this was nothing more than sensible team orders, but McLaren can hardly have imagined the furore which the implementation of such a prudent strategy would provoke once the race was over.

Come practice and qualifying at Melbourne's Albert Park circuit, Hakkinen and Coulthard proved to be the class act of the field. With an unruffled assurance, Mika lapped in 1m 30.010s to take pole position from Coulthard by the scant margin of 0.043s, leaving Michael Schumacher's Ferrari trailing in third place by another seven-tenths of a second.

It was the second pole position of Hakkinen's career, achieved despite having to abort a couple of laps due to heavy traffic. Coulthard also felt he'd not taken best advantage of his situation. 'On two corners round the back of the circuit in particular, I had a touch too much understeer,' he confessed, 'and on the last two runs I couldn't quite get clean runs together.'

Prior to the race, David agreed that whoever led through the first corner would be permitted to run unchallenged at the head of the field. The Scot thought the money was already in the bank, confident that his own splendid record of fast starts would see him win this particular contest. In fact he fluffed his getaway and Hakkinen got to the first corner comfortably ahead. From then on, it looked like no contest.

Hakkinen led through the first refuelling stop, but his hopes seemed to be dashed after a mix-up in radio communication saw him waved through the pits when he came in the end of lap 36. He stopped on schedule four laps later, resuming 33.5s behind Coulthard. After Coulthard's second stop, Hakkinen was only 13.3s adrift and closed dramatically in the closing stages.

For a few tantalising laps it looked as though the two McLarens might make a race of it all the way to the flag, raising the uncomfortable spectre of the Senna/Prost collision in the 1989 Japanese Grand Prix. However, after a lengthy conversation over the pit-to-car radio link, Coulthard understood that Hakkinen's first visit to the pit lane had been a mistake. With that in mind, he eased his pace and allowed his team-mate to overtake in front of the pits with only two laps to go.

'What David did today was remarkable,' said Hakkinen after the race. 'I have been in F1 for many years and seen a great deal. What he did today was really gentlemanly, unreal and fantastic.'

The cynics had a field day and, on the morning after the race, the Melbourne daily newspapers went in to bat heavily on the side of those punters who'd bet their hard-earned dollars on Coulthard emerging victorious. Particularly annoyed was Australian GP promoter Ron Walker who issued a lofty statement. This read: 'It is not my place to discuss any punitive action, it is not my area of responsibility, but we have to seek clarification on this matter.

'It is not the right of team owners to decide who is going to win. I don't think you have heard the end yet. I think that Max Mosley will advise on this the moment he lands in London.'

Walker's fax elicited a cautious response from the sport's governing body which rightly pointed out that team orders were as old as the sport itself and it saw no immediate need to censure McLaren. However, it did fire a very firm warning shot on the general subject of team orders.

It announced that the stewards at all future grands prix will be informed that 'any acts prejudicial to the interests of any competition' should be penalised severely under the terms of the international sporting code.

'All we have done is draw attention to provisions which have been in the rules for decades,' said Mosley, 'but everybody should remember that this is a drivers' contest, not just a team championship.'

Be that as it may, the McLaren team was inundated with messages of support during the days which followed their 1–2 triumph at Melbourne. Yet it was the comments of his old boss Sir Jack Brabham, speaking on a local television station in Australia, which really touched Ron Dennis. In his day, before cynicism ruled, said Brabham, Coulthard would have been regarded beyond question as a gentleman.

As far as McLaren's rivals were concerned, for Goodyear, Melbourne was an uncomfortable experience, although not as bad as it looked at first glance. If McLaren was taken out of the equation, Giancarlo Fisichella's Benetton B198 was the next fastest Bridgestone runner, seventh on the grid some 1.7s away from Hakkinen's pole time.

By the end of the race, Heinz-Harald Frentzen survived to take third place in his Goodyear-shod Williams ahead of Eddie Irvine's Ferrari after Michael Schumacher's Italian machine had been sidelined by a blown engine early in the chase. World Champion Jacques Villeneuve limped home fifth, his Williams hobbled by dramatically high oil temperature caused by leaves blocking his radiator intakes, which also affected his gearchange mechanism, while Johnny Herbert completed the top six after a vigorous run in his Sauber-Ferrari.

There were also techno-political problems which threatened to embroil the McLaren-Mercedes enclave. Despite the fact that FIA technical delegate Charlie Whiting had given the green light to the team's secondary braking system, which had been used on the Mercedes-engined cars since the middle of last season, suddenly the Ferrari camp seemed to be spearheading an orchestrated programme of complaints about this particular technical tweak.

The system, which stabilises the car in corners by means of reducing braking load on the outer rear wheel, was controlled purely by the driver. Its use could also lessen high speed understeer, pulling the nose of the car into the corner. Similar devices had also been developed by Williams and Jordan, but the newly resurgent McLaren-Mercedes team was the main target of these dissenters who wanted the system banned.

Initially Ferrari Technical Director Ross Brawn sent a memo to Whiting – copied to all the other teams – outlining his objection. It was based on the premise that the McLaren secondary braking system was effectively an additional steering aid.

This line of argument was initially rejected. Undaunted, Ferrari, aided by Arrows, encouraged several other teams to sign a document objecting to the system on the basis that the rules require one pedal to control at least two brake circuits on an F1 car. That was also rejected.

The FIA's representative indicated that he was satisfied that the system was in conformity with the rules. However, he added that this was his own personal view and that any competing team was free to challenge his interpretation by lodging an official protest. None did so. Not on this occasion.

The net result of all this controversy was to send Mika Hakkinen and David Coulthard into the Brazilian Grand Prix at Sao Paulo's Interlagos circuit firmly on their guard. Yet the off-track events during practice and qualifying at least served to emphasise that the performance advantage of the MP4/13 could not be attributed to one single technical element.

On this occasion, F1's most impressive double act at least spared its rivals any excessive display of team orders and rivals Michael Schumacher and Alexander Wurz (Benetton B198) were able to finish on the same lap as the silver machines.

Hakkinen accelerated straight into the lead from pole position with Coulthard tucking in behind as the pack braked for the first corner. Right behind them Heinz-Harald Frentzen's Williams slotted into an immediate third place with Eddie Irvine getting ahead of his Ferrari team leader Michael Schumacher as the pack jostled into the first corner.

The race, as such, ended with the first lap. Hakkinen and Coulthard were already a couple of seconds clear of Frentzen's Williams and it took until lap nine before Schumacher forced his way ahead into fourth place.

'I don't think there was ever any chance of my catching Mika after he got ahead at the start,' said Coulthard. 'I would like to have been first rather than second, but I made a slow start on the uphill gradient away from the line and that was that. Unless he had a problem I wasn't going to get close to him, particularly as I had traction problems out of the last couple of corners of the lap.'

The McLarens both harnessed a one stop strategy to consolidate their advantage and finished the race almost a minute clear of Schumacher's Ferrari. 'That was absolutely the best we could hope for,' said Michael, 'but Ferrari has some more developments in the pipeline for the Argentine Grand Prix in two weeks time when I hope to give these guys a bit of a chase, otherwise they will both fall asleep.'

However, the most outstanding single driving effort of the race came when Wurz, driving only his fifth grand prix in the Benetton, audaciously outbraked Frentzen into the tight left-hander after the pits. He may have benefitted from Bridgestone tyres, but his whole performance was a breath of fresh air and he fully deserved fourth place ahead of Frentzen and Fisichella.

The McLaren team's domination of this second round of the World Championship came as the best antidote imaginable to a wearying weekend of controversy. This began when, as expected, on the Thursday before the race Ferrari orchestrated an official protest against the secondary braking system.

In deference to the possible outcome of this protest, McLaren disengaged the system from the start of the first practice session, as did Jordan and Williams who had similar systems on their cars which had been the subject of parallel protests.

The three teams concerned did not hear the outcome of the stewards' deliberations until the start of Saturday morning's free practice session when the protests were upheld. It was a decision which flew in the face of opinions offered by the FIA's Charlie Whiting who had consistently advised McLaren while the team was developing and building the new car that he believed the system to be legal.

What was even more frustrating was the amount of time and effort the whole McLaren team went to in order to put a well reasoned and detailed defence of the system, only for the stewards – Nazir Hoosein, Radovan Novak and Elcio de Sao Thiago – to brush it aside and request a summary of its features on a single A4 sheet.

The official view was that the primary purpose of the secondary braking system was steering rather than braking, so it was banned and the teams concerned decided to let the matter rest rather than prolonging the controversy by lodging an appeal. However McLaren expressed their astonishment in a well moderated bulletin which read: 'The West McLaren Mercedes team is extremely surprised by the decision of the stewards of the 1998 Brazilian Grand Prix to uphold the protest regarding its braking system.

'The team has worked closely with the FIA to establish the legality of this system, providing full and precise details over the last six months. Correspondence received from the FIA dated 5th November 1997, 21st November 1997, 19th January 1998, 5th March 1998 and 7th March 1998 all supported the legality of the McLaren braking system.

'Whilst the team seriously questions the process by which the stewards' decision was taken, it has decided not to appeal against their decision and create further controversy which might lead to the results of the Brazilian Grand Prix being deemed provisional, pending the outcome of an appeal.

'The stewards' decision is, however, contrary to all the views previously expressed by the FIA. It is accepted however that the stewards of the Brazilian Grand Prix have reached an opinion which will mean that the McLaren braking system should not be used during this event.

'The team had informed the stewards on Thursday that it would, in order to minimise further controversy, disable the system fitted to its cars. In the light of this decision the system has not, and will not, be employed at any time throughout the weekend.

'The West McLaren Mercedes team strongly believes that the FIA technical department should be the ultimate determining technical authority in respect of the interpretation of the F1 technical regulations. The team will therefore seek to discuss this matter with the FIA in order to clarify this decision and ultimately determine whether the McLaren braking system may be used in future events of the 1998 Formula 1 World Championship.

'Given the controversy which has been generated around this issue both prior to and during this event, the West McLaren Mercedes team does not wish to make any further press statement on this issue.'

It was a firm response, yet one which many observers felt was totally reasonable given the unusual circumstances surrounding the episode. For their part, the stewards did not take such an indulgent attitude. They felt that McLaren clearly did not accept the authority of the international rules and should consequently be reported to the sport's governing body.

Yet at the end of the day, what McLaren had proved was that the business of efficient F1 car design did not centre on any individual aspect of the technical package, but a shrewd blend of competitive features. Robbing the McLarens of their secondary braking system did nothing to blunt their competitive edge. The rest of the field would simply have to try harder.

Come the Argentine Grand Prix at Buenos Aires, the opposition did just that. Sure enough, Coulthard's title hopes were boosted by the sixth pole position of his career, his first at the wheel of a McLaren-Mercedes. The Scot opened his account at the Autodromo Oscar A. Galvez with a flawless performance during Friday's free practice session to end up half a second ahead of Schumacher's Ferrari with Hakkinen third, despite a wayward slide in the closing stages of the session.

Schumacher and Hakkinen eventually qualified second and third fastest, Mika reporting that none of his runs worked out as he had planned: 'I had some problems coming out of the corners and made a couple of driving mistakes on my second and third sets. It started well, but I lost the back end in a couple of corners. It was a bit of a disaster, but I'm very happy for David.'

Even so, it was Schumacher who had initially set the pace, raising the prospect of some serious opposition for the McLaren-Mercedes team in the longer term, although it soon became clear that the opposition had some way to go before Coulthard and Hakkinen were decisively toppled from their current domination.

After a heavy rain shower during the Friday morning mid-session break, Schumacher treated the spectators to a dazzling display of throttle control as he lapped the tight little circuit in a series of spectacular opposite lock slides, yet this was only an amusing side show to the main business of the day.

The real question was whether or not the latest wider front Goodyear tyres, making their race debut at this event, could transform the fortunes of teams such as Ferrari, Williams and Jordan in a straight fight against the Bridgestone-shod McLarens on a dry track surface.

The McLaren drivers treated the first practice session with considerable restraint, reasoning that there was no purpose to be served by cleaning up the dusty track surface with a succession of unnecessary laps. But they were no less effective for that.

In the paddock there was more frenzied speculation, this time based round rumours that Ferrari would protest the McLaren team's alleged use of a 'regenerative power system'. But it fell flat even before the cars took to the circuit.

There had been whispers that McLaren had developed a means of harnessing energy produced under hard braking and using it to generate electrical power which would take over the operation of the engine driven fuel and water pumps for brief spells. If used, such a system had the potential to unlock around an additional 70bhp from the Mercedes engine for short spurts during a race or qualifying.

Unfortunately for those detractors who seemed hell-bent on unmasking some magic formula for the McLarens' speed, Ron Dennis confirmed that such a system had indeed been developed – but never run in a car. 'In any case, within the last month the FIA has indicated that such systems are not legal,' he said.

Schumacher was in an extremely confident mood before the start, although he made only a moderate getaway to trail Coulthard and Hakkinen into the first corner. Midway round the second lap Schumacher darted ahead of Hakkinen to close in quickly on Coulthard's leading McLaren. The Finn, thinking of the long game, let him through.

David was already hampered by a slightly 'lazy' downchange mechanism on his McLaren-Mercedes which meant there was a small delay each time he pulled for a gear. Mid-way round lap four he momentarily ran wide under braking, allowing Michael to close in dramatically.

Next time round, David repeated the performance, running slightly wide on the entrance to the tight right-hander at the end of the long back straight. In a trice Schumacher – showing the aggression that had blackened his reputation in Jerez last year – had his right-hand wheels up the inside kerb as he sliced through. But the Ferrari's left front wheel caught the McLaren's right rear, launching Coulthard into the air from whence he spun to a halt, engine thankfully still running.

The Scot rejoined in sixth place, later admitting that he felt pretty angry about the whole episode 'but these things happen.' Then he added: 'In this instance it wasn't for me to give anything, because I was in front. He damaged my car just in front of the rear wheel. As I see it, he accelerated and understeered into me.'

Schumacher's version was understandably different. 'I went inside, but David seemed to close the door and there was nowhere to go,' he insisted. 'I didn't feel I had to lift off because I felt I had the momentum.'

Thereafter the race settled down into a two-way contest between Hakkinen and Schumacher, the Finn running a one-stop schedule to the Ferrari driver's two. The key moment would be whether or not Mika could get ahead of Michael when the Ferrari went into the pits for the second time. He failed by 2.7s, although a few laps earlier he had lost over 4s being baulked by the dawdling Heinz-Harald Frentzen.

Hakkinen also lost seven seconds on lap 68, with only four to go, when a rain shower brushed the circuit, frustrating his efforts to capitalise on Schumacher's error two laps earlier when the Ferrari ace slid onto the gravel trap just prior to the start/finish line.

Even allowing for the fact that the McLarens' Bridgestone tyre compound was a little too hard for the conditions, the outcome of the race was certainly a close run thing.

In third place, Eddie Irvine did a good job in the second Ferrari, battling hard with the Benetton of Alexander Wurz in the closing stages of the race. Although Wurz briefly got ahead, he promptly spun which allowed Irvine to get back ahead once again.

Fifth place fell to Jean Alesi's Sauber-Ferrari, the Frenchman managing to continue at unabated speed despite one of his car's secondary side-mounted wings being accidentally ripped off during a refuelling stop. He crossed the line just over one second ahead of the frustrated Coulthard who at least gained a single point for his efforts.

'I think this circuit tends to suit my style a little more than Mika's,' he said, 'but I think the advantage is likely to swing back and forth between us over the next few races. Trouble is, Mika found more circuits which seemed to favour his style than I did through last year!'

Once the race was over, Michael Schumacher visited the McLaren team garage where he was welcomed with a bear hug by Norbert Haug. Behind closed doors he had a brief talk with Coulthard about their incident, after which they agreed to differ. For David, it was an annoying setback. Having played second fiddle to Hakkinen in the first two races of the season, he had been looking to the Argentine GP as his personal moment. Instead, he came away with only sixth place.

That put him third in the Drivers' Championship with half Hakkinen's total of 26 points. He could only take comfort from Adrian Newey's view that Buenos Aires was always going to be a difficult track for the McLaren-Mercedes and look forward to the San Marino Grand Prix at Imola with a sense of gently mounting anxiety.

A fortnight later Coulthard brilliantly revived his World Championship prospects by winning the San Marino GP. This proved a doubly satisfying victory, for not only did he start from pole and lead all the way – despite, latterly, having engine trouble – he also beat the Ferraris of Schumacher and Eddie Irvine conclusively into second and third places.

From the touchlines, Coulthard seemed to be taking it easy, slowing his pace in the closing stages of the race to conserve his McLaren MP4/13, even though the German was closing dramatically in his wake. The reality was that Coulthard's car was suffering from a seriously overheating gearbox, the symptoms of the problem which had already eliminated his team-mate from second place with a broken transmission only 17 laps into the 62-lap race.

The problem caused an anxious Ron Dennis periodically to stroll from his position on the pit wall to the back of the garage to check the electronic telemetry system. Coulthard was simply told to ease up and change gear as carefully as possible during the second half of the race.

'I wanted to run at a pace that wasn't too hard on the brakes or the engine, so I was just trying to maintain the gap to Michael,' he explained, unaware of the depth of his own car's technical problem.

'I was perfectly comfortable to let that gap be reduced, because I knew that I could have gone a little faster if necessary. I knew Mika had stopped, but I didn't ask why because I didn't want to be worrying about it for the rest of the race.'

During the Saturday's hour-long qualifying session, Coulthard had worked hard to secure the seventh pole position of his career. Hakkinen qualified alongside him to clinch the third all-McLaren front row so far this season.

Yet neither driver under-estimated the challenge threatened by Michael Schumacher's Ferrari F300 – the German driver, in jaunty mood throughout the weekend, was straining every sinew to make the best possible use of a more powerful V10 engine and a new aerodynamic package. He qualified third, but Hakkinen blocked him out on the run to the first corner, holding him back in third place as the two McLarens consolidated an initial advantage at the head of the field.

After Hakkinen's retirement, Coulthard continued to retain his lead over Schumacher through his two scheduled refuelling stops, the Ferrari fleetingly closing to within two seconds of the McLaren before making its own second visit to the pits. In the end, Coulthard allowed his advantage to dwindle over the final few laps, taking the chequered flag 4.5sec ahead of his arch rival. At a stroke, it seemed as though we now had a three-way battle for the world title. Hakkinen, 26 points; Coulthard, 23 points; Schumacher 20 points. In the Constructors' table it was McLaren-Mercedes, 49 points, Ferrari, 31 points.

Nobody else was within realistic sight. But for how long could the Woking team retain that advantage?

Appendix 1

Biographical details of McLaren World Championship drivers

1974
Emerson Fittipaldi (Brazil)
Born 12 December 1946, Sao
  Paulo.
144 grands prix, 14 wins, 6 pole
  positions, 6 fastest race laps.

1976
James Hunt (Great Britain)
Born 29 August 1947, South
  London; died 15th June 1993,
  Wimbledon.
92 grands prix, 10 wins, 14 pole
  positions, 8 fastest race laps.

1984
Niki Lauda (Austria)
Born 22 February 1949, Vienna.
171 grands prix, 25 wins, 24 pole
  positions, 25 fastest race laps.

1985, '86 and '89
Alain Prost (France)
Born 24 February 1955, St
  Chamond.
199 grands prix, 51 wins, 33 pole
  positions, 41 fastest race laps.

1988, '90 and '91
Ayrton Senna (Brazil)
Born 21 March 1960, Sao Paulo;
  died 1 May 1994, Bologna.
161 grands prix, 41 wins, 65 pole
  positions, 19 fastest race laps.

Appendix 2

McLaren Drivers' Championship placings since 1966

Year	Placing	Driver	Year	Placing	Driver
1966	14th	Bruce McLaren	**1982**	2nd=	John Watson
1967	14th	Bruce McLaren		5th	Niki Lauda
1968	3rd	Denny Hulme	**1983**	6th	John Watson
	5th	Bruce McLaren		10th	Niki Lauda
1969	3rd	Bruce McLaren	**1984**	1st	Niki Lauda
	6th	Denny Hulme		2nd	Alain Prost
1970	4th	Denny Hulme	**1985**	1st	Alain Prost
	14th	Bruce McLaren		10th	Niki Lauda
1971	9th=	Denny Hulme	**1986**	1st	Alain Prost
	9th=	Peter Gethin		6th	Keke Rosberg
		(drove for McLaren,	**1987**	4th	Alain Prost
		but scored points		6th	Stefan Johansson
		only after mid-season	**1988**	1st	Ayrton Senna
		switch to BRM)		2nd	Alain Prost
1972	3rd	Denny Hulme	**1989**	1st	Alain Prost
	5th	Peter Revson		2nd	Ayrton Senna
	12th	Brian Redman	**1990**	1st	Ayrton Senna
1973	5th	Peter Revson		2nd	Alain Prost
	6th	Denny Hulme	**1991**	1st	Ayrton Senna
1974	1st	Emerson Fittipaldi		4th	Gerhard Berger
	7th	Denny Hulme	**1992**	4th	Ayrton Senna
1975	2nd	Emerson Fittipaldi		5th	Gerhard Berger
	7th	Jochen Mass	**1993**	2nd	Ayrton Senna
1976	1st	James Hunt		11th	Michael Andretti
	9th=	Jochen Mass	**1994**	4th	Mika Hakkinen
1977	5th	James Hunt		7th	Martin Brundle
	6th	Jochen Mass	**1995**	7th	Mika Hakkinen
1978	13th=	James Hunt		10th	Mark Blundell
	13th=	Patrick Tambay		NC	Nigel Mansell
1979	9th	John Watson		NC	Jan Magnussen
	NC	Patrick Tambay	**1996**	5th	Mika Hakkinen
1980	10th=	John Watson		7th	David Coulthard
	15th	Alain Prost	**1997**	3rd=	David Coulthard
1981	6th	John Watson		4th=	Mika Hakkinen
	18th	Andrea de Cesaris			

Appendix 3

McLaren Constructors' Championship placings since 1966

Year	Placing		Year	Placing
1966	7th=		**1982**	2nd
1967	8th		**1983**	5th
1968	2nd		**1984**	1st
1969	4th		**1985**	1st
1970	4th=		**1986**	2nd
1971	6th		**1987**	2nd
1972	3rd		**1988**	1st
1973	3rd		**1989**	1st
1974	1st		**1990**	1st
1975	3rd		**1991**	1st
1976	2nd		**1992**	2nd
1977	3rd		**1993**	2nd
1978	8th		**1994**	4th
1979	7th		**1995**	4th
1980	7th=		**1996**	4th
1981	6th		**1997**	4th

Appendix 4

McLaren Formula 1 World Championship grand prix victories

Race/venue	Driver	Car type-engine
1968		
Belgian/Spa-Francorchamps	Bruce McLaren	M7A-Ford DFV
Italian/Monza	Denny Hulme	M7A-Ford DFV
Canadian/Mont Tremblant	Denny Hulme	M7A-Ford DFV
1969		
Mexican/Mexico City	Denny Hulme	M7A-Ford DFV
1972		
South African/Kyalami	Denny Hulme	M19A-Ford DFV
1973		
Swedish/Anderstorp	Denny Hulme	M23-Ford DFV
British/Silverstone	Peter Revson	M23-Ford DFV
Canadian/Mosport Park	Peter Revson	M23-Ford DFV
1974		
Argentine/Buenos Aires	Denny Hulme	M23-Ford DFV
Brazilian/Interlagos	Emerson Fittipaldi	M23-Ford DFV
Belgian/Nivelles-Baulers	Emerson Fittipaldi	M23-Ford DFV
Canadian/Mosport Park	Emerson Fittipaldi	M23-Ford DFV
1975		
Argentine/Buenos Aires	Emerson Fittipaldi	M23-Ford DFV
Spanish/Montjuich Park	Jochen Mass	M23-Ford DFV
British/Silverstone	Emerson Fittipaldi	M23-Ford DFV
1976		
Spanish/Jarama	James Hunt	M23-Ford DFV
French/Paul Ricard	James Hunt	M23-Ford DFV
German/Nurburgring	James Hunt	M23-Ford DFV
Dutch/Zandvoort	James Hunt	M23-Ford DFV
Canadian/Mosport Park	James Hunt	M23-Ford DFV
USA East/Watkins Glen	James Hunt	M23-Ford DFV

1977

British/Silverstone	James Hunt	M26-Ford DFV
USA East/Watkins Glen	James Hunt	M26-Ford DFV
Japanese/Fuji	James Hunt	M26-Ford DFV

1981

British/Silverstone	John Watson	MP4-Ford DFV

1982

USA West/Long Beach	Niki Lauda	MP4/1B-Ford DFV
Belgian/Zolder	John Watson	MP4/1B-Ford DFV
USA/Detroit	John Watson	MP4/1B-Ford DFV
British/Brands Hatch	Niki Lauda	MP4/1B-Ford DFV

1983

USA West/Long Beach	John Watson	MP4/1C-Ford DFV

1984

Brazilian/Rio de Janeiro	Alain Prost	MP4/2-TAG turbo
South African/Kyalami	Niki Lauda	MP4/2-TAG turbo
San Marino/Imola	Alain Prost	MP4/2-TAG turbo
French/Dijon-Prenois	Niki Lauda	MP4/2-TAG turbo
Monaco/Monte Carlo	Alain Prost	MP4/2-TAG turbo
British/Brands Hatch	Niki Lauda	MP4/2-TAG turbo
German/Hockenheim	Alain Prost	MP4/2-TAG turbo
Austrian/Osterreichring	Niki Lauda	MP4/2-TAG turbo
Dutch/Zandvoort	Alain Prost	MP4/2-TAG turbo
Italian/Monza	Niki Lauda	MP4/2-TAG turbo
European/Nurburgring	Alain Prost	MP4/2-TAG turbo
Portuguese/Estoril	Alain Prost	MP4/2-TAG turbo

1985

Brazilian/Rio de Janeiro	Alain Prost	MP4/2B-TAG turbo
Monaco/Monte Carlo	Alain Prost	MP4/2B-TAG turbo
British/Silverstone	Alain Prost	MP4/2B-TAG turbo
Austrian/Osterreichring	Alain Prost	MP4/2B-TAG turbo
Dutch/Zandvoort	Niki Lauda	MP4/2B-TAG turbo
Italian/Monza	Alain Prost	MP4/2B-TAG turbo

1986

San Marino/Imola	Alain Prost	MP4/2C-TAG turbo
Monaco/Monte Carlo	Alain Prost	MP4/2C-TAG turbo
Austrian/Osterreichring	Alain Prost	MP4/2C-TAG turbo
Australian/Adelaide	Alain Prost	MP4/2C-TAG turbo

1987

Brazil/Rio de Janeiro	Alain Prost	MP4/3-TAG turbo
Belgian/Spa-Francorchamps	Alain Prost	MP4/3-TAG turbo
Portuguese/Estoril	Alain Prost	MP4/3-TAG turbo

1988

Brazil/Rio de Janeiro	Alain Prost	MP4/4-Honda turbo
San Marino/Imola	Ayrton Senna	MP4/4-Honda turbo
Monaco/Monte Carlo	Alain Prost	MP4/4-Honda turbo
Mexican/Mexico City	Alain Prost	MP4/4-Honda turbo
Canadian/Montreal	Ayrton Senna	MP4/4-Honda turbo
USA/Detroit	Ayrton Senna	MP4/4-Honda turbo
French/Paul Ricard	Alain Prost	MP4/4-Honda turbo
British/Silverstone	Ayrton Senna	MP4/4-Honda turbo
German/Hockenheim	Ayrton Senna	MP4/4-Honda turbo
Hungarian/Budapest	Ayrton Senna	MP4/4-Honda turbo
Belgian/Spa-Francorchamps	Ayrton Senna	MP4/4-Honda turbo
Portuguese/Estoril	Alain Prost	MP4/4-Honda turbo
Spanish/Jerez	Alain Prost	MP4/4-Honda turbo
Japanese/Suzuka	Ayrton Senna	MP4/4-Honda turbo
Australian/Adelaide	Alain Prost	MP4/4-Honda turbo

1989

San Marino/Imola	Ayrton Senna	MP4/5-Honda
Monaco/Monte Carlo	Ayrton Senna	MP4/5-Honda
Mexican/Mexico City	Ayrton Senna	MP4/5-Honda
USA/Phoenix	Alain Prost	MP4/5-Honda
French/Paul Ricard	Alain Prost	MP4/5-Honda
British/Silverstone	Alain Prost	MP4/5-Honda
German/Hockenheim	Ayrton Senna	MP4/5-Honda
Belgian/Spa-Francorchamps	Ayrton Senna	MP4/5-Honda
Italian/Monza	Alain Prost	MP4/5-Honda
Spanish/Jerez	Ayrton Senna	MP4/5-Honda

1990

USA/Phoenix	Ayrton Senna	MP4/5B-Honda
Monaco/Monte Carlo	Ayrton Senna	MP4/5B-Honda
Canadian/Montreal	Ayrton Senna	MP4/5B-Honda
German/Hockenheim	Ayrton Senna	MP4/5B-Honda
Belgian/Spa-Francorchamps	Ayrton Senna	MP4/5B-Honda
Italian/Monza	Ayrton Senna	MP4.5B-Honda

1991

USA/Phoenix	Ayrton Senna	MP4/6-Honda
Brazilian/Interlagos	Ayrton Senna	MP4/6-Honda
San Marino/Imola	Ayrton Senna	MP4/6-Honda
Monaco/Monte Carlo	Ayrton Senna	MP4/6-Honda
Hungarian/Hungaroring	Ayrton Senna	MP4/6-Honda
Belgian/Spa-Francorchamps	Ayrton Senna	MP4/6-Honda
Japanese/Suzuka	Gerhard Berger	MP4/6-Honda
Australian/Adelaide	Ayrton Senna	MP4/6-Honda

1992

Monaco/Monte Carlo	Ayrton Senna	MP4/7A-Honda
Canada/Montreal	Gerhard Berger	MP4/7A-Honda

Hungarian/Hungaroring	Ayrton Senna	MP4/7A-Honda
Italian/Monza	Ayrton Senna	MP4/7A-Honda
Australian/Adelaide	Gerhard Berger	MP4/7A-Honda

1993

Brazilian/Interlagos	Ayrton Senna	MP4/8-Ford HB
European/Donington Park	Ayrton Senna	MP4/8-Ford HB
Monaco/Monte Carlo	Ayrton Senna	MP4/8-Ford HB
Japanese/Suzuka	Ayrton Senna	MP4/8-Ford HB
Australian/Adelaide	Ayrton Senna	MP4/8-Ford HB

1997

Australian/Melbourne	David Coulthard	MP4/12-Mercedes
Italian/Monza	David Coulthard	MP4/12-Mercedes
European/Jerez	Mika Hakkinen	MP4/12-Mercedes

1998

Australian/Melbourne	Mika Hakkinen	MP4/13-Mercedes
Brazilian/Interlagos	Mika Hakkinen	MP4/13-Mercedes
San Marino/Imola	David Coulthard	MP4/13-Mercedes
Spanish/Barcelona	Mika Hakkinen	MP4/13-Mercedes

Bibliography

Henry, Alan, *Ayrton Senna* (Hazleton Publishing, 1988 and 1992)
    Niki Lauda (Hazleton Publishing, 1989)
Hilton, Christopher *Ayrton Senna: The Hard Edge of Genius* (Patrick
Stephens Limited, 1990)
Lauda, Niki, written in collaboration with Herbert Volker; translated
from the German by E. J. Crockett *To Hell and Back: An
Autobiography* (Stanley Paul, 1986)
Nye, Doug *McLaren: The Grand Prix, Can-Am and Indy Cars*
(Hazleton Publishing, 1984 and 1988)
Roebuck, Nigel *Alain Prost* (Hazleton Publishing, 1990)
Young, Eoin *Bruce McLaren, The Man and his Racing Team* (Eyre &
Spottiswoode, 1971; reprinted by Patrick Stephens Limited, 1995)

Autocourse
Autosport
Motoring News

Index